Praise for

CHOOSE *YOUR* CUSTOMER

and Jonathan L. S. Byrnes
and John S. Wass

Choose Your Customer provides real-world, practical, and actionable advice for companies to survive and thrive in the New Digital Age. A terrific blueprint to successfully go to market and win against the digital giants.

> —**Roger Fradin,** Chairman of Resideo and former Vice Chairman of Honeywell International

This book provides a tried-and-true, data-driven, logical approach to developing and executing a successful strategic transformation in today's threatening high-risk environment.

> —**Ben Shapiro,** Malcolm P. McNair Professor of Marketing Emeritus at Harvard Business School

Jonathan and John provide compelling examples to understand true profitability by product and customer, using the most atomic level of data: actual sales transactions. They describe useful frameworks to turn analytical insights into initiatives and management alignment, clearly defining a strategy, including what not to do. This book is a road map of initiatives that will drive a 20 to 30 percent profit improvement.

> —**Massimo Russo,** Managing Director and Senior Partner at Boston Consulting Group and Fellow of the BCG Bruce Henderson Institute

Choose Your Customer explains how to develop and manage new innovative, win-win relationships with your customers that target and meet their specific, evolving needs. This is critical to success in competing against the powerful digital competitors and aggressive investor-backed companies that are disrupting every industry. Every manager will benefit from reading it.

  —**Mike Kaufmann,** CEO of Cardinal Health

Dr. Byrnes is probably the world's foremost authority on profit mapping and *effective* supply chain management, and all of Profit Isle's work should be required reading for managers of and investors in any supply chain–related business. In *Choose Your Customer*, Jonathan and John provide terrific advice on how a company should compete against the digital behemoths by using transaction-based profit metrics to recognize (and then align the organization around) its true customer profit core. If you're still thinking that maximizing efficiency is a key imperative for your business, then you REALLY need to read this book.

  —**Sam Darkatsh,** Managing Director at Raymond James Equity Research

Choose Your Customer is a great master plan for companies to better understand their customers and align to improve performance. It is a readable, commonsense framework for managing your business better in today's digital world. A must-read for today's managers in a world of disruptive competitors.

  —**Ron Sargent,** former Chairman and CEO of Staples, Lead Director at Kroger, and Director at Wells Fargo and Five Below

Choose Your Customer is an important book that tells managers how to compete successfully against the onslaught of digital giants that is transforming business today. It is essential reading for CEOs, CFOs, and other managers who need to reposition their companies for success. Business school students and all managers will benefit from the book's explanation of how to become value entrepreneurs.

  —**Vijay Govindarajan,** Coxe Distinguished Professor of Management at Tuck School of Business at Dartmouth and *New York Times* and *Wall Street Journal* bestselling author of *The Three-Box Solution*

With profitability as its North Star, this book provides the vision and definitive game plan for how to reposition your business to compete successfully in the future. The authors articulate the sweep of disruptive market transitions today, and then surgically offer prescriptive, actionable steps company leaders can—and must—take to win. Favorite quote: "Most businesses are doing what they should have been doing 5 to 10 years ago." Amen.

—**Thomas Gale,** CEO of *Modern Distribution Management*

Choose Your Customer is the indispensable guide for companies looking to thrive and prosper in today's disruptive environment. This book is just what distributors need today. Using practical tips and rich examples, Byrnes and Wass will challenge you to strategically manage your customers, data, business processes, and management team in pursuit of strategic dominance.

—**Patricia Lilly,** Chief Thought Leadership Officer of the National
Association of Wholesaler-Distributors

I believe that Jonathan and John are pioneers in the area of strategy and profitability management. They have used their deep expertise to bring together a very insightful and practical approach for companies to lead, transform in this new era of digital disruption, and drive value for the consumer. This book has really shaped my perspective in this space: it is a must-read for all executives, managers, and students.

—**Gautam Kapur,** VP of Consumer Strategy and Innovation at
Fidelity Investments

Choose Your Customer is that rare book that combines academic rigor with practical experience. Byrnes and Wass describe why the digital giants are threatening conventional physical businesses, and then provide the tools to fight back. A necessary resource for any CEO looking to collect the granular sales and profit information that can turn their supply chains into a source of competitive advantage.

—**Eric Ball,** General Partner at Impact Venture Capital,
former SVP and Treasurer at Oracle, and author of
Unlocking the Ivory Tower

Through their groundbreaking Profit Isle methodology, Jonathan and John have fundamentally changed the lens with which we view profitability and the levers we use to drive improved performance in our company. They taught us that optimizing our supply chain actually starts at the very beginning—with targeting the right customers. I would encourage any CEO or CFO looking to drive a step function change to read this book.

—**Erik Gershwind,** President and CEO of MSC Industrial Direct

If you own or run a business, you must read this book. Byrnes and Wass show us that all customers are not created equal. Every business must identify and nurture profitable relationships and neglect those customers who lose you money. Their model of how to segment your customers provides you with the tools necessary to increase your profitability and boost employee morale.

—**Denis Kelly,** Vice Chairman of Scura Partners and former Head of Mergers and Acquisitions at Prudential Securities

Driving profitable growth is critical for long-term survival. It goes beyond simply defining your value proposition and identifying sources of competitive advantage. It includes prioritizing the game changers and aligning human and financial capital accordingly. In this book, Jonathan and John combine practical advice with a scalable framework to help leaders understand where and how to take action and create a playbook for winning.

—**Mike Duffy,** CEO at FleetPride, former CEO of C&S Wholesale Grocers, and former President of Hospital Solutions and Global Supply Chain at Cardinal Health

In today's highly segmented markets dominated by big digital giants, Byrnes and Wass show step-by-step how to zero in on the lucrative opportunities that abound, if you only know where to look. It's a quick read, thought-provoking, and informative how-to manual, and go-to source for concrete, actionable insights.

—**Dan Furman,** Managing Director of State Street Global Advisors, State Street Corporation

An outstanding book, *Choose Your Customer* shares significant new insights about how a firm can effectively evaluate and manage its profit core in today's increasingly heterogeneous markets. The authors keenly understand the critical importance of granular profit knowledge, i.e., via transaction-based profit metrics and analytics that recognize that individual product/customer/service/delivery channel combinations are often unique and must be evaluated and managed as such. They carefully dissect the many ways in which today's Age of Diverse Markets, increasingly dominated by digital giants, differs markedly from the mass market era, and how today's executives must think and manage differently to successfully compete. The book is packed with great ideas linked perceptively to practice both within firms and within those firms' supply chains. It will occupy a worthy place on the bookshelves of top managers.

> —**Roy Shapiro,** Philip Caldwell Professor of Business Administration
> Emeritus at Harvard Business School

Kudos to Jonathan and John for continuing their quest to help us focus on "where the money is" via smart and logical analytics. Their magic lies in taking the complexity of millions of transactions, and distilling the data into actionable moves to drive profit and focus on the right customers. There is no substitute for this level of segmentation and stratification.

> —**Mitch Williams,** President and CEO of Construction Supply Group
> and Six Sigma Master Black Belt

Choose Your Customer is an authoritative guide with actionable advice that can transform a looming financial disaster into a beacon of business success. The authors discuss the coronavirus pandemic and provide a prescription for survival and prosperity. Their decades of research and business experience permeate this book.

> —**Samuel Goldhaber,** MD, Associate Chief and Clinical Director of the
> Division of Cardiovascular Medicine at Brigham and Women's Hospital
> and Professor of Medicine at Harvard Medical School

Choose Your Customer is superb. It should be part of every MBA curriculum in the country.

> —**Charles Davis,** Cameron Professor Emeritus at the
> University of St. Thomas

New competition from digital giants is not going away. But as your business landscape changes, so does that of your customer. This book lays out a sensible and methodical way to embrace the forces of change and to become the partner your customers need now.

> —**Chris Holt,** former Leader of Global Healthcare at Amazon

A road map that starts with the customer and ends deep inside your company, bringing higher profits and stronger strategic positioning, *Choose Your Customer* offers a must-have toolkit for the new Age of Data-Driven Precision Marketing.

> —**Richard Daly,** CEO of DNAnexus

As markets fragment and digital giants take over important customer segments, supply chain managers must coordinate with their sales and marketing counterparts. Such coordination aims to target the segments that will produce sustained profit growth, while assembling and providing customers with the innovative packages of products and services that will enable them to win. *Choose Your Customer* presents a systematic, proven methodology to accomplish this.

> —**Yossi Sheffi,** Elisha Gray II Professor of Engineering
> Systems at MIT and Director of the MIT Center for
> Transportation and Logistics

The key for all distributors is to identify your value proposition and then align the business to capitalize on how to sell this profitably. In *Choose Your Customer*, Jonathan and John have developed a program and system that allows the distributor to analyze the profitability of each customer, enabling it to drive the strengths of the company and recognize the profit levers unique to each customer. This not only benefits the distributor but, in most cases, the customer as well, which contributes to an even stronger long-term partnership.

> —**Pat Larmon,** Director of Huttig Building Products, Bodycote, Diversified Foodservice Systems, Pestell Nutrition Management, and QC Supply and former CEO and Director of Bunzl Distribution

This is a book about strategy to pragmatically win the war of profitability. It offers real-life scenarios we face in the ultracompetitive business world. The context is relatable to all levels of management.

> —**Craig Brown,** VP of Glass at Maverick Transportation

Through compelling examples, Byrnes and Wass show how businesses can boost their profits, even in a turbulent environment, by choosing their customers well and creating value for them. This lucidly written book offers easy-to-follow steps for developing and executing such a win-win strategy. It is an invaluable read for all managers.

> —**Bala Chakravarthy,** Professor of Strategy and Leadership Emeritus at IMD

This vital resource reveals smart, actionable, and transformative insights that not only point you to where the profits lie but show you how to unlock and sustain them. I've read, quoted, and infused Byrnes's wisdom in my company for years, and see this book as a lifework that can accelerate your skills and successes by decades.

> —**Luke Zaientz,** CEO of Reigning Champs

Jonathan and John's book comes in a very important period of transition from mass markets to diverse markets. Digital giants are capable of marketing anything directly to customers, which brings them advantages over traditional companies. *Choose Your Customer* addresses this weakness, empowering leaders at traditional companies to sustain competitive advantage and profits. The authors clarify how profit data supports thoughtfully choosing customers; suggest different strategies on how to align the company to capture, dominate, and grow its target segments; and explain how to manage complex internal business processes. This book is a must-read for all modern managers who want not only to accelerate focused growth but also to enable their companies to respond to a rapidly evolving environment.

—**Ioannis Koliousis,** Associate Professor of Supply Chain Management at Cranfield University

CHOOSE *YOUR* CUSTOMER

CHOOSE *YOUR* CUSTOMER

HOW TO COMPETE AGAINST
THE DIGITAL GIANTS AND THRIVE

JONATHAN L. S. BYRNES
and
JOHN S. WASS

Mc
Graw
Hill

NEW YORK   CHICAGO   SAN FRANCISCO   ATHENS   LONDON
MADRID   MEXICO CITY   MILAN   NEW DELHI
SINGAPORE   SYDNEY   TORONTO

1 2 3 4 5 6 7 8 9   LCR   26 25 24 23 22 21

ISBN 978-1-264-25709-6
MHID   1-264-25709-0

e-ISBN 978-1-264-25710-2
e-MHID   1-264-25710-4

Design by Lee Fukui and Mauna Eichner

Library of Congress Cataloging-in-Publication Data

Names: Byrnes, Jonathan L. S., author. | Wass, John S., author.
Title: Choose your customer : how to compete against the digital giants and
   thrive / Jonathan L.S. Byrnes and John S. Wass.
Description: New York : McGraw Hill, [2021] | Includes bibliographical
   references and index.
Identifiers: LCCN 2020053390 (print) | LCCN 2020053391 (ebook) | ISBN
   9781264257096 (hardback) | ISBN 9781264257102 (ebook)
Subjects: LCSH: Consumer behavior. | Customer relations--Management. |
   Corporate profits.
Classification: LCC HF5415.32 .B97 2021 (print) | LCC HF5415.32 (ebook) |
   DDC 658.8/12--dc23
LC record available at https://lccn.loc.gov/2020053390
LC ebook record available at https://lccn.loc.gov/2020053391

McGraw Hill books are available at special quantity discounts to use as premiums and sales promotions or for use in corporate training programs. To contact a representative, please visit the Contact Us pages at www.mhprofessional.com.

To my family: Marsha, Dan, Kristin, Edison,
Steve, Nicole, George, Adrian, and Warren
—JLSB

To my wife, Kimberly, and our children,
Taggart, Oliver, and Noah
—JSW

CONTENTS

ACKNOWLEDGMENTS

We are very grateful to Profit Isle's employees and clients for their very helpful comments and suggestions, and to our students and teaching assistants at MIT for helping to develop and refine the concepts in this book.

Esmond Harmsworth, our literary agent, was extremely helpful in positioning and structuring this book and in guiding us through the publishing process. Many thanks to Casey Ebro, our editor at McGraw Hill, for overseeing the editing and publishing process and to Kevin Commins for his valuable suggestions.

In addition, several individuals have been extremely helpful to us in developing the concepts and techniques in this book and have helped make this book possible: Gerry Allan, Craig Brown, Toni Choueiri, Dick Daly, Sam Darkatsh, Charles Davis, Lisa Dolin, Mike Duffy, Dan Furman, Erik Gershwind, Sam Goldhaber, Fred Hooper, Mitchell Jacobson, Ed Jamieson, Ken Sewall, Ben Shapiro, Roy Shapiro, and Jim Zimmerman.

Our MIT colleagues Chris Caplice, George Kocur, Jim Rice, and Yossi Sheffi have always been an important source of wisdom and support. Dan Bigman, Leigh Buchanan, Tom Gale, Trish Lilly, John Peter, Vince Ryan, Sean Silverthorne, and Dirk Van Dongen have provided important guidance in refining the book's concepts.

Sadly, Bill Copacino and Don Rosenfield, who provided friendship and guidance in many ways, have passed away all too soon.

We are very grateful for the many readers of our articles and listeners to our speeches and webinars for their constructive suggestions and advice.

Many other friends and colleagues have been enormously helpful, and we are very grateful for their wisdom and kindness. We happily acknowledge their contributions, and we accept full responsibility for any errors or shortcomings in the book.

INTRODUCTION

The genesis of this book is a meeting that we recently had with the CEO of a multibillion-dollar distributor. He had just met with his management team about how Amazon and the other digital giants had entered his business and were steadily vacuuming up market share.

This was the third meeting we had that week with CEOs of major companies asking us the same questions:

- How can I defend my company against these aggressive digital giants that have overwhelming digital capabilities and a price-cutting mentality?

- I'm cutting my costs across the board, but my profitability is dropping—what else can I do?

- How can I identify and invest in growing my real profit core—my business segments that will provide high growth—and remain profitable and defensible against my new competitors?

- How can I align my organization around my profit core and build dominance in my target market segments?

As we outlined our experience helping companies overcome these issues, our thoughts turned to a seminal management committee meeting that we had had with the top managers of one of the largest hospital supply companies several years earlier.

The company's vice presidents gathered around a broad mahogany table in the company's boardroom. The president sat at the head of the table.

As the operating review progressed, each vice president in turn said, "I made budget." When they got to the president, he looked at them and said, "That's great. I'm the only one who didn't make budget."

WHAT HAPPENED?

As we dug into the situation, we saw that the vice president of sales had increased revenues, but the new customers had ordered products that were not stocked in the local distribution center. The vice president of operations was measured on a set of standard costs; he had to source these products from a distant warehouse, and he had beaten his budget by negotiating a lower freight rate.

The company had increased budgeted revenues and decreased budgeted costs, but it had lost profits. This was not supposed to happen, and they did not see it until it was too late.

We had just completed a project that developed the first vendor-managed inventory, which we describe in Chapter 1. In a nutshell, the company developed the capability to provide a new service with which it could deliver products directly to the patient care areas and clinics of its hospital customers. In the process, we found that the company's actual cost of the products depended on both the products themselves and the cost of the related services. But this cost not only varied from customer to customer but also from product to product within a customer—depending on the location of each product's destination and other factors.

This was both a huge opportunity and a major problem. The opportunity was that the company was carving out a new business that was completely defensible against price-cutting competitors who had a lower cost structure because they simply dropped their products off at the hospital's receiving dock.

The problem was that the hospital supply market was fragmenting rapidly, as different customers wanted different packages of products and related services—while the company was set up to sell and deliver only a narrow set of products and services. The company needed to realign its market positioning (account selection), organization, and management processes with this new rapidly evolving segmentation.

Moreover, when we tried to calculate the profits from the new system, we found a big problem: the company's traditional accounting system could not match each revenue increment with the actual cost of producing it because the traditional accounting categories, like revenue and cost, were too broad. When we simply spread the costs across the order lines, we got a wildly inaccurate picture—much like the hospital supply company president's discovery in his management committee meeting. Their traditional metrics and key performance indicators (KPIs) showed their average profitability but not their true, granular, rapidly shifting profit landscape.

And this was happening in company after company.

After some head scratching, we developed a completely new way to analyze profitability, which we call *transaction-based profit metrics and analytics*: we carefully assign the correct costs to each transaction (invoice line) based on each transaction's actual costs, essentially creating an all-in P&L for each order line. For example, if a customer walked into a store and bought two pencils, an eraser, and a ruler, we produced three distinct all-in P&Ls, one for each transaction. Because each order line had a set of unique identifiers (for example, customer, product, store, sales rep, delivery), we could create a powerful data set that would combine and recombine the relevant transactions on a monthly basis to show the actual profitability of every nook and cranny of the company—especially their rapidly shifting Profit Peaks and Drains that were hidden by their average metrics.

This profit segmentation dynamically shows a company's true profit landscape, and it forms the basis for a powerful new and completely different way to analyze and manage a company—one that provides the basis for successfully competing with the digital giants (and which is central to Jonathan's graduate and executive courses at MIT).

We developed a solution in Profit Isle, our software-as-a-service (SaaS) profit solutions company, to rapidly produce this analysis at high volumes, enabling managers to immediately focus on creating their highest-payoff actions. We have analyzed tens of billions of dollars of client revenues using this solution, supporting management teams that have produced sustained

10 to 30 percent year-on-year profit increases, even in the presence of competition from the digital giants.

When we stepped back and thought about how the digital giants' data-driven precision marketing was disrupting industry after industry, and the increasingly critical need for company profit metrics to match the rapidly changing business environment, we saw that company after company in industry after industry was undergoing a fundamental shift in the way that it needed to be managed.

In essence, we have entered a new era of business: we are experiencing the end of the mass market era, and accelerating into a new era, which we call the Age of Diverse Markets. The objective of this book is to explain how to manage and thrive in this new era by aligning your organization around your profit core (both current profits and your projected defensible market positioning) to build dominance in your target market segments.

BOOK OVERVIEW

After the first section, "The End of an Era," which provides historical context, this book has three main sections, matching the three essential management steps you need to take to succeed in this new era of diverse markets and digital giants: Part II, "Choose Your Customer," Part III, "Align Your Company," and Part IV, "Manage to Win."

Choose Your Customer

Chapter 1, "Today's Flood of Change," describes this sea change and explains what is changing. Not only is the basic management process changing, but the new era is also characterized by a broad shift in technology that has created a massive opportunity for a set of digital giants like Amazon to emerge and grow to dominate important segments of our economy.

This chapter outlines how managers must change their management process to reposition for success in the new era. While the mass markets era created an opportunity for limited product segmentation (for example, regular Coke versus Diet Coke), the Age of Diverse Markets is characterized by much more extensive and complex segmentation involving both products and related services.

The good news is that there are plenty of opportunities to grow and thrive in the new era, but it requires that management use true profit data to thoughtfully **choose** its target customers; **align** the company to capture, dominate, and grow its target segments; and **manage** its increasingly complex internal business processes to accelerate its focused growth and respond to its rapidly evolving market segment needs.

Simply improving the efficiency of what a company always has done is a recipe for disaster.

Chapter 2, "Navigate the Currents of Change," identifies and analyzes the currents of change that are transforming industry after industry, ushering in the Age of Diverse Markets. The chapter describes how these currents will differentially affect new entrants and incumbent firms.

Chapter 3, "Build Your Strategic High Ground," focuses on granular profit analytics, one of the most important manager capabilities in the Age of Diverse Markets. The objectives are to explain how to analyze a company's Profit Peaks, Profit Drains, and Profit Deserts and to give managers a practical understanding of how to build a set of management processes that put this information into action.

Chapter 4, "Manage to Thrive in a Period of Crisis," analyzes the impact of the current pandemic on companies, and it describes how managers can build a set of processes to grow customer loyalty, manage supply chain shock waves, and accomplish productive downsizing. The goal is to enable managers to develop a program that will provide cash flow and profits during the crisis period, while building a strategy and set of management processes that will produce long-term sustainable success in the prolonged period that follows.

Align Your Company

Chapter 5, "Create a Winning Customer Value Footprint," explains how to identify and meet your target customers' deep needs by creating extended products and developing deep strategic product management capabilities.

Chapter 6, "Own Your Customer High Ground," focuses on the processes of selecting and managing customers, including pricing and strategic partnerships. The fundamental nature of a key account (that is, a Profit Peak customer) is changing dramatically, so it is critical that you choose your customers carefully so you are devoting resources to customers who fit your capabilities and strategic direction and who will join you in building win-win relationships that give you both strategic dominance and long-run sustained profit growth.

Chapter 7, "Develop the Right Customer Relationships," discusses how to build the supply chains and channels that will enable you to effectively structure your customer relationships. The objective of this chapter is to explain how to design and manage this complex process.

Manage to Win

Chapter 8, "Manage at the Right Level," focuses on one of the most important enablers of company success. To succeed, managers at all levels of a company must shift their focus and management processes from the old command-and-control Age of Mass Markets practices to those that will enable them to develop and manage the decentralized initiatives needed to win in today's Age of Diverse Markets. This chapter explains how managers at the three key levels of management— top management, upper management, and operating management—can make this transition.

In the final chapter, "Become a Value Entrepreneur," we describe the evolving capabilities that will be the hallmarks of successful managers of the future. This set of capabilities, which we call *value entrepreneurship*, is rooted in the three key imperatives: choice, alignment, and management. We explain how managers can develop and perfect these new skills through both training and leadership experiences.

The future holds a very exciting, rewarding, and productive opportunity for the next generation of managers. This book guides you in building a proven, pragmatic pathway to success.

PART I

THE END OF AN ERA

1

TODAY'S FLOOD
OF CHANGE

everal years ago, the front page of the *New York Times* reported that two
Columbia University geophysicists had found clear evidence of ancient
villages lying beneath hundreds of feet of water on the seabed of the
Black Sea. Their investigations, later narrated in a fascinating book, *Noah's
Flood*, revealed that a sizable portion of what is now the Black Sea had once
been a giant freshwater lake, filled with meltwater from Asian glaciers.*

About 7,600 years ago, as the last ice age waned and the waters rose, the
Mediterranean Sea breached a high mountain barrier, and a monumental
flood rushed through the Bosporus valley, running through what we know
today as Istanbul. Ocean water poured into the lake with historical force,
destroying and submerging all life in the area, and formed the Black Sea.
This was the actual event that storytellers memorialized as the biblical flood.

Today, business is transitioning from one major era, the Age of Mass
Markets, to another, which we call the Age of Diverse Markets. The two ages
could not be more different, and the change is as inevitable and disruptive

---

* William Ryan and Walter Pittman, *Noah's Flood* (New York: Simon & Schuster, 1998).

as the flood that created the Black Sea. While the transition began some time ago, it is rapidly accelerating, and the seismic shift is leaving managers scrambling for a practical pathway to succeed in a new, very different world.

A NEW ERA

The Age of Mass Markets, which extended through most of the prior century, was characterized by fast-growing homogeneous markets. Railroads and roads integrated diverse geographic markets, and many large national enterprises emerged. This was the age of the "generals"—General Electric, General Foods, General Motors, General Dynamics—and this management paradigm continued into the 1980s and 1990s, with big-box retailers like Walmart, Best Buy, and Staples.

These companies were characterized by massive economies of scale in nearly every business function (production, distribution, advertising, and so on), which ensured that as they increased their sales, their unit costs dropped, giving them ample profits to invest in getting more sales and in further reducing their costs by increasing the efficiency of their production and distribution systems. Both prices and distribution costs were relatively uniform, so reporting tools based on averages—like aggregate revenues, costs, and gross margins—were sufficient.

The key management imperative was to get big fast. The rules of thumb were that all revenues were good and all costs were bad. Companies segregated their functional departments to individually optimize their revenue-maximizing or cost-minimizing objectives, and they coordinated them at the top through periodic planning sessions and period-end financial reports.

Today's Age of Diverse Markets, which began its widespread acceleration around 2000, is completely different. Today, there are very few mass markets, while there are more and more diverse markets where product offerings, pricing, and service packages are uniquely configured, if not by individual customer, than at least by highly segmented target markets.

Today, markets are heterogeneous and fragmenting down to the individual customer in many cases. Throughout our economy, pricing is becoming much more varied, both within market segments and even between one customer and the next. In parallel, the cost to serve each customer is becoming increasingly diverse, depending on the customer relationship, product-service mix, and other factors. This change has already overtaken the business-to-consumer (B2C) markets, and it is rapidly transforming the business-to-business (B2B) markets as well.

In the Age of Mass Markets, products were "king." To a large extent, companies succeeded by selling the same products to as many customers as possible. In the Age of Diverse Markets, in contrast, customers are "king." Companies succeed by microtargeting particular customers and tightly specified market segments and providing them with tailored packages of products and related services.

In the prior era, companies won with top-down management processes that kept their revenue-maximizing and cost-minimizing functions separate. Today, companies win by choosing customers who fit their strategic positioning and serving them with highly integrated sets of products and services that are delivered through decentralized organizations and processes—while at the same time remaining flexible and adaptable to all types of change. In the past, managers needed only aggregate metrics, while today, they need to understand the relationship between revenue and cost for literally every product sold to every customer every time.

The rise of the digital giants originated with their ability to market directly to customers, which enabled them to create microsegments and to configure offers to individuals at scale using Big Data and algorithmic recommendations based on captured customer information.

Today, as the Age of Diverse Markets tsunami rushes in, industry after industry is being disrupted by digital giants like Amazon, Uber, Google, Facebook, Apple, and Alibaba and by savvy incumbents that have staked out a strategic high ground and generated sustained profit growth.

The wave is gathering speed and is pushing through the consumer landscape and into the B2B markets. Amazon is experimenting with placing Alexa, its voice-controlled device, throughout hospitals and in key manufacturing plants where supplies are ordered and used. Uber's rapidly growing Uber Freight is displacing many traditional trucking companies. Google acquired Fitbit, spearheading the company's move into the personal health and medical industry. The time frame for managing significant business change is three to five years, so organizations that are under siege from these forces must devise and initiate a response very quickly. The digital giants are moving fast, and even the pandemic crisis has not slowed them down.

As we wrote this book, the COVID-19 pandemic was raging throughout the world. The crisis accelerated the relentless drive toward digital commerce and diverse markets, which made it even more urgent for companies to reposition for long-term success to compete with the digital giants. In Chapter 4, "Manage to Thrive in a Period of Crisis," we explain how to create short-term profits and cash flow during a crisis, while at the same time repositioning for the long run. The steps that you need to succeed in a crisis—whether it's COVID-19 or anything else—are the same that you need to prosper when it ends.

The biggest problem in business today is that all too many managers are not embracing the Age of Diverse Markets success elements that will enable them to prosper. Instead, they are doubling down on tactical innovations and tuning up old practices from the Age of Mass Markets—usually with diminishing results. Savvy managers, on the other hand, are realizing that the new disruptors are not winning by doing old things better but instead, by doing new things that incumbent companies are simply not capable of doing with their current business practices.

The key to success in the Age of Diverse Markets is choosing your customer. This has three imperatives:

- **Choose:** Define a defensible strategy that your company can dominate, choose the customers who fit, and say no to those who do not.

- **Align:** Identify and build the capabilities that will enable your company to achieve high sustained profitability with your chosen customers in your target strategic group (that is, the set of firms pursuing the same strategy), and focus your resources to quickly excel in your strategic direction.

- **Manage:** Develop your organization so your managers can seamlessly coordinate to identify and support your chosen customers, and to meet their diverse and rapidly evolving needs.

The objective of this book is to explain the currents of change that are creating today's disruptive tsunamis and to give managers a realistic pathway to success—one that involves managing in a new, creative, data-driven, and much more interesting way. In our experience across a range of industries, we have seen successful companies achieve long-term industry strategic leadership and sustain 10 to 30 percent annual profit growth—even while so many of their peers have run aground, victims of the devastating competition from the digital giants.

THE CASE OF EDISON FURNITURE

Perhaps the easiest way to explain the enormous pressures on business today—and how to overcome them—is with an example. We begin with a story about one of the oldest businesses undergoing a forced reinvention: the furniture business.

The retail furniture industry is facing an upheaval. Mattresses are a major profit generator. However, focused new competitors, including specialty off-price retailers, "mattress in a box" internet retailers, and manufacturers opening their own retail stores are grabbing market share from traditional multiline incumbents. The company we will name Edison (this is an actual company, but we are disguising the name) was under pressure from all sides. A majority of its customers were demanding that it match or beat the competitors' prices, so it responded by running TV ads featuring low prices.

There appeared to be no way out of this price war, which the company seemed destined to lose because its higher cost, brick-and-mortar stores were competing with the internet sellers' much lower costs.

In response, Edison decided to look more carefully at its data. Using transaction-based profit metrics and analytics, it created what was essentially a full, all-in P&L for every transaction (that is, invoice line: literally, every time a product was bought by a customer, which we will explain in the next chapter)—to determine which parts of its business were making or losing money. When they saw the results, they nearly fell off their chairs:

- About 18 percent of their customers, which we call their Profit Peak accounts, accounted for about half of their revenues but produced over 130 percent of their profits.

- About 30 percent of their customers, their large money-losing Profit Drains, accounted for about one-third of their revenues but drained off about 50 percent of the profits earned by the rest of the company.

- About half of the company's customers were Profit Desert customers who accounted for about 20 percent of the revenues and produced less than 10 percent of the profits.

When Edison's managers saw this, they immediately understood that their price war strategy was a response to the profit-draining customers' demands, while they were essentially ignoring their critical high-profit customers.

In fact, a few months earlier, they had conducted a marketing survey that had concluded that two-thirds of their *high-revenue* customers (a group that included both large Profit Peak and Profit Drain customers) were price shoppers. However, when Edison's managers saw the new transaction-based profit information, they realized that this new survey was fatally flawed because it neglected to discover how many of these customers were high-profit customers, and it failed to investigate what those high-profit customers really wanted. Were they just shopping on price, like the profit-draining customers, or were they looking for something else?

In response, Edison sent a short, quick survey to a sample of its high-revenue customers, but it carefully segregated the Profit Peak customers' responses from those of the profit drainers. What they saw was startling: each group was homogeneous, but the two customer groups could not be more different:

- The Profit Peak customers were very store loyal. They liked to shop at the store, and they often had a trusted sales rep who guided their purchases. They referred their friends and family to the store (and that is how they had found it), and while they were not wealthy, they were relatively insensitive to prices.

- The profit drainers, on the other hand, were classic price shoppers. They often started shopping at one of the company's stores, then went comparison shopping at the off-price and internet retailers. They finished by returning to the company's store to demand that it match the lowest price they had found and deliver the strong service that Edison was known for.

This led Edison to change its competitive positioning to respond to the onslaught of low-cost, low-service internet competitors. It focused on building its business with the Profit Peak customers in several ways:

- It fed the Profit Peak customers' identities into its Salesforce customer relationship management system, so that they were recognized as soon as they entered the store and were sent immediately to their favorite sales rep, who had on his or her iPad a history of the customers' buying preferences, both for style and accessories like high-profit warrantees.

- The Profit Peak customers were offered special services, including after-hours appointments with their favorite sales reps and customer concierge services to help with appointments, answer questions, and respond to requests.

- Edison instructed its best product managers to develop "store brand" private-label products, which were much more profitable than branded products and which the high-profit customers actually preferred.

- The sales reps were instructed not to negotiate price discounts with the profit-draining customers, whom they could recognize from the notations in the Salesforce system.

- Advertising themes changed from low prices to high service and quality "store brand" products, and the company started holding regular "friends and family" after-hours wine and cheese parties for its Profit Peak customers and their guests.

- Delivery services were changed to focus customer service on high-profit customers. The director of delivery noted that about one-third of the drivers were very good at customer service, while the other two-thirds of the drivers simply liked to drive.

He stationed the service-sensitive drivers in neighborhoods where the Profit Peak customers lived and had the other drivers shuttle trucks of furniture to them. This freed the master drivers to do all the Profit Peak customer interactions, including noting other furniture needs and preferences that they could report to the sales reps, who would follow up.

The best news was that when Edison Furniture looked at the currents of change that were buffeting the industry, it saw that it had carved out a defensible, high-growth, high-profit strategic group that the powerful digital and off-price competitors could not enter with their low-price, low-service strategies.

Edison's executives noted that their high-profit customers required more costly service, but they realized that this was a great investment as the extra cost was easily justified by the accelerated profits. They also realized that simply maximizing *revenues* by pursuing profit-draining customers was causing them to lose money hand over fist.

Edison's management made the brave strategic decision to abandon the revenue from its Profit Drain customers and to stop their old practice of meeting the lowest price in the market. They were pleasantly surprised to find that a significant number of the Profit Drain customers eventually purchased from Edison at full price anyway so they could get Edison's legendary great service.

Importantly, since most of the key elements of this strategy were already present in the company, it could manage the transition to the new strategy by using its current resources. Management was delighted to find that the new strategy generated significant new cash flow from the start, which paid for the additional changes needed to complete their strategic shift.

Edison succeeded because it **chose** its customers by identifying its high-profit, defensible strategic group; it **aligned** its resources around the processes and technologies that supported its chosen customers; and it **managed** the coordination of its key functional areas—sales, products, and customer relationships—to meet its customers' needs and not to maximize all revenues and minimize all costs.

Edison's customer profit segmentation—dividing the customers into Profit Peaks, Profit Drains, and Profit Deserts—was essential to **choosing** its strategic group. When Edison's managers used their transaction-based profit metrics and analytics to determine the actual all-in profit of every customer (and product, store, and so on), they saw that their customers clustered naturally into these three profit segments. Figure 1.1 provides a *profit map* (that is, a summary characterizing a set of profit segments) of Edison's customers.

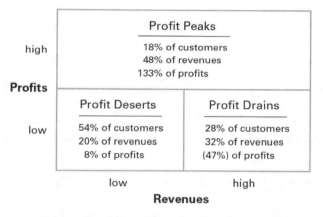

Figure 1.1 Edison Furniture's Profit Segments

Once Edison's managers examined the company's profit map, they determined that their Profit Peak accounts formed an existing and defensible core set of customers that would endure in the transformed industry (as the currents of change played out), so they could anchor their choice of strategic group in this customer set. As a result, they could figure out the tactics that would enable them to secure and grow their Profit Peaks, convert as many Profit Drains as possible into Profit Peaks, and focus on lowering the cost to serve their Profit Deserts. This gave them a clear game plan for **aligning** and **managing** the company.

THE CASE OF BAXTER

A second example of how companies can reinvent their priorities, beat back competition, and discover astonishing new sources of profit comes from the medical industry, specifically a hospital supplier named Baxter.

We highlight this case because it was one of the landmark innovations that started the transition to the Age of Diverse Markets and because it shows how Baxter, in its healthcare business market, paralleled the situation that Edison faced in its B2C market: intense competition, pricing transparency, and a seemingly no-win situation. Like Edison, Baxter had to shift its focus from selling traditional products to creating innovative ways to meet its customer needs. And, just as it was for Edison, choosing its customers and realigning its organization were the keys to Baxter's success.

Baxter was stuck in the mud. The company sold a variety of hospital supplies, like intravenous (IV) solutions and plastic sets to deliver drugs and fluid to patients. The business was wracked with constant price wars; a five-year hospital contract would hinge on whether the price was, say, $1.05 versus $1.03 per liter. The decision-makers were hospital pharmacists, who were price buyers.

Baxter's management found that its core strategy of selling commodity products with minimal and identical services to all customers was creating chronic price wars with giant competitors that were doing the same thing. The company needed a way to break out of this shrinking strategic box and redefine its business.

Baxter assembled a small team to investigate how to raise its profitability. The team carefully examined the company's sales and operating costs. They saw that the company was quite efficient; it appeared that there was little that could be done.

Then the team had an inspired thought: all their cost-reduction work had naturally focused on the activities within Baxter's "four walls," just as their competitors were doing. During a brainstorming session, the team had a quirky thought: they wondered what happened to the products within the hospital from the time they were received until they were administered to the patients. They thought that this information might provide a way to break out of their shrinking strategic box. Surprisingly, the team had little knowledge of these activities.

Soon, the team fanned out to visit several hospitals, pursuing their hunch that they might find something useful. They were amazed to find that in hospital after hospital, the products flowed through a series of internal supply chain steps, many of which replicated those that took place in

Baxter. Moreover, the steps were poorly organized and were accomplished at volumes that were too small to achieve even a minimum efficient scale.

The team conducted a study at a major hospital to measure the cost of each supply chain step. They divided the supply chain into a set of discrete steps (for example, deciding what to order, determining how much to order, transmitting the order) and interviewed all relevant hospital personnel (for example, purchasing personnel, materials management personnel, nurses) to determine how much time each person spent on each step in a typical week. They scaled these numbers by the loaded labor rate to calculate the hospital's supply chain cost by activity and department, giving them transaction-based profit information.

The study's results shocked everyone on the team and in the hospital: for many important products, the total cost of the supply chain activities exceeded the cost of the supplies. Departments that were not thought to be involved in supply chain activities, like nursing, constituted a surprisingly large proportion of the costs. For the nurses in particular, the time and cost of supply chain activities nearly equaled the cost of patient care—an immensely important insight in this period of skilled nursing shortages.

No one had even imagined that this picture would emerge. Careful studies in multiple hospitals confirmed that this was the norm.

The cost landscape of hospitals surprised and amazed all those involved. To illustrate, if the cost to the hospital of a liter of IV solution was about $1.00, the total cost by the time it was administered to a patient was about $7.00, and of the $6.00 difference representing the cost within the hospital, about half, or $3.00, was avoidable. While the suppliers and the hospital were bickering over a few pennies, about $2.00 to $3.00 in cost reductions were hidden but addressable through process improvements.

When the hospitals' top managers saw this cost picture, they came to Baxter and essentially said: "We just have two questions: First, can you really do this? And second, can we trust you?" As one of the largest and most reliable hospital suppliers, Baxter could authentically answer yes to both questions. Besides, Baxter's managers had the advantage of creating the new system, and their careful efficiency calculations showed them the exact ways to reduce costs that later imitators never saw.

This new strategy allowed Baxter's managers to shift the decision-maker buying their products from the price-oriented pharmacist to the hospitals' top managers. For the first time in many years, they found themselves in the driver's seat of their hospital relationships.

Based on the comprehensive hospital study information, verified in a number of hospitals, the team suggested a new system that would integrate the supply chains of Baxter and the hospitals. Baxter called it the "stockless system" (now called "vendor-managed inventory," or VMI), later rebranded as ValueLink. It still is a critical element in Cardinal Health's hospital supply services (this portion of Baxter's business was eventually spun off and later purchased by Cardinal Health).

Under the stockless system, a Baxter materials management coordinator was resident in each hospital. The coordinator was not a sales rep but rather, a floor supervisor from Baxter's distribution center (DC). Using a new, efficient protocol, the coordinator counted the products in each of the hospital's patient care areas and clinics and transmitted the order information for each patient care area and clinic to Baxter using a handheld device.

At the Baxter DC, a special section of the warehouse was devoted to the stockless system. It was carefully designed for picking individual items like two boxes of bandages, which are called "eaches," in contrast with the main sections of the DC that were set up to handle bulk items like cases and pallets. After receiving the hospital orders at the DC, a dedicated set of DC personnel packed each order into a set of special totes, with each tote addressed to the specific hospital patient care area or clinic that generated the order.

At the end of the day, the totes were loaded onto delivery trucks and brought to the hospitals. They were received using *statistical receiving* (that is, inspecting a sample of high-value products), made possible by highly audited Baxter shipping verification protocols, and then moved to the respective patient care areas or clinics at night. The Baxter coordinators put the products away and returned the totes to the stockroom for transportation back to Baxter the next day.

The new stockless system resulted in three major benefits: one expected, another a surprise, and a third completely unexpected.

First, the stockless system *reduced the hospital's supply chain costs by over 30 percent.*

It reduced costs in several ways: by eliminating the redundancies between Baxter and the hospitals; by substituting the use of Baxter's systems operating at efficient scale; and by identifying and rectifying inefficiencies in the prior hospital operations (for example, eliminating the massive amount of time nurses had been spending going to the stockroom to get missing supplies).

Baxter had found a way to escape from its shrinking strategic box by "building a bigger box around its business," which opened a new world of possibilities for expanding what we call its *customer value footprint* (that is, the value that a company provides to a customer). In the process, Baxter redefined its business.

Second, the Baxter managers were surprised to find that *their own operating costs dropped by over 30 percent.*

Baxter now controlled the hospital order pattern. Baxter's managers could balance the hospital inventories with the ordering pattern by building a little more stock of inexpensive supplies, which helped reduce order frequency; by spotting early trends and proactively building inventories to avoid expediting costs; and by directing hospital staff to alternative stocking locations within the hospital when needed.

Third, and completely unexpectedly, *Baxter's product sales rose by over 35 percent, even in the most highly penetrated hospitals in the country.*

This massive sales increase was driven by the efficiency and performance of the stockless system, which greatly eased the burden on all the hospital personnel involved, especially the nurses. Just as important, a very strong working relationship—rooted in ongoing problem solving and jointly finding ways to improve the system—developed between the head nurses and the Baxter coordinators. This effectively made Baxter the preferred vendor.

When it became clear that the stockless system was a major revenue generator, the sales reps, who previously tried to keep the team out of their important accounts, did an about-face. They quickly tried to get all their accounts to the head of the line for the new system because they expected huge commissions on the big sales increases.

It soon became clear that the company needed a more systematic way to decide which accounts would get the new system and a way to prioritize the accounts in light of Baxter's limited capacity to implement the new system. For the first time, Baxter had to choose its customers—and this ran completely counter to its established practice of treating all customers alike.

The answer was what we call *market mapping*—matching customers to the relationships that they *should have*, not necessarily to the relationships that they initially want.

The market mapping process involves sales managers, marketing managers, and supply chain managers. Once the market mapping team decides on the right relationship that the company should have with a customer, it is the job of the sales rep, often in combination with the supply chain manager and other members of the multicapability account team, to sell the account into that relationship over time.

In targeting accounts for these relationships, the team found four key factors: (1) the amount of the potential profits at stake; (2) the operating fit; (3) the account's willingness and ability to partner; and (4) the account's buyer behavior (that is, relationship versus transactional). The team also saw that it needed to define a small number of alternative relationships— which we call a *relationship hierarchy*—for accounts for whom full integration did not fit.

Through this process, Baxter was able to align its sales process, product-service mix, and organizational processes to fit the respective needs of its various target customers.

A second big issue that arose was whether to offer the service only for products that the hospital bought from Baxter or to offer the service for all hospital products. This discussion was heated, with the sales and product managers adamant that the service was a critical incentive for selling Baxter products and should be offered only for Baxter products.

Baxter's president thought about this issue and reasoned that the stockless system was creating a pipeline flow into the hospitals that helped hospitals reduce costs, eliminate redundant personnel, and free up nurses' time. Unless Baxter handled all the hospitals' products, the hospitals could not achieve the full cost savings and efficiency improvements made possible by the stockless system. Therefore, stockless had to handle all hospital products.

A related question arose: should Baxter charge for the stockless system, or should the company offer it as a "perk" to large-volume customers?

Again, the sales and product managers argued that it should be considered a sales incentive and be made available at no cost to big accounts.

The president turned down this argument, explaining that because hospitals would have to make significant internal changes to implement the system, charging for the system would force them to acknowledge the value they would be receiving. Moreover, it would provide an incentive to make the changes.

With these important strategic decisions in hand, Baxter rolled out the stockless system using multicapability teams tailored for each target hospital. As expected, the teams encountered some operating issues, but importantly, the system produced major benefits.

Stepping back, what did this fundamentally new way of doing business signify for managers?

The stockless system, just like other forms of close supplier-customer integration and cooperation, heralded a major shift in the nature of business and contributed to the Age of Diverse Markets.

First, it unleashed huge new profits by eliminating the inefficiencies that lay hidden for decades between companies, rather than addressing only issues within companies.

Second, the stockless system created decisive strategic differentiation. It enabled Baxter to integrate with its most important customers, which fostered very strong operating ties. Baxter created a new, lucrative strategic group, which was defensible against both traditional and digital competitors. Moreover, this strategy invited and underpinned critical hospital strategic initiatives.

For example, prior to this partnership, hospitals were reluctant to develop remote facilities and clinics because they lacked confidence in their managers' ability to support these complex operations. The Baxter partnership gave them confidence to do this, which transformed hospital strategies. Competitors with arm's-length strategies (for example, only shipping in bulk to hospitals' receiving docks), even digital giants with Big Data, could not possibly match Baxter's rapidly evolving customer value footprint.

Third, this innovation was not about the products. It was all about Baxter developing enduring strategic advantage and financial gains from its customer-oriented go-to-market innovations—one of the hallmarks of the new Age of Diverse Markets.

Fourth, when Baxter used transaction-based profit information to guide its own business, it discovered its prices and cost to serve varied widely depending on the customer relationship, the service package, and other salient factors. Without its granular new transaction-based profitability information, Baxter managers would not have been able to select the right target accounts, match those customers to the right relationships by aligning their cost to serve with the customer's profit potential, and develop the right custom-tailored packages of products and services to fit their target market segments and customers.

Like Edison, Baxter succeeded because it **chose** its customers by identifying those who fit its high-profit, defensible strategic group; it **aligned** resources around the processes that supported its chosen customers; and it **managed** the coordination of its key functional areas—sales, products, and customer relationships—to meet its customers' needs. Like Edison, Baxter understood that the old model of maximizing all revenues and minimizing all costs was a losing proposition.

WHO WINS BIG

Today, every market is changing rapidly with most companies reducing their supplier base by 40 to 60 percent. The all-important question of who stays and who goes is rarely made on product characteristics alone, or even price. The decision on who wins big and who gets pushed out is almost always determined by a supplier's go-to-market capabilities—namely, the ability to choose its customers, to produce more essential customer value through an innovative value footprint, and to create new profits and strategic advantage *for the customers*.

The overriding management issue is that this change in business eras is creating a critical need for a shift from broad-market targeting to focused-segment—and even customer—selection. In today's Age of Diverse Markets, "choose your customer" is the most important theme.

In order to succeed, companies have to abide by the three imperatives we highlighted before: (1) **Choose:** Define a defensible strategic group that your company can dominate, and select the most lucrative customers within it; (2) **Align:** Identify and build the capabilities that will enable your company to achieve high sustained profitability in your target strategic group; and (3) **Manage:** Develop your organization to enable your managers to seamlessly coordinate to meet your chosen customers' diverse and rapidly evolving needs.

This shift, in turn, requires much more granular profit information—in essence, a full P&L on every transaction—and a shift to an organization that can create and supply tightly coordinated packages of products and services aimed at a company's increasingly divergent market segments, and even individual customers.

In a nutshell, this is the key to success today. But most managers have been blinded by their experience in the fading Age of Mass Markets in which all revenues are assumed to be good and all costs are seen to be bad. This is the overriding management problem that our book is designed to address.

THE CURRENTS OF CHANGE

In Chapter 2, we describe in detail the currents of change that are ushering in the Age of Diverse Markets. Managers must understand and address these changes in repositioning their organizations. The five currents propelling this tsunami of change are these:

- **Rapid technology innovation:** Technology is revolutionizing industry after industry. Think about this: computers, mobile commerce, and even the internet were not in widespread use until the tail end of the prior century. Now smartphones have more computer power than was packed into the *Apollo* spacecraft. Drones and self-driving cars are on the near horizon, and less-known but equally revolutionary technologies like robotics and *additive manufacturing* (in which devices are "built" with powdered metal under heat treatment, rather than "sculpted" by metalworking parts) are capturing increasing market share. At the same time, artificial intelligence (AI) and machine learning are enabling managers to optimize their companies and customer relationships in powerful new ways—in many cases, getting every transaction right every time. All these are making the mass customization of products and services both possible and competitively necessary.

- **New buyer behavior:** New forms of buyer behavior are emerging, upending traditional sales and marketing relationships. In addition to the new internet retailers and distributors bringing powerful B2C processes like omnichannel retailing (which takes a lot of experience to perfect), disruptive companies and their millennial customers are moving toward higher levels of price transparency and service expectations. Managers responding to the former must offer carefully constructed sets of products and services, creating hard-to-follow packages, while managers facing the latter must create new forms of mass customization, especially involving highly integrated customer relationships. Managers have to create alternative approaches that the internet competitors and other disruptors cannot follow.

- **Channel boundaries breaking down:** In industry after industry, channel boundaries are blurring, and new players with new strategies and capabilities, including powerful network effects, are rising to dominance. While Amazon is the poster child for this, consider CH Robinson, a major national transportation carrier. For years, it moved most of the fruit flowing from the Pacific Northwest to markets around the nation. A few years ago, CH Robinson decided that since it had a dominant position moving fruit, which was a low-profit business, it should become a distributor and take ownership of the fruit, which is the high-profit part of the business. The company contracted with several major food companies to use their brands, and today if you buy Tropicana, Welch's, or Mott's fresh fruit, you are buying food that was distributed by CH Robinson.

- **New metrics and analytics:** In the Age of Mass Markets, product prices and cost to serve were relatively uniform from customer to customer. In today's Age of Diverse Markets, all this has changed: prices and cost to serve vary widely from customer to customer, and even within a customer. Transaction-based profit metrics and analytics allow managers to see exactly where they are making money and where they are losing it—and this detailed understanding of customer, product, and process profitability enables managers to create sharply focused and highly effective initiatives.

- **New company capabilities:** Companies have not been standing still either. Managers are making tremendous leaps forward in marketing, sales, and supply chain management. In marketing, Big Data enables managers to pinpoint evolving buyer patterns customer by customer and product by product in real time, allowing them to create compelling segment-specific "extended products" (that is, a full set of products and services that provide a unique customer value footprint, like Baxter's stockless system, in which physical products were delivered to the hospitals' internal points of use). In sales, electronic data interchange (EDI) offers important cost savings; customer relationship management (CRM) systems focus sales resources; and dedicated multicapability teams specialize in providing packages of products and related services to a company's respective profit segments. In supply chain management, the internet of things (IoT) and other digital innovations are speeding up responsiveness, while new forms of vendor-customer integration are allowing managers to build closer ties and switching costs with key customers.

BUILD YOUR STRATEGIC HIGH GROUND

The pervasive fear felt by so many incumbent company managers is rooted in the false assumption that the currents of change, of which Amazon is emblematic, will completely disrupt industries and leave no place to hide or prosper.

In fact, hundreds of studies of industry profitability in the industrial organization economics literature show the opposite. The most profitable overall industry configuration is one with a relatively small number of competitors, with each having a different strategy and each being very profitable—some serving small customers, others serving large customers; some offering arm's-length service, others building integrated customer relationships; and so on. In fact, contrary to popular belief, the industry model of a big winner and a lot of losers consistently provides low overall profits to all industry participants.

Today, the winning strategy is "choose your customer." For example, while Amazon is destroying many traditional brick-and-mortar businesses, the company has dominant strengths along only a few dimensions: arm's-length digital services mostly to small customers with prodigious network effects. This leaves a large, lucrative, open playing field.

In Chapter 5, we describe how Zara, a Spanish retailer, created a dominant strategy in "fast fashion" by **choosing** customers who wanted the latest styles; **aligning** their marketing, merchandising, and supply chain activities around those customers' needs; and **managing** their organization to produce this focused offering.

The overwhelmingly important problem for all too many managers in incumbent firms is that they are stuck in the obsolete strategic paradigm of the fading Age of Mass Markets in which the primary goal is to maximize all revenues while minimizing all costs. In essence, they are choosing all possible customers, which is no choice at all.

This objective is completely wrong today because transaction-based profit metrics and analytics consistently show that only a small portion of revenues are highly profitable (where the cost to serve aligns with the customer's profit potential). These metrics and analytics show that the cost to serve high-profit customers is often higher than average because giving them high service is a great investment.

In most companies today, traditional metrics, such as aggregate revenues, costs, and margins—which show managers *whether* their companies are profitable—actually prevent managers from understanding *where* they are profitable. While this granular profit knowledge was unnecessary in the Age of Mass Markets (with its homogeneous prices and costs), in today's increasingly heterogeneous markets, this is a life-or-death problem.

Continuing to act on the obsolete assumption that all revenues are good and all costs are bad leads all too many managers to dilute and waste resources trying to hold on to all of their business, rather than choosing their customers and focusing on building their high-profit, defensible business in their target strategic group. This is the single most important issue in business today, and most managers do not even see it.

THREE IMPERATIVES

How can managers choose their customers and build their strategic high ground? What information, processes, and organization do they need to compete effectively against the digital giants? The answer lies in the three imperatives that form the theme of this book.

Choose

In order to succeed against the digital giants and other aggressive competitors, you must have a different strategy rather than trying to beat them at their own game. To succeed against competitors with strategies similar to yours, you must get all the details of your business right.

In order to define a defensible strategic group that your company can dominate, three principles are critical:

- **It is all about customer value.** The customer value you create both positions you against your competitors and provides the basis for compensatory pricing. For example, Chapter 5 contains the section "Win the Customer Value War," which says to turn the price war into a customer value war, and when you have the lead, step on the gas. While the digital giants have some strong advantages, there is plenty of room left to create a unique customer value footprint that will provide long-term strategic dominance and sustained high profitability—just as Walmart is doing now with its healthcare initiative (providing healthcare and related services *in their stores*).

- **Strategy is defined by what you say no to.** If you treat all revenues as equally desirable, you don't have a strategy. Strategy is about choices. Amazon competes along only a few dimensions in which it can provide a unique customer value footprint with strong network effects, and it avoids strategies where it can't provide unique customer value. The same is true of Walmart, Facebook, FedEx, Apple, and all the rest. Most importantly, if you don't have a detailed understanding of where your business is making and losing money (through transaction-based profit metrics and analytics), you can't select the right strategic group that will provide you with high sustained profit growth, even in the face of massive changes that are transforming the industrial landscape. This is the root cause of so many companies failing today.

- **You have to be best at something.** If you are not the best at creating a winning customer value footprint and focusing your resources on developing your target market, you are destined to be overtaken by a competitor who is. This is a moving target—the pace of change is accelerating, so fast response is an increasingly critical competitive advantage. If you are not constantly improving your customer value footprint and refining your customer targeting, you will be left in the dust by competitors who are. Just look at Amazon's new initiatives to place Alexa in hospitals and manufacturers. The ability to innovate your customer value footprint at high speed must be a core capability of your company—but it is impossible to do if your company is targeting all revenues indiscriminately. This is what separates the winners from the losers.

Align

Alignment is the second imperative. You have to identify and build the capabilities that will enable your company to achieve high sustained profitability in your target strategic group. This has three core components that must be tightly coordinated and not managed independently:

- **Products:** This book explains the process of developing effective extended products. These can range from delivering products directly to hospital clinics through vendor-managed inventory, to providing well-specified customer-specific programs of maintenance for precision ball bearings, to posting product review and Q&A sections on the digital giants' websites. Extended products are an essential part of an effective strategic response to digital giants and other disruptive competitors that can address only a specific dimension of the available market. After all, how could an internet competitor replace Baxter's deep relationship with the head nurses?

- **Customers:** As markets become increasingly heterogeneous, customer needs are fragmenting. In the Age of Mass Markets, companies could provide a narrow range of products with minimal customization services to the entire market. Today, companies must understand the needs of specific segments of their markets for integrated products and services, and they must be able to deliver packages of well-targeted, well-coordinated products and services to each segment. This requires focused initiatives in selecting and managing accounts, and not simply providing a homogeneous set of products to as many customers as possible—or trying to defend against the digital giants by digitally offering arm's-length products to the same customers. As your product-service packages get more complex, price optimization must become much more sophisticated, reflecting not just price maximization but also in many cases trading price for operating-cost reduction.

- **Relationships (supply chain and channels):** As customer needs get increasingly diverse and customer integration becomes more critical, supply chains must become more diverse and specialized as well. Companies need to develop multiple parallel supply chains reflecting the growing disparity in customer importance, product criticality, degree of integration, and other factors. This is an extremely efficient configuration, and it creates a hard-to-follow competitive advantage. Similarly, as companies open more channels (that is, forums through which companies engage their customers) ranging from stores, to direct sales, to distributor sales, to internet sales, companies can achieve critical differentiation by using omnichannel management to coordinate their channel offerings and employing artificial intelligence and machine learning to anticipate and shape customer buyer behavior.

The objective of strategy is to aim and align the company. The choice of a strategic group aims the company, and the alignment imperative ensures that the three core areas—products, customers, and relationships—are not only managed well but are also tightly coordinated to devise and offer the right sets of integrated products and services to the right customer segments in the right way. As markets become increasingly heterogeneous, this becomes a critical issue for companies. Without transaction-based profit metrics and analytics, managers cannot identify and target the right strategic group and align their resources and activities to capture their focus market segments and customers.

This book provides essential advice at two levels: things that you *have* to do to compete with the digital giants and other aggressive new competitors, and things that you *should* do to maximize your profitability within your chosen strategic paradigm.

Manage

Organizational effectiveness is the third imperative. As markets become more fragmented and heterogeneous, managers must coordinate in diverse, segment-oriented, or even customer-specific, teams to understand and meet increasingly divergent customer needs.

In a recent MIT supply chain management executive program class, Jonathan started by declaring that focusing on improving the efficiency of your supply chain was the worst thing that a supply chain manager could do. The class, which included about 80 top executives from the United States, Europe, and Asia, gasped in response.

After a lengthy pause, Jonathan asked, "Are all of your orders equally profitable to serve?" The participants shook their heads. "What determines which orders you have to fulfill?" The answer was simply that once a sales rep booked an order, it had to be fulfilled. "So, what determines which orders the sales reps book?" The answer from the class was that the sales reps were paid to bring in any business that added to revenues, regardless of the profitability—in other words, that was how they "chose" their customers. The bottom line was that the cost to serve was someone else's problem—and that someone else was sitting in the MIT executive classroom.

Jonathan then explained that he opens his graduate supply chain management and strategy course by asking the class, "What do you think is the objective of this course?"

Usually, the students politely answer, "To teach us supply chain management, of course," to which he responds, "No, it is to make you *effective* supply chain managers—and if you waste resources fulfilling unprofitable orders, you are not being effective. Your job is to link with your counterparts in sales, marketing, and finance and use transaction-based profit metrics and analytics to determine which orders will be profitable—even in the presence of digital giants and other aggressive competitors—and then structure your supply chain to fulfill them. This is an issue of choosing your customer: clearly identifying your target strategic group and teaming with your colleagues to align all of your activities to achieve that objective."

Organizational effectiveness has two dimensions: business processes and organization structure.

BUSINESS PROCESSES

In Chapter 3, we discuss the four cornerstone business processes that are essential for success:

- **Strategic positioning and risk management:** Transaction-based profit metrics and analytics enable managers to evaluate and reshape their companies' competitive positioning and risk profile as the currents of change transform their respective industries.

- **Profit river management:** *Profit rivers*, major segments of a company that have similar management imperatives, are a company's prime sources of profit or loss. Typically, they have three characteristics: (1) each is important, (2) each is relatively homogeneous and somewhat different from the others, and (3) each has a natural cross-functional management constituency.

- **Transition initiative management:** These initiatives are essential in repositioning a company for increased profitability and success in its transforming industry.

- **Profit-driven process management:** Transaction-based profit information is necessary to maximize the performance of a company's core set of business processes that are essential for managing customer, product, and supply chain activities.

Together, these four cornerstone business processes enable managers to maximize their companies' performance in the near term, in the long term, and in the transition period in between.

ORGANIZATION STRUCTURE: MANAGING AT THE RIGHT LEVEL

One of the most thorny and difficult management problems is managing a level too low, as we explain in Chapter 8. This occurs when a manager is promoted and spends an inordinate amount of time tuning up the work of his or her subordinates. Not only do the subordinates lose the opportunity to improve but, more importantly, the manager's new work does not get done

In the Age of Mass Markets, managing by tuning up subordinates' work was in fact the most important thing a manager could do. In that era, markets were stable and homogeneous, and most interfunctional coordination took place at the top of the company in periodic planning sessions.

Managers were largely left with the task of tuning up their subordinates' technical skills at maximizing revenues or minimizing costs.

Today, the situation is completely different. Markets are increasingly fragmented, diverse, and fast changing. The key to success is to form multi-capability teams that can create and produce sophisticated packages of products and services to meet the needs of respective target segments and even individual customers. This need to respond fast enough to emerging or changing customer needs must be every manager's prime focus. The company's organization and processes have to foster this mindset. This is one of the most important keys to success in the Age of Diverse Markets

In essence, companies today need to be managed at three levels: top management, upper management, and operating management.

Top Management

Since the time frame for managing major change in companies today is about three to five years, top management's highest priority is to design the company as it will need to be in three to five years and to bolt a transition plan in place—and not to focus inordinately on tuning up the current day-to-day business. As we have seen, the biggest challenge facing companies is to choose a strategy that will enable the company to achieve industry dominance and accelerating profit growth for a decade or more. The parallel issue is to form an aligned organization composed of multicapability teams that can discern and fulfill the evolving needs of the company's increasingly fragmented, diverse, rapidly changing target customers. This is the essence of top management's job.

This is a particularly challenging task for most top managers who have spent their careers in functional stand-alone departments of mass market companies, and it is an underlying reason why so many major incumbent firms are failing to keep up with newer competitors.

Upper Management

The upper management team, primarily directors and some vice presidents, should be the locus of both ongoing strategic positioning and alignment. In our experience, this is best accomplished through a multi-capability committee, which we call the Managing Profitable Growth (MPG) Committee. Responsible for successfully putting the company's strategy into action, the MPG Committee must be furnished with regular profit scans using transaction-based profit metrics and analytics. With an understanding of the company's internal profit landscape, these managers can gauge the impact of the currents of change on the company's segments in terms of current and prospective strategic defensibility and sustainable profitability. This forms the basis for building and managing a transition plan, including forming and overseeing multicapability teams to address the evolving needs of target segments and customers.

Operating Management

The sales and operating managers run the company's day-to-day sales and operations. In the Age of Mass Markets, this meant focusing on a single department, like sales or distribution. But in the Age of Diverse Markets, this means teaming with one's counterparts from other functional areas to design and provide the integrated package of products and services that will meet the target segments' and customers' needs. The difference could not be more marked, and communications and coordination throughout the company must undergo major changes to adapt successfully.

•   •   •

The enormous chasm between managers' jobs at all three levels in the fading Age of Mass Markets versus the current Age of Diverse Markets means that the Manager of the Future has to have a very different skill set, and even personality to succeed.

THE MANAGER OF THE FUTURE: VALUE ENTREPRENEUR

In the past, managers were more or less technical specialists with single-dimension capabilities. The caricature is that sales reps were "lone sharks swimming in the ocean," while marketing managers sat in conference rooms poring over broad-market statistics and focus group results to design products, and supply chain managers were largely confined to their warehouses ensuring error-free shipments.

Today, all of that has changed. Each manager needs a base of broad multidisciplinary technical skills, but more importantly, he or she needs deep insight into understanding evolving customer needs. After all, if a company does what a customer requests, it is a good supplier; but if the company does what the customer really needs (even if the customer does not see it yet), it is a long-term strategic partner. And once a customer team understands customer needs, it must be very skilled in change management—that is, managing change within the customer—and in coordinating in unique and dynamic ways to meet evolving customer needs.

It all starts with choosing your customer, or, as we put it, selecting your strategic group and then aligning and organizing your functional capabilities to meet your diverse and rapidly changing customer needs.

The Manager of the Future must be adept at what we call Value Entrepreneurship, which we define as teaming with peer managers to constantly push the envelope of the company's customer value footprint in its diverse target market segments in a tight but flexible way. We explain this in Chapter 9.

This profile has enormous implications for management education, training, and career tracking. The book describes this emerging need in detail, and in the process it provides a portrait of the Manager of the Future and a concrete program for managers to develop their skills and experience to succeed in today's Age of Diverse Markets.

The ultimate purpose of this book is to enable managers at all levels—both current and prospective managers—to understand how to manage in today's revolutionary business era, and to give them a clear, practical pathway to success.

THINGS TO THINK ABOUT

1. What competitive pressures over the next three to five years are causing you to reevaluate your business?

2. Have you selected your customers strategically in light of your new competitive threats?

3. Are you still trying to compete on your traditional strength?

4. Have you identified and prioritized the transformational resources you will need to win in your new environment?

PART II

CHOOSE YOUR CUSTOMER

2

NAVIGATE THE CURRENTS OF CHANGE

Sunday, December 7, 1941. Admiral Chester Nimitz was attending a concert in Washington, DC. He was paged and told there was a phone call for him. When he answered, he heard the voice of President Franklin Delano Roosevelt on the phone.

He told Admiral Nimitz that he (Nimitz) would now be commander of the Pacific Fleet. Admiral Nimitz flew to Hawaii to assume command of the Pacific Fleet. He landed at Pearl Harbor on Christmas Eve, 1941. There was a spirit of despair, dejection, and defeat, as if the United States had already lost the war.

On Christmas Day, 1941, Admiral Nimitz was given a boat tour of the destruction wrought on Pearl Harbor. Big sunken battleships and navy vessels cluttered the waters. As the tour boat returned to dock, the young helmsman of the boat asked, "Well, Admiral, what do you think after seeing all this destruction?"

Admiral Nimitz's reply shocked everyone. "The Japanese made three of the biggest mistakes an attack force could ever make, or God was taking care of America. Which do you think it was?"

HOW TO WIN THE BATTLE
AND LOSE THE WAR

Shocked and surprised, the helmsman asked, "What do you mean by saying the Japanese made three of the biggest mistakes an attack force could ever make?"

Nimitz explained:

Mistake 1: "The Japanese attacked on Sunday morning. Nine out of ten crewmen of those ships were ashore on leave. If those same ships had been lured to sea and been sunk, we would have lost 38,000 men, instead of 3,800."

Mistake 2: "When the Japanese saw all those battleships lined up in a row, they got so carried away sinking those battleships that they never once bombed our dry docks opposite those ships. If they had destroyed our dry docks, we would have had to tow every one of those ships to the mainland to be repaired.

"As it is now, they are in shallow water, and they can be raised. One tug can pull them over to the dry docks, and we can have them repaired and at sea by the time we could have towed them to the mainland. And I already have crews ashore anxious to man those ships."

Mistake 3: "Every drop of fuel in the Pacific theater of war is on top of the ground in storage tanks five miles away over that hill. One attack plane could have strafed those tanks and destroyed our fuel supply."

"That's why I say the Japanese made three of the biggest mistakes an attack force could make, or God was taking care of America."

Whether this story is factual or merely a very compelling urban legend, it offers important strategic lessons that are critically relevant in today's Age of Diverse Markets.

STRATEGIC PERSPECTIVE

We thought about this anecdote during a recent meeting when we were reviewing a company's situation with its CEO.

A competitor had signed an agreement with a digital giant to resell its products on the giant's website. The company's VP of marketing argued that signing a similar agreement with a digital giant would give the company a powerful new channel to reach more customers and it would lower its cost of sales—which in turn would enable it to lower its prices. What should the company do?

The seemingly obvious answer was to match the competitor so as not to lose any market share. The market had been changing rapidly, with powerful new competitors and changing customer behavior. The competitor had indeed made tactical gains that raised concerns. But it was not at all clear that simply following the competitor would produce a long-term strategic win.

The real question was whether this potential move would win the battle at the expense of losing the war. Would it provide a long-term strategic advantage, or would it merely embed the company in a never-ending series of price wars? What would Admiral Nimitz do?

In our discussion, three problems became clear: (1) At best, by signing on with a digital reseller, the company would only achieve parity with the competitor. (2) At worst, the digital giant would gain a deep understanding of the company's products and customers, potentially setting up the reseller as a voracious competitor that could offer the company's best products directly to its best customers—cutting the company out of the process. (3) The company didn't have the scale and experience to make its own digital capabilities world-class.

Instead, the CEO decided to explore other strategic directions that would position the company for strategic dominance and long-term profitability. As the hockey great Wayne Gretsky famously said, "Skate to where the puck is going, not where it has been."

In the course of the discussion, we developed several potentially viable strategic alternatives. The CEO assigned a small team the task of spending a few weeks with several customers to investigate how the company could create a new value footprint that would be meaningful and defensible against the digital giants and other new competitors.

Working with their customer counterparts, the team developed a set of services to help the customers set and dynamically manage their branch inventories. This was an especially critical issue for their customers in this fast-changing industry. At the beginning of the product life cycle, it was important to quickly determine what was selling strongly in particular branches, and at the end of the life cycle, it was necessary to avoid inventory markdowns.

The management team had the insight and discipline to step back and make a strategic assessment of the currents of change, and not just make tactical changes to respond to immediate competitive threats. Admiral Nimitz would have been proud!

What's especially important about this situation, and so many others like it, is that the rush of events—whether it's concerns about keeping up with a competitor's tactics or, conversely, enjoying the satisfaction of tactical gains—can essentially blind a company's management team to the broader, more subtle opportunities to develop a creative strategy that will position it to win in its transformed industry.

Paradoxically, the broader the industry change taking place, the greater the opportunity to win big by positioning into the new environment—in other words, skating to where the puck will be. Conversely, companies that focus on tuning up their long-standing tactics and business processes will quickly fall further and further behind. In today's Age of Diverse Markets, winning the war is the top management imperative.

Managers often feel they don't have time to concentrate systematically on their deeper, more value-laden opportunities because they are so busy trying to keep up in the tactical battles. They are frustrated that they do not have the right metrics and analytics to identify, prioritize, and harvest their most important strategic opportunities, so they are left with the task of choosing among fragmented and often function-specific projects that bubble up from departmental managers.

In short, most managers instinctively focus on how to win the battle, rather than how to win the war of staying on top as their industry transforms. They are so focused on their near-term Age of Mass Markets key performance indicators (KPIs), like broad-based sales growth and cost reductions, that they lose the opportunity to build a lasting, winning position in their industry.

This chapter is about understanding the currents of change that are transforming every industry. The next chapter explains how to create the cornerstone management processes that will enable you to accelerate your profitability and reposition your company to succeed in your transformed industry.

Companies now are at a crucial pivot point. The time frame for paradigmatic change is three to five years, from conception to development to implementation to fruition. Today, managers have time to rebuild their strategies and operations to succeed in their changing industries. For most companies, next year will almost be too late to start the process.

THE MAKING OF AN ERA

On rare occasions, a relatively small number of underlying currents of change converge into a single powerful force, changing the fundamental nature of business and completely altering the context and strategic imperatives of companies. This is called a *paradigm shift*.

The Age of Mass Markets was created in the late 1800s and early 1900s when rail, water, and road transportation enabled local markets to integrate into national mass markets. This agglomeration of volume converged with innovations in manufacturing, marketing, and distribution—like assembly line production; mass media like newspapers, radio, and broadcast television; and national networks of distributors—to create massive economies of scale. In this context, the most important strategic imperative was to get big.

All this began to change a few decades ago. The change was largely driven by technology. Computers came into widespread use, the internet was developed, and both wireless networks and narrowcast technologies like cable TV were deployed. These innovations accelerated companies' ability to reach out directly to customers and microsegment markets, and to accumulate data so that they could microtarget customers. Manufacturing innovations like small-batch production, robotics, process automation, and additive manufacturing broke down economies of scale, enabling companies to produce niche products and services targeted at individual segments and even at individual customers.

The digital giants were born in this era. Using data from every click and developing social networks, Facebook, Amazon, Google, Apple, and others created innovations that personalized direct customer sales, transforming B2C markets. Today, they are shifting focus to B2B markets, the last bastion of the Age of Mass Markets.

In parallel, a generation of millennial buyers grew up with strong digital capabilities and an expectation of increasing mass customization in products and selling. In response, traditional channel structures broke down, with manufacturers bypassing distributors and with powerful B2C and other innovative companies entering B2B businesses, often with sophisticated new AI and machine-learning capabilities. At the same time, companies like Baxter took advantage of the new technologies to develop strong integrative ties with their premier customers.

These changes upended the homogeneous price and cost to serve of mass market companies, as both prices and cost to serve began to vary by customer and even within customers. This required a new set of metrics—transaction-based profit metrics and analytics—that matched each increment of revenue (each order line) with the cost of producing it. Companies required new business processes and organization structures to manage the diversity of products and markets that they faced.

While getting big was the strategic imperative in the Age of Mass Markets, the strategic imperative of the Age of Diverse Markets is to adroitly manage complexity. Today, successful companies must be expert at **choosing** their customer, **aligning** their resources, and **managing** their organization to target and meet the needs of the most lucrative, defensible parts of the emerging market in their transforming industry.

CURRENTS OF CHANGE

The objective of this chapter is to present a brief summary of the currents of change that are transforming business today. This is important because managers must not only position their companies for success today but also reposition their business, if necessary, for future success at the same time. Figure 2.1 presents an overview of the forces that are transforming business today.

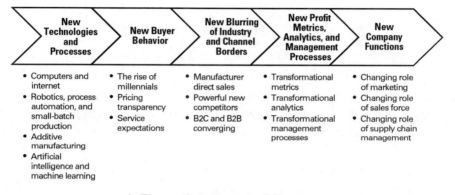

Figure 2.1 Currents of Change

New Technologies and Processes

Technology is always changing, creating new opportunities and risks. The action issue for managers is gauging and managing the impact of these changes on your company's current and future profitability. Transaction-based profit metrics and analytics are the keys to developing this critical understanding.

Computers and the Internet

Today, virtually all companies are involved in "digital transformation." Generally, this involves replacing semi-manual processes, like accounts receivable processing, with automation, and it also involves supplementing traditional processes, like customer relationship management (CRM), with digital tools like SalesForce, or developing new capabilities, like digital channels. The possibilities are endless.

The key question managers must answer is this: which capabilities are most important today? Four areas stand out:

- Supporting integration with your Profit Peak customers

- Enabling efforts to convert your Profit Drain customers into Profit Peaks, usually by improving a specific operating-cost deficiency like product mix or overly frequent ordering

- Reducing the cost to serve your Profit Desert customers, generally by automating the customer service interface

- Using your transaction-based profit metrics and analytics to model the currents of change in order to develop your transition strategy and to identify and mitigate related risks as you reposition your company to capture the strategic high ground in your transformed industry

For a select set of companies today, like Facebook and Apple, developing a *platform business* (that is, anchoring an ecosystem of customers and providers of complementary products and services) with strong network effects is a winning strategy. However, there are many other paths to lasting high-profit strategic growth.

Robotics, Process Automation, and Small-Batch Production

Robotics have already transformed a number of industries, ranging from manufacturing to telecommunications to service provision. For example, robotics and related automation have led to a massive capital-for-labor substitution in manufacturing, resulting in a significant on-shoring of US manufacturing capacity. In parallel, innovations in process automation and small-batch manufacturing have broken down the economies of scale in several industries.

An important application of robotics has been in supply chain operations. For example, Amazon bought Kiva, a state-of-the-art robotics company that brought robotic capabilities to the warehouse floor, giving Amazon the economic efficiencies to scale its operations rapidly and broadly, which in turn allowed it to expand its business at a rapid rate.

Today, robots are already remarkably inexpensive and dexterous. A robot under human remote-control operation can already fold sheets, fluff pillows, and make dinner. The only missing ingredient is an AI "brain" to replace the human operator, and this capability is developing fast.

Additive Manufacturing

Additive manufacturing, also called *3-D printing*, is a process of "building" an item by shaping a powdery, malleable substance (either metal or non-metal) to a specified design and hardening it, usually by treating it with heat. This contrasts with traditional *subtractive manufacturing*, in which a tool removes material from a piece of raw material to "sculpt" a finished or semifinished product.

Additive manufacturing offers several advantages over traditional subtractive manufacturing, including (1) the ability to join the manufacturing process to computer-aided design for rapid prototyping and testing; (2) highly flexible production schedules, with the possibility of very short production runs; and (3) the ability to produce pieces with complex geometry without the need to join multiple parts into the finished product.

Present estimates of additive manufacturing market penetration cluster around 5 to 10 percent of the market, with noteworthy penetration in areas as diverse as aircraft engine parts, medical device parts, and toy parts. As a relatively new technology, there is a general expectation that with experience and volume, costs will decline quickly and applications will increase as well. There is a consensus, however, that simple, high-volume, mass-produced parts will continue to be produced using subtractive manufacturing.

If it turns out, as initial evidence seems to indicate, that customers use additive manufacturing to self-manufacture complex, high-value products and parts, it may well be the case that a supplier's Profit Peak customers and products will be impacted disproportionately. For example, if 15 percent of a supplier's business is generated from Profit Peak customers and products, and the company experiences a 6 percent overall business reduction due to additive manufacturing, but two-thirds of this reduction occurs in the Profit Peak segment, the company's profitability will be reduced by over 25 percent.

Artificial Intelligence and Machine Learning

This is an increasingly important and vital capability. In essence, artificial intelligence (AI) and machine learning are mathematical processes that enable a vast number of rapidly changing factors to be analyzed and optimized instantaneously and with extreme effectiveness.

Today, companies are primarily using AI and machine learning toward the objective of *maximizing revenue*. The big untapped opportunity, however, is applying these techniques toward the objective of *maximizing profits*. This has not been previously possible because a machine-learning algorithm can optimize only for a quantity that can be measured and fed back into the algorithm, and transaction-based profit information has not been available until now.

For example, if a company has thousands of customers buying thousands of products across several channels, and many customers' purchase patterns are evolving, artificial intelligence and machine-learning techniques can calculate what the company should offer to each customer each time in order to maximize the likelihood of profitable growth. As the customer population responds to these offers and their responses are fed back into the algorithms, the mathematical techniques will "change themselves" to become more effective.

These techniques will result in true mass customization of customer marketing and customer service.

New Buyer Behavior

Buyer behavior is transforming in fundamental ways, creating a major impact on all areas of business. The ubiquity of personal computers, mobile devices, and the internet, coupled with a proliferation of readily available, focused applications, has bred a generation of customers who simply assume a much greater level of information availability and customized services than previous generations expected.

The Rise of Millennials
The rise of millennials has led to completely new forms of buyer behavior. Millennials are avid internet users, which has created compelling new value points, like Amazon's product reviews, as well as direct ordering from manufacturers and out-of-region distributors.

Increasingly, millennials are bringing this mentality and behavior to business purchasing. A recent UPS Survey of Industrial Buying Dynamics found that one-third of industrial buyers were millennials and that they greatly valued choice, convenience, and customization. They had a great desire to experiment with different ways of conducting business electronically and were very willing to source products overseas. They invested significant time and effort into online research, gathering information from social media channels and mobile apps—and they tended to cut out the middlemen and buy directly from manufacturers and online marketplaces.

The survey found that most industrial suppliers were out of step with millennials' evolving requirements and needed to eliminate the traditionally drastic distinction between B2B and B2C best practices.

Pricing Transparency

Millennials are conditioned to expect price visibility from their internet experiences. This is a very big issue. The classic ways to combat pricing transparency (and the resulting price wars) are by offering discounts based on product mix and volume and by crafting combinations of products and services into hard-to-compare packages. To an extent, these selling tactics are still effective, but the internet now offers powerful, accessible alternatives such as unbundled online discounts and Q&A reviews, both of which provide service equivalents.

Some services, including various forms of supplier-customer integration like Baxter's vendor-managed inventory, still have the capability to knit nearly unbreakable bonds between a supplier and customer. However, supply chain integration and other forms of intercompany coordination are much more difficult to develop than it may appear at first glance. They require great care in qualifying accounts, partner selection, and relationship development and management. This will leave lagging companies vulnerable to more sophisticated competitors.

Service Expectations

The shift to millennials' buyer behavior has led some sophisticated companies to develop dual marketing and service capabilities. They continue to offer traditional sales rep calls, order cycles, and support for older purchasers. However, they join this with internet-oriented sales and marketing programs, coupled with rapid service, product feature customization, and product selection suggestions for millennials.

As an example of this evolving duality in buyer purchase behavior, we recall participating in a meeting of major financial institution chief marketing officers. One speaker described how his firm, a forward-thinking retail pharmacy chain, had developed a millennial-oriented positioning that was essentially "health central," with integrated internet-based consumer health information, and on-site services and products.

The company complemented this powerful new capability with its traditional retail pharmacy offerings and promotions, appealing to both the emerging new millennial consumers and their traditional customers. As the traditional customers increasingly changed their buyer behavior toward new digital offerings, they had a comfortable transition path within their local pharmacy. The result: sales rose remarkably.

New Blurring of Industry and Channel Borders

As a result of technology developments and the emergence of millennial buyers, the strong walls that for years separated industries and channels are falling, blurring traditional roles, and bringing powerful new competitors like Wayfair and Google with unique, well-honed capabilities, often based on strong network effects, into direct competition with traditional retailers, distributors, and even manufacturers (through their growing private-label offerings).

Manufacturer Direct Sales

Many manufacturers have had minor direct sales functions, typically to major accounts. In the past, these were limited by the threat that powerful distributors, who handled the bulk of their business, would retaliate and favor competitors. Today, this bulwark of distributor power is breaking down, as manufacturers are acquiring more power and establishing direct channels to more and more of their customers.

Across the board, company after company is establishing the capability of selling direct to its customers. The internet has made this fundamental transformation possible. In fact, many customers actually prefer to get information directly from manufacturer websites and to order directly from the producer. Many producers have websites, marketing materials, and direct customer service capabilities that far surpass those of traditional distributors. For example, powered by this new demand, Nike, Apple, and others have even established direct retail captives.

Powerful New Competitors

Amazon, with its disruptive business model, is the poster child for the internet-based blurring of industry and channel boundaries. Amazon, along with a host of similar competitors, is winning not by simply doing better what traditional sellers always have done but rather by doing completely new things that traditional retailers and distributors are hard-pressed to do.

For example, Amazon can bring its very sophisticated consumer capabilities to industrial customers in several ways. The company has developed powerful customer interfaces that drive customer traffic through ordering and customer service in extraordinarily convenient ways. These capabilities range from Alexa's voice or image ordering, to Amazon Go stores with their advanced scanning systems that enable purchasing without checkout, to effective cluster analytics that can create offers to customers based on their past and evolving purchase patterns ("If you liked that, try this").

If Amazon were to transform these advanced ordering systems and install them in business customers' stockrooms and other purchasing areas, it would be very difficult for all but the strongest, most sophisticated distributors to follow.

Similarly, Amazon is now offering two-hour delivery service to its Prime customers in many densely populated areas. If Amazon were to create mixed truckloads of consumer and business products, it would have the density to dramatically increase its route profitability, even with two-hour delivery windows. In terms of pricing, the company could offer its business products at reduced margins, and it could make up the profits on the consumer goods, or vice versa.

B2C and B2B Converging

The inexorable convergence of B2B and B2C is blurring formerly separate traditional channels and market segments. This creates huge new opportunities and competitive threats to traditional incumbent sellers.

Most sellers are developing the capability to offer their products and support services in a few different ways, often through direct sales, telesales, and internet selling, generally employing the same distribution channels to fulfill orders from any sales channel. In traditional companies, these channels are generally managed separately.

The most effective way to manage them, however, is by using the truly integrated processes of *omnichannel management*, which is another name for the ability to offer sales and related services on an integrated basis to customers through different forums like brick-and-mortar stores, the internet, direct sales, and telesales.

The key to successful omnichannel management is to follow—and guide—your Profit Peak customers from channel to channel as they pursue their interests, and not just to manage the offerings of individual channels on a largely stand-alone basis.

Most sellers have little experience with true omnichannel management; ordering capabilities and product listings are their primary offerings. Experienced B2C companies, like L.L.Bean and others, on the other hand, have invested large sums to develop extremely sophisticated systems that bridge store and internet, track and profile their customers, and move them from channel to channel based on their evolving consumer behavior.

Omnichannel management is also critical in managing your accounts. In fact, in one major retailer with whom we worked, over 60 percent of the accounts were Profit Desert customers, compared to about 15 percent who were Profit Peak customers. The problem was that buried within the Profit Desert accounts were a number of customers (perhaps 20 percent) that had the potential to grow to Profit Peak customers, but they were largely ignored because there were so many small accounts that the company had no way to identify them. As a default, the company treated all Profit Desert customers in an arm's-length, one-size-fits-all manner.

The solution was for the retailer to profile its Profit Peak accounts using a quick, inexpensive, internet survey. Armed with the survey results, the retailer began to systematically probe its Profit Desert customers using social media and digital marketing, searching for behavior that indicated that a customer had the potential to become a Profit Peak customer. When a Profit Desert customer was identified as a potential Profit Peak, the customer was given an intensive program of omnichannel promotions to begin to increase and shape its buying pattern. Moving even 10 to 20 percent of the Profit Desert customers up to Profit Peak profit levels had the potential to almost double the company's net profits.

This whole area—profiling and shaping customer behavior as it constantly evolves across omnichannel networks—is a prime application for artificial intelligence and machine learning, creating even more competitive advantage for those who can develop these advanced capabilities.

New Profit Metrics, Analytics, and Management Processes

Transaction-based profit metrics and analytics, along with profit management processes, enable managers to identify, prioritize, and implement the *profit levers* (that is, systematic actions that improve profitability) that will be discussed throughout this book. These powerful new capabilities enable companies to successfully adapt to the tremendous changes that are upending their markets.

This section discusses transaction-based profit metrics and analytics. Chapter 3 explains the profit management processes that translate this information into results.

One of the most common problems in managing profitable growth is that some companies develop a set of profit metrics (often with incorrect broad cost allocations, rather than transaction-based profit metrics) and simply assume that their managers will use those metrics to look up the profitability of their customers and products and do the right things. This is a major error.

Profit metrics are a starting point, but they are not useful without a set of powerful, intuitive profit analytics and profitable growth processes. In this chapter and the next, we describe a set of analytics and processes that are custom designed and field-tested to convert profit metrics into actionable information, producing consistently high levels of sustained profitable growth.

Transformational Metrics

Accounting courses teach that there are two types of accounting: financial reporting and management control. The objective of financial accounting is to report accurately the performance of a firm, or a major part of the firm. The objective of management control is to give managers profit information that is essential for their decision-making.

The problem, mentioned earlier, is that financial reporting information is aggregated; all the revenues are combined, either in total or in broad categories, and the same is true for costs.

Because financial reporting information is so well curated—and was so widely used for management control decisions in the Age of Mass Markets—managers simply assume that they should continue using it as the basis for management control.

In response to the need for profit metrics that would accommodate the wide variance in prices and costs, we created the transaction-based profit metrics and analytics we mentioned earlier based on an all-in P&L, which we call a *profit stack*, for *each and every transaction (invoice line)*, which is necessary because the transaction is the financial atom of the company.

Once the transactions for a period are costed into profit stacks, they are embedded in a powerful data structure that allows a manager to see, at any level of detail or aggregation, exactly where the company is making money, where it is losing money, and why each occurs. Armed with this information, a manager can identify profit levers and then create processes and initiatives to get more high-profit business and reverse the losses on profit-draining business.

The Problem with Gross Margin

Our extensive work with transaction-based profit metrics and analytics has shown us that gross margin (GM), one of the most widely used management metrics, is seldom correlated with net profits. This common management assumption is an artifact of the Age of Mass Markets, and it prevents most companies and financial analysts from making effective, profit-maximizing decisions.

The problem with gross margin as a predictor of net profits can be seen in the example provided in Figure 2.2. The conclusion: gross margin does not predict net profit. There is no logical function that could relate these factors.

	Revenues ($000)	Gross Margin ($000)	Net Profit ($000)
Rep 1	1,349	346	216
Rep 2	664	131	(25)
Rep 3	2,773	328	64
Rep 4	3,920	556	217

Figure 2.2 Sales Rep Comparison Example
Note: The numbers used in this example are disguised
actual data from a very successful company.

Figure 2.3 demonstrates the same conclusion using different data. Here, we show data, which is relationally correct but highly disguised, from a very successful, well-run company. The vertical axis shows the net margin (NM)

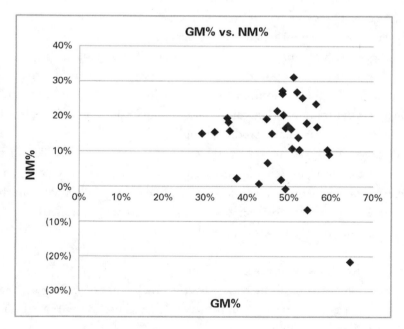

Figure 2.3 No Correlation Between Gross and Net Margins
Note: The numbers representing product categories are disguised
actual data from a very successful company.

of a set of product categories, while the horizontal axis shows the gross margin. The data points are the mapping of each product category by these dimensions.

If gross margin were correlated with net margin, we would expect to see the data points lining up in a pattern that resembled a straight line, with high gross margin and high net margin at one end, and low gross margin and low net margin at the other. Instead, the data points are scattered in a randomlike pattern.

There are two important reasons why gross margin does not predict net profits: (1) Several important sets of critical costs—sales and marketing costs, operating and supply chain costs, and overhead costs—are not included in the gross margin calculation, and these costs are decisive in today's business environment (that is, large *relative to net profit*, creating strong profit leverage) in which the cost to serve varies widely from customer to customer, and even within customers. (2) A fundamentally different metric, *revenue per line*, is a very important profit lever (because the cost of selling and distributing an order is dependent on the number of lines, not the number of units), but it is seldom tracked and managed.

Transaction-based profit metrics are necessary to understand the performance of highly customized transactions that are common in today's business environment. They can be cross-referenced in numerous dimensions, including customer, product, supply chain, and channel.

They will even show you exactly where a current of change, like a new competitor with omnichannel experience, will reduce your profits, and where a new capability like additive manufacturing will enable you to increase your profitability. Today, transaction-based net profit metrics make the difference between success and failure.

Transformational Analytics

Transaction-based profit metrics make possible a full range of profit analytics that are much more powerful, granular, and useful than traditional analytics.

Consider marketing as an example. The objective of traditional marketing analytics is to increase revenues. This may seem obvious, but some revenues are very profitable while others rapidly drain profits.

In contrast, transaction-based profit metrics and analytics enable companies to identify and target Profit Peak customers and products, again maximizing profitable growth—without sacrificing revenue growth rates. The same logic and process holds for sales reps, stores, branches, and every other element of a company's business.

This process creates a lot of profit leverage. For example, in many companies, increasing the number of Profit Peak customers by 10 to 15 percent, while converting 20 percent of the Profit Drain customers to Profit Peaks, will increase the company's overall net profits by surprisingly large amounts, often 50 percent or more.

In most companies today, this profitable core is very underresourced, both because Profit Peak customers are not complainers and because traditional mass market profit metrics make it impossible to identify them.

Cost Reduction

Cost reduction provides another landmark example of the power of transaction-based profit analytics. In virtually all supply chain projects, the objective is to reduce costs. The analytical process is to identify the costs that are above average and reduce them to at least average levels. What could be wrong with this?

The answer is that neither simply reducing higher-than-average costs nor reducing costs across the board will maximize profitability. The reason is that the Profit Peak customers are often more costly to serve—and rightly so because the extra customer service costs are a great investment.

Transformational Management Processes

We cannot emphasize strongly enough the importance of developing a set of ongoing management processes that regularly and systematically convert transaction-based profit metrics and analytics into systematic, ongoing programs of accelerated profitability. This is the subject of Chapter 3.

It is helpful to take a lesson from the quality process. Unless the concepts are systematically institutionalized, the process will not produce systematic results. In an important sense, managing profitable growth is analogous to the quality process. In transaction-based profit systems, every activity of the company is directly linked to one measure: profitability.

New Company Functions

Critical external factors are changing industries in fundamental ways and, in response, many companies are transforming their core functions of marketing, sales, and supply chain management.

Changing Role of Marketing

Accelerating improvements in social media and digital marketing are enabling sophisticated companies to precisely target their Profit Peak customers (and those Profit Desert customers with the potential to become Profit Peaks) and to promote the right product to the right customer at the right time.

Beyond this, social media and digital marketing are creating enormously powerful opportunities to offer extended products and mass customization, based both on sensing and shaping customer behavior on a transaction-by-transaction basis using AI, machine learning, and omni-channel management.

Changing Role of the Sales Force

Traditionally, sellers had a simple formula: employ a force of experienced sales reps deployed most often on a geographic basis. This was an artifact of the older-route sales process. The sales reps educated and supported customers, and they took orders.

Today's selling processes look nothing like the past ones. The most effective companies shape their account management processes to fit the needs of their profit segments. Profit Peak customers are served by dedicated multicapability teams skilled in change management and intercompany integration. Profit Drain customers are served by other dedicated multicapability teams experienced in identifying and rectifying cost-to-serve problems. Profit Desert customers, on the other hand, are served by automated process and menu offerings.

In parallel, electronic ordering, either through electronic data interchange (EDI) or through website ordering, has rapidly grown in volume and importance. In one particularly advanced company, over 60 percent of the orders arrive electronically.

Electronic ordering certainly offers lower order costs. However, it can produce hidden costs and cause other problems.

When a customer orders electronically, the distributor loses the advantage of constant customer touch through a rep's or a call center operator's relationship with the customer's purchasing counterpart. This strong bond is very important, and so is the opportunity to pick up trends and gossip that are critical to the sales process. In fact, in one internal distribution company study, management found that the delivery truck drivers had by far the best customer knowledge, and the order takers (not the sales reps) were second.

This inside knowledge and these warm relationships are essential to cross-selling and upselling products, to getting the customer to accept substitute products, and to managing the product mix while continuing to grow revenues.

The other disadvantage of employing electronic ordering is that the companies who do so lose the ability to manage demand (that is, the customer's order pattern). They have to react to the order pattern that comes to them without human contact, and in the process, they lose the all-important opportunity to reduce the frequency and volatility of orders. It turns out that this is one of the most important profit levers—one that is almost always unseen, unmeasured, unmanaged, and almost painless and costless for both the distributor and the customer to improve. Importantly, excessive small orders are costly not only for the vendor but also for *the customer*, who has to order, receive, put away, and distribute the product internally.

For example, we are aware of one example of a very well-run distributor whose sales reps were under pressure to install vending machines in as many customers' premises as possible. The sales reps told the customers that with vending machines, they would not have to carry much inventory because they could order replenishments frequently, even every day.

The result was an endless flood of small orders with the handling cost far higher than the gross margin. Yet because the revenue and gross margin rose substantially—these were the success metrics that the distributor watched—the sales reps were celebrated. This celebration lasted until the distributor's transaction-based profit metrics and analytics showed that the real *net profit* on this important segment of business was in fact a major loss.

The solution was simply to add clauses to the vending contracts limiting the replenishment ordering frequency to reasonable levels, which turned a major loss into a handsome net profit and reduced the customers' costs at the same time.

Another distributor developed this unlikely, but highly effective process: when they receive an electronic order from a Profit Peak customer, a customer service rep calls the customer to thank the customer and to scout for opportunities to cross-sell and upsell, as well as to manage the order timing.

Changing Role of Supply Chain Management

Supply chain management is transforming as radically as is sales. For years, supply chain managers focused largely on managing the physical operations within their facilities, including order taking, DC operations, inventory, replenishment, and related activities.

Today, all this is changing. Order taking, as we saw in the prior section, is migrating to electronic modes, chiefly EDI and internet, and DC operations are becoming both highly automated and commoditized. Increasingly, third-party logistics (3PL) capabilities are growing, rendering distributor internal operations expertise a nice-to-have rather than a core necessity.

However, supply chain activities are growing in very important areas.

Leading companies are increasingly integrating their supply chains with their Profit Peak customers. This requires that their supply chain managers have both sophisticated skills at scattered-site management and close alignment with their internal sales and marketing counterpart managers for account qualification, account selection, and account management. We will discuss this much more extensively in Chapter 7.

Another area of contemporary distributor supply chain growth is in the materials management aspects of supply chain management—primarily directing and managing product flow patterns. This requires building very close ties between supply chain managers and their counterpart product and/or category managers in order to determine the optimum flow of products through procurement, through the DC network, and onward to the customers.

Demand management is a third area of increasing supply chain importance. We earlier described the very important opportunity to increase order size and reduce order volatility. But again, we note that this critically important profit lever, like so many others, is almost always unseen, unmeasured, and unmanaged, unless the company utilizes transaction-based profit metrics and analytics.

STRATEGIC CORNERSTONES

Today, the powerful change currents outlined above are creating a cyclone of revolutionary change in virtually every industry.

These currents are systematically transforming every company's profit landscape. The key to success is to project these changes onto your customer and product base in order to identify and secure your *future* Profit Peaks, to avoid your *future* Profit Drains, and to minimize your *future* Profit Deserts. The next chapter explains how to do this.

In light of the tsunami that is disrupting industry after industry, managers have three essential strategic cornerstones:

- **Choose your customer—both current and future.** Focus on winning the war. Understand that your company needs paradigmatic change, not tactical improvements, and insist that this mentality permeate your whole company.

- **Align around new capabilities.** The time frame for change is three to five years at best before more aggressive, astute competitors—or competitors with activist investors at the helm—take your profitable core. Next year may be too late to start planning and doing *profit-showcase projects* (that is, opportunities to explore new innovations and "learn by doing"—like the initial Baxter project described in Chapter 1).

- **Manage your transition.** The highest priority is to double down on your profitable core, your Profit Peaks—the customers, products, supply chain, and channels that provide virtually all your profits—and to build and secure your *future* Profit Peaks.

Turning around Profit Drains is helpful, but your highest priority is securing and aggressively growing a lasting set of Profit Peaks.

Together, these will enable you to navigate the currents of change and chart a course to success, both in today's business and in your transforming industry. This will ensure that you are the master of your fate, while your competitors are left feeling like the victims of their circumstances.

THINGS TO THINK ABOUT

1. How has the behavior of your Profit Peak customers changed? How will it change over the next three to five years? Are your Profit Peak customers buying from nontraditional sellers?

2. What new technologies are affecting your market now? In three to five years?

3. Do you have the granular profit information you need to make decisions and focus your resources?

4. Is your company transforming as fast as your markets?

3

BUILD YOUR STRATEGIC HIGH GROUND

Several years ago, we worked with one of the nation's largest, most successful telephone companies in the early days of regulatory change, when new competitors were first entering the market.

We had the privilege of working with the executive vice president (EVP) of this telephone company, helping guide the company's transformation into its new world of competition. We had earlier worked with the prior EVP, who had just retired.

The prior EVP was legendary in the industry. Every morning, when he arrived, he had on his desk a "trouble report" showing outages throughout the system. If the responsible lower-level manager did not clear the trouble in two hours, a report was escalated to the regional vice president, and if the trouble was not cleared in four to eight hours, it wound up on the EVP's desk.

First thing in the morning, at 5:00 a.m., the EVP would call the responsible manager. No one ever wanted to take that call. Then the EVP personally would call the customer to apologize. That is how the company was run.

Think about how the EVP defined his job. Certainly, it was very important for a telephone company, especially in the very early days of wireless and private networks, to be extremely reliable, but a lot was happening in the background that was pushed aside. This telephone company had in its territory one of the largest, most important cities in the country.

At this time, a competitor, a large capable construction company, had targeted the downtown area of the city and was laying optical fiber spines along all the main streets—which were lined by skyscrapers full of the company's Profit Peak customers. The competitor hired a number of young sales reps who went door to door along each main street and avenue selling the new service, and they were steadily capturing the telephone company's most lucrative customers.

Meanwhile, the prior EVP was managing the telephone company as if it were a monopoly—replacing the oldest assets first and marketing to increase sales equally in all areas, regardless of whether an area was a highly competitive urban business district or a rural region. The result: profits dropped through the floor. In essence, this was Mass Markets Age management confronting an emerging Age of Diverse Markets business environment.

MANAGING THE
TELECOMMUNICATIONS REVOLUTION

The prior EVP retired, and a new EVP was named. The new EVP saw that managing the telephone company in the old monopolistic, mass market way was leading to the loss of the company's best customers.

In response, he reorganized the company by dividing it into five regional units: two focused on the company's major cities, two focused on the rings of suburbs that surrounded these major cities, and the remaining unit focused on the company's rural and semi-rural regions. He divided the company's organization into multifunctional business teams (each had marketing, sales, engineering, operations, and finance capabilities), with each team managing a region. His logic was that the regions were becoming very different from one another, so they needed to be managed in disparate ways.

The EVP charged each regional management team with dividing its region into a set of about 20 smaller geographically defined "business blocks," such as a particular downtown business area, a busy suburb, or a specific rural area. He created a planning process in which each regional team analyzed each of its business blocks using transaction-based profit metrics and analytics. A planning team in each region first determined the profitability of every component of each business block and then estimated the likely competitor inroads, along with the telephone company's potential marketing initiatives (competitors would avoid areas in which the company was investing heavily on marketing).

The planning team projected the expenditures and profits for several scenarios for each business block, then selected the set of plans that would produce the best short-term and long-term results, along with a transition plan to guide their market development efforts. The company's CFO gathered these plans from the regions, compared the results to the company's needs, and suggested revisions where needed. This decentralized process became the company's primary financial planning and analysis process.

THREE IMPERATIVES

The telephone company's new process embodied the three imperatives we highlighted in Chapter 1: **choosing** the target customers, **aligning** the company's capabilities to capture and manage these customers, and **managing** through a decentralized organization featuring multifunctional teams, each focused on a unique set of customer needs. Transaction-based profit metrics and analytics were central to this process. This is emblematic of successful companies in the Age of Diverse Markets.

The EVP wisely aligned the company's organization with its geographic regions because the company's assets were primarily regional, competitors were entering the market regionally, and the regions were very different from one another. Other companies, however, might divide their organizations to align with customer market segments (for example, machine shops versus trucking companies) or product categories (for example, equipment versus consumables), or network effects, which combine both.

We call each major grouping, like the telephone company's regions, a *profit river*, and we call each focused grouping within a profit river, like a business block, a *profit stream*. As markets become fragmented at an accelerating pace, having a clear understanding of a company's profit rivers and profit streams, and aligning its organization and management processes with them, is a critical success factor.

THE CASE OF
ADRIAN ENTERPRISES

Adrian Enterprises, a disguised actual company, sells process control equipment. It had a problem: its revenues were rising, but its profits were falling. The company appointed a team to figure out why this was happening and how to rectify it.

The company had two main customer groups: university laboratories and suppliers to semiconductor fabrication plants (fabs). The sales reps strongly favored the university laboratories over the semiconductor fab suppliers because the laboratories had much higher gross margins.

Using transaction-based profit metrics and analytics, the team looked carefully at the company's customer profitability landscape. When they created separate profit stacks for the semiconductor fab suppliers and the university laboratories, the team was surprised to see that the company was making a huge amount of money on the fab suppliers and was losing its shirt on the university laboratories.

When they investigated why this was happening, they saw that the semiconductor fab suppliers had very low selling and customer support costs because they negotiated annual blanket contracts; had low shipping costs due to stable, predictable order patterns; had no returns; and had no need for ancillary services like engineering or technical support.

The university laboratories, on the other hand, were extremely costly to serve. Nearly every order was for a unique experiment—and every experiment required significant sales and engineering time. In addition, this segment generated many returns and unpredictable orders.

The answer was to define each of these customer segments as a profit river (and particular types of fab suppliers and university laboratories as profit streams) and to create a closely aligned, high-impact sales and support capability for each.

They decided to devote a lot more sales resources to obtaining the low gross margin, high net profit semiconductor fab business. Then they had an inspired thought: hire and train a set of graduate students in each major university to be "product representatives" who could help the researchers identify the right equipment, pay them $10 to $15 per hour, and let them serve free pizza to the researchers.

The fab supplier business skyrocketed, the laboratory business became much more profitable, and the company's net profits went through the roof.

Again, the three imperatives were the keys to success: **choosing** the right customers, **aligning** the functions to meet the specific characteristics and needs of each profit river (customer segment), and **managing** the organization to meet each profit river's disparate needs. Again, transaction-based profit metrics and analytics were essential to the success of the process.

FOUR STEPS TO BUILD YOUR STRATEGIC HIGH GROUND

For this approach to succeed, you need to see your business's *profit landscape*—the detailed set of profits and losses that total your overall profitability. Transaction-based profit metrics show you the all-in net profit of every segment of your company and provide the foundation for a powerful set of processes that enable you to choose your customer, align your functions, and manage your organization.

In order to build your strategic high ground, four cornerstone business processes are especially important:

Choose Your Customer

1. **Strategic positioning and risk management:** Profit maps and profit contours, which we will discuss shortly, enable managers to evaluate and reshape their companies' competitive positioning and risk profile as the currents of change transform their respective industries.

Align Your Functions

2. **Profit river management:** Profit rivers are a company's prime sources of profit or loss. Typically, they have three characteristics: (1) each is important, (2) each is relatively homogeneous and somewhat different from the others, and (3) each has a natural cross-functional management constituency.

3. **Transition initiative management:** These initiatives are essential in repositioning a company for increased profitability and success in its transforming industry.

Manage Your Organization

4. **Profit-driven process management:** Transaction-based profit information is critical to maximize the performance of a company's core set of business processes essential for managing customer, product, and supply chain activities.

Together, these enable managers to maximize their companies' performance in the near term, in the long term, and in the transition period in between.

Strategic Positioning and Risk Management

Profit contours are essential for managing strategic positioning and risk. A *profit contour* shows the joint profitability of two intersecting dimensions of a company, like customers and products, or stores and product categories.*

Figure 3.1 shows the profit breakdown of a disguised distribution company that we will call Kimberly Products. The three customer segments

---

* See also: Ben Shapiro and Jonathan Byrnes, "Bridge the Gap Between Strategy and Tactics," *Harvard Business School Working Knowledge*, November 3, 2003. Also see: Ben Shapiro and Jonathan Byrnes, *Bridge the Gap Between Strategy and Tactics with the Magic Matrix*, Harvard Business School Publishing Working Paper, 2003 (Note #9-999-008).

(Profit Peaks, Profit Drains, and Profit Deserts) are on the vertical axis, while the three product segments are on the horizontal axis. This company is very profitable overall.

	Products			
	Profit Deserts	Profit Drains	Profit Peaks	All Products
Profit Peaks	<1% of revenues (4%) of profits	27% of revenues (26%) of profits	32% of revenues 167% of profits	59% of revenues 137% of profits
Profit Drains	1% of revenues (11%) of profits	9% of revenues (49%) of profits	11% of revenues 18% of profits	21% of revenues (42%) of profits
Profit Deserts	1% of revenues (11%) of profits	10% of revenues (9%) of profits	9% of revenues 25% of profits	20% of revenues 5% of profits
All Customers	2% of revenues (26%) of profits	46% of revenues (84%) of profits	52% of revenues 210% of profits	100% of revenues 100% of profits

(Left axis label: **Customers**)

Figure 3.1 Three-Segment Profit Contour of Kimberly Products' Customers Versus Products

This company's profit contour shows a remarkable concentration of profits and losses. Profit Peak customers buying Profit Peak products generate 32 percent of the company's revenues, but fully 167 percent of the profits, while Profit Drain customers buying Profit Drain products produce only 9 percent of the revenues but erode 49 percent of the profits.

This profit contour invites a number of important questions—some relating to the current business paradigm and others relating to the transforming industry. In the former, managers can ask what factors in the profit stacks of their Profit Drain customers are causing the huge losses. In the latter, managers can ask whether their current Profit Peak customers are vulnerable to particular currents of change, ranging from additive manufacturing to incursion of B2C companies with network effects that are skilled in omnichannel management. All these questions, and more, are easily answered by transaction-based profit analytics.

Profit contours are extremely important for strategic positioning. Let's look at the example of another disguised furniture retailer, which we will call Northwest Interiors, with revenues of about $700 million and profits of about $65 million. Figure 3.2 shows this company's customer and product profit maps.

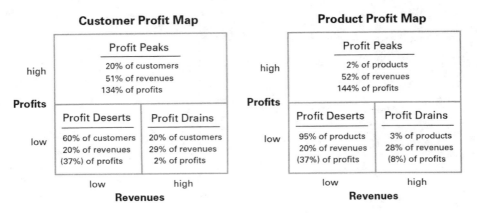

Figure 3.2 Northwest Interiors Profit Maps

Here are the customer segments:

- **Profit Peak customers:** About 20 percent of the customers produce 51 percent of the revenue and 134 percent of the profit.

- **Profit Drain customers:** About 20 percent of the customers produce 29 percent of the revenue and only 2 percent of the profit.

- **Profit Desert customers:** About 60 percent of the customers produce 20 percent of the revenue but *erode* fully 37 percent of the profits.

Here are the product segments:

- **Profit Peak products:** Only 2 percent of the products produce 52 percent of the revenue and fully 144 percent of the profits.

- **Profit Drain products:** Only 3 percent of the products produce 28 percent of the revenue and erode 8 percent of the profits.

- **Profit Desert products:** Fully 95 percent of the products produce 20 percent of the revenue and *drain* a whopping 37 percent of the profits.

Figure 3.3 shows the distribution of profits by the intersections of Northwest Interiors' customer segments and product segments.

Products

	Profit Deserts	Profit Drains	Profit Peaks	All Products
Profit Peaks	8% of revenues 9% of profits	11% of revenues 12% of profits	32% of revenues 113% of profits	51% of revenues 134% of profits
Profit Drains	8% of revenues (14%) of profits	9% of revenues (6%) of profits	12% of revenues 22% of profits	29% of revenues 2% of profits
Profit Deserts	4% of revenues (32%) of profits	8% of revenues (14%) of profits	8% of revenues 9% of profits	20% of revenues (37%) of profits
All Customers	20% of revenues (37%) of profits	28% of revenues (8%) of profits	52% of revenues 144% of profits	100% of revenues 100% of profits

Customers (axis label)

Figure 3.3 Three-Segment Profit Contour of Northwest Interiors' Customers Versus Products

This figure shows the strong concentration of Northwest Interiors' profits and losses. Profit Peak customers buying Profit Peak products generate 32 percent of the company's revenues but contribute fully 113 percent of the profits. Surprisingly, Profit Drain customers buying Profit Peak products account for only 12 percent of the revenue but produce *22 percent of the profits.*

Interestingly, Profit Drain customers buying Profit Drain products account for only 9 percent of the revenues and erode only 6 percent of the profits. However, Profit Desert customers buying Profit Desert products contribute a minor 4 percent of the revenue but *erode* fully 32 percent of the profits.

With a relatively quick investigation, the company's managers determined how to significantly increase and sustain the company's Profit Peak business and dramatically diminish the Profit Desert losses (which were primarily in returns, delivery fee discounts, and handling costs for low-ticket items like bedding and housewares).

Strategic Positioning

Most strategic analyses are based on an assessment of a company as a whole. This is an artifact of the Age of Mass Markets. So-called strengths-weaknesses-opportunities-threats (SWOT) analysis, and even Michael Porter's powerful Five Forces framework, illustrate this approach.* Profit contour analysis significantly *enriches* these analytical models because it shows the composition of a company's component segments and activities, allowing managers to see their underlying patterns of profitability, which have historically been hidden by aggregate, average metrics.

Companies are not monolithic. For example, profit contour analysis indicates how much a company would be helped by better positioning (for example, which segments are helped, which would suffer profit erosion in the absence of repositioning, and which are well positioned already). It also indicates how difficult, costly, or time-consuming the transition will be (for example, what proportion of the products or vendors have to be changed). This is especially important in addressing the specific problems and opportunities that the currents of change pose.

For example, Chapter 2 explains how an increase in additive manufacturing could have either a minor or huge impact on a company's profitability, depending on whether the customers who are vulnerable to displacement by additive manufacturers are primarily Profit Peaks. Every current of change has a similar differential impact on particular segments of a company.

Profit contours rooted in transaction-based profit metrics provide fact-based answers to strategic questions like these: Which stores will be most affected by a vendor bankruptcy (as a function of the product mix and

---

* Michael Porter, *Competitive Strategy* (New York: Free Press, 1980).

substitute preferences of the store's Profit Peak customers)? Which services will be endangered or helped by new developments in artificial intelligence and machine learning?

Not only do profit contours provide essential information when formulating strategy, but they also enable a company to track its repositioning progress with a remarkable degree of exactitude. Managers can watch the erosion rate of vulnerable Profit Peak customers and products, literally day by day, and they can then focus their resources for initiating their repositioning transition on specific customers, products, stores, or even sales reps.

These granular issues are critical for strategic positioning: **choosing** your customer, **aligning** your organization with your company's emerging Profit Peak customer needs, and **managing** the company both during the transition period and in its transformed industry.

In analyzing possible strategic groups in both your current and transformed industry, it is very instructive to focus on the value-to-cost relationship of your major profit segments: Profit Peaks, Profit Drains, and Profit Deserts. The key questions are, How can you improve your customer value footprint, reduce your cost, or both, creating a new basis for competitive advantage? The cases we present throughout this book illustrate this process.

For example, Edison Furniture increased its value footprint for its Profit Peak customers, while Baxter both increased its value footprint and reduced its cost for its Profit Peak customers. In Chapter 9, we provide a more comprehensive range of examples, all from cases in this book.

Bad Profits

Recently, we had a lengthy conversation with the vice president of finance of a major company. She was immersed in the capital budgeting process and wanted to explore ways to evaluate investment proposals.

Our conversation started with a discussion of the cost of capital, which is an important ingredient in evaluating investments. She was going through the periodic process of ranking investment opportunities by their projected returns, taking into account the cost of capital in order to select and fund the most lucrative opportunities.

Throughout this book, we argue that all revenues are not equally profitable—some produce high profits, and some actually produce losses. But are all profits equally desirable?

The surprising answer is no—and the key to understanding the difference between "good profits" and "bad profits" is demonstrated in Figure 3.4.

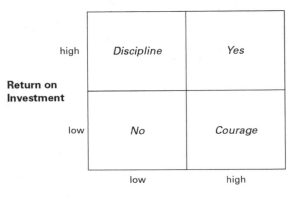

Figure 3.4 Investment Decision Matrix

The desirability of an investment is not just a function of the likely returns but also a function of the strategic relevance (whether the investment moves the company's strategy forward). This is especially important in today's Age of Diverse Markets when the currents of change are transforming key aspects of every industry.

Two quadrants of the matrix are easy to evaluate; the other two take some thought. The upper right, high returns and high strategic relevance, is an obvious winner. The lower left, low returns and low strategic relevance, clearly is a poor bet.

Consider the upper left quadrant: high returns but low strategic relevance. This quadrant is quicksand. These investments look very attractive, but they take the company's capital and focus away from its main line of business. All too many companies have unclear and unproductive positioning because they lack the discipline to say no to attractive-looking investments that don't fit. Ultimately, companies that pursue these types of investments get picked off by highly focused competitors. These are the investments that produce bad profits.

Think about the lower right quadrant: low returns but high strategic relevance. These are investments that would show up at the bottom of a simple capital budgeting ranking, but they are essential to moving the company forward. Here, the watchword is *courage*, a character trait that is especially critical in today's transforming business world.

For example, several years ago we met with the top officers of another major telephone company when telephone companies first began to develop video capabilities that could compete with cable TV. The company had a study that showed that an early investment in video would not pass the company's investment hurdle rate. The question was whether to invest.

After discussion, the officers saw that the real question was *not* whether this initial video investment produced high enough returns. Instead, the right question was which customers should they choose. Did the company want to remain the dominant communications channel into millions of customers, or was it willing to open the door for a host of competitors to get a foothold in their customers—especially the early adopting Profit Peaks customers. Fortunately, the management team made the right decision.

The moral of the story is that while investments in the upper left quadrant produce bad profits, investments in the lower right produce "good losses."

How is this possible? Investments are virtually always part of larger business or strategic initiatives. The correct frame of analysis is the overall initiative, not just the component investment.

Within this strategic context, capital budgeting is a useful way to evaluate alternative ways to accomplish a strategic goal (for example, which machine to choose to accomplish a given task), but it is inappropriate to use capital budgeting to determine strategy.

This is why it is so important that CFOs and other top finance managers be broad-gauge strategic thinkers, as well as disciplined business managers—especially during this Age of Diverse Markets. This is the power of choosing your customer wisely.

Risk Management

In most companies today, risk assessment and management are largely a qualitative process. The core analytical tool is a *heat map*. Managers develop heat maps by identifying the main operating elements of their companies and then assessing whether each element is likely to be affected by an identified risk factor.

For example, a company's sales force is a critical operating element, so it probably would be ranked high in importance. The risk of massive resignations in the sales force or of technology replacing sales reps probably is low. So on a risk heat map, on which the horizontal axis represents an element's importance and the vertical axis represents an element's risk of damage (and potential impact), the data point for sales will be in the lower right quadrant, as shown in Figure 3.5.

Figure 3.5 Example of a Risk Heat Map

Here's another example. Assume that the same company has its main warehouse located in an area that is prone to be hit by major hurricanes. The importance is high, and the risk is high (reflecting the somewhat high risk of being shut down and the extreme damage that a shutdown would cause). This also is shown in Figure 3.5.

In a third example, the company may have a DC in the Northeast. The importance of this DC is gauged at medium because in a pinch, the products could be moved into the area from DCs in nearby regions or through a set of cross-docks from the main warehouse. The risk is assessed at medium, primarily from a possible unionization that would increase the DC's operating costs. Figure 3.5 shows this as well.

The point here is not that a risk heat map is useless but that it is very qualitative and vague.

Profit contours, on the other hand, enable managers to identify and quantify the exact impact of risk factors on their specific customer segments, product families, stores, and other business elements.

More importantly, virtually all risk analyses ignore the most important risk: loss of core profitability. For example, we recently met with the CEO of a major company. He showed us his latest heat map risk analysis. His risk management team had identified several factors as priority risks, including potential price pressure from a rising digital competitor, along with certain operational and systems risks. These potential threats raised concerns.

We had recently completed a profit landscape analysis and profit strategy for his company. We found that about 4 percent of the customers provided over 70 percent of the company's net profits, and when these same customers bought the most profitable 3 percent of the company's products, this customer and product segment provided about 60 percent of the total net profits.

We asked the CEO whether he considered this profit concentration to be a business risk. He replied with a strong yes. The number of customers in this segment amounted to a few thousand, and a quick query showed that the sales reps serving these all-important customers were distributed almost randomly among the company's segments of sales rep performance—in fact, many more were served by underperforming reps than by Profit Peak reps.

When we dug further into the company's Profit Peak customer segment, we found that most of these customers were significantly integrated with the supplier through vendor-managed inventory and other innovations, they had a strongly coordinated planning process, and they were long-time customers with broad portfolios of products. Interviews with the sales reps showed that these customers were very receptive to service innovations. Moreover, they were not price sensitive because the products constituted only a small proportion of the customers' cost of goods sold and were critical to the quality of the customers' products.

A new digital competitor was trying to pick up market share by price-cutting on products that were relatively undifferentiated and sold to customers who were bargain hunters. In fact, the CEO's company had lost some of its Profit Desert and Profit Drain customers to this competitor, while most of its Profit Peak customers had remained loyal.

The glaring question was why this company's exhaustive risk management process, which involved interviews with all the company's top officers as inputs into the heat map, had not picked up its customer *profit risk profile*. The direct answer was that this profile, which initially was concerning (with its concentration of profits), but was shown upon examination to be quite low, was "hidden" from the company's traditional risk metrics—although it was glaring once the company adopted transaction-based profit metrics and analytics.

The sources of risk can reside within the industry's current strategic paradigm, or they can stem from breakout currents of change—or even *force majeure* events like the pandemic crisis. A current competitor lowering prices exemplifies the former, while a new innovation (like Apple moving from its computer platform to take over the phone, music, and camera industries) or a new business model (like Southwest Airlines' revolutionary low-cost, low-price strategy) exemplifies the latter.

Profit contours show a risk management team the exact location of their company's Profit Peaks and Profit Drains. They provide a mechanism for precise quantification and modeling of various risk-increasing scenarios and for identifying and modeling various risk-reducing actions.

Profit River Management

The objective of profit river management is to give top management a small set of natural business units (we think of these as *profit-based strategic business units*, or SBUs) to monitor and manage that are critical to the company's success. The company should coordinate and align its functions to meet the needs of each profit river.

For example, N. Oliver Designs, a disguised retailer, has six profit rivers:

- Profit Peak stores
  - Profit Peak categories
  - Other categories
- Profit Drain and Profit Desert stores
  - Profit Peak categories
  - Other categories
- Profit Peak customers and prospects
- Profit Drain and Profit Desert customers

Note that these profit rivers overlap each other; this provides a valuable set of complementary perspectives. Alternatively, management could define its profit rivers so that they have no overlap and together constitute the whole company's bottom line.

Profit rivers often cross functional boundaries, and they almost always have profit generation (or loss reduction) as a defining characteristic. They are major rivers of business that flow through the functional areas, and functional area managers are responsible for coordinating and aligning in order to meet each river's needs in a specifically appropriate way. Profit rivers should not simply be a company's traditional business units carried forward from the prior Age of Mass Markets.

The following sections describe the characteristics of each of N. Oliver Designs' profit rivers.

Profit Peak Categories in Profit Peak Stores

In these high-profit stores, this group of product categories accounts for about $470 million in revenues and $59 million in profits. The high-profit (Profit Peak) products *within this group of categories* (bear in mind that a product *category* is composed of many products, some highly profitable, others not) contribute $274 million in revenues and $66 million in profits, while the low-profit (Profit Drain and Profit Desert) products *in this group* contribute $196 million in revenues but lose a surprising $7 million.

This group of categories in this set of stores constitutes the highest-profit-leverage sales channel in the company. Its natural management constituency is composed of relevant managers from store operations, category management, supply chain management, and several other functions.

Other Categories in Profit Peak Stores

In these high-profit stores, this group of product categories contributes about $355 million in revenues but only $8 million in profits. The high-profit products *in this group* contribute $140 million in revenue and $21 million in profits, while the low-profit products contribute $215 million in revenues but lose $13 million.

This broad group of categories produces strong revenues but contributes relatively low profits, even though the stores in this group are the strongest earners in the company. The natural constituency set of managers is composed of largely the same set of relevant store operations managers and supply chain managers as above, but different category managers, plus other selected functional managers.

Profit Peak Categories in Profit Drain and Profit Desert Stores

In this group of low-profit stores, this set of high-profit product categories produces $234 million in revenues and $18 million in profits. The high-profit products *in this group* account for about $130 million in revenues and $25 million in profits, while the low-profit products contribute $104 million in revenues but lose $7 million.

This group of products produces moderate revenues and moderate profits. The natural constituency is composed of a different set of store managers than the profit rivers above, but the same relevant category and supply chain managers, plus selected others.

Other Categories in Profit Drain and Profit Desert Stores

In these low-profit stores, this group of product categories contributes $158 million in revenues but loses $8 million. The high-profit products account for $69 million in revenues and produce a surprising $8 million in profits, while the low-profit products contribute $89 million and *lose* a whopping $16 million.

The natural constituency for this group consists of the relevant store managers and supply chain managers as above, but a different set of category managers, plus other relevant managers.

Profit Peak Customers and Prospects

This group of customers overlaps with the profit rivers above because they shop in virtually all stores for all product categories. However, this profit river's specific focus on this very important set of customers, and its priority on the extremely critical tasks of identifying, obtaining, and developing prospective customers for this group, suggests that it be accorded its special profit river status.

This group of customers generates a very strong $615 million in revenues and $130 million in profits. The high-profit products bought by this group generate $378 million in revenues and $102 million in profits, while the low-profit products bought by this group account for $236 million in revenues and a strong $28 million in profits. *Importantly, note that even the low-profit products bought by these premier customers produce strong profits.*

The natural constituency of managers involved in this group has some overlap with the profit rivers above, but also has a unique and important set of involved managers.

Profit Drain and Profit Desert Customers

This group of customers overlaps with the first four profit rivers, but it requires a very different focus and a different set of activities. These customers are very important, but for very different reasons from those in the profit river above: they are underperformers who must be improved, either by increasing their profit contribution to the Profit Peaks level (or at least to break even), or by differentiating the service they receive to reduce the cost to serve to compensatory levels. As above, the natural constituency set of managers has some overlap with those above, but the activities involved are very separate and different.

This group of customers is much more problematic. They generate $602 million in revenues but lose $53 million. Importantly, the high-profit products bought by these customers account for $234 million in revenues and a reasonably strong $18 million in profits, while the low-profit products bought by these customers produce $368 million in revenues but lose an amazing $71 million. This certainly warrants an intensive focus because it is a critically important profit drain.

Profit River Structure

This profit river structure provides N. Oliver Designs with a set of six extremely important business segments, some overlapping. Each has a specific, unique situation, a unique set of profit levers, and a unique set of profit opportunities and imperatives. The relevant functional areas need to organize and align in an appropriate way to manage each profit river (and profit stream) effectively.

Together, these profit-based SBUs provide management with a concise, but comprehensive, set of focal points to understand and judge the integrated effects of the company's initiatives and activities for managing profitable growth.

Transition Initiatives Management

A *transition initiative* is a project that is undertaken by a team of managers over a period of a few months to address a profit improvement or strategic repositioning opportunity that transaction-based profit metrics and analytics uncovers. These opportunities might involve improving current operating and sales processes, or they may address needs to develop new capabilities as the currents of change transform the industry.

Generally, a company should undertake two or three initiatives at a time. As an initiative is completed, another can be added. This allows the teams to focus on a few specific, high-impact issues without disrupting the ongoing business. The company should assess its portfolio of transition initiatives each quarter. We will explain this process in more detail in Chapter 8.

For example, N. Oliver Designs identified four candidate initiatives that together promised to add about $50 million *per year* to the company's bottom line, a 75 percent increase in profitability:

- Refocus advertising toward Profit Peak customers: $14.2 million.

- Train sales associates to accelerate Profit Peak orders and customers: $11.5 million.

- Consolidate vendors to raise Profit Drain and Profit Desert products' profitability: $8.9 million.

- Begin to adjust the store portfolio: $15.4 million.

Refocus Advertising Toward Profit Peak Customers

Traditionally, the company's sizable advertising program was aimed at the broad market, with a focus on newspaper flyers and similar wide-market vehicles. Diverting even a relatively small fraction of this to highly targeted Profit Peak customers and prospects would provide great profit leverage to increase the Profit Peak customer count; to increase their Profit Peak product purchases; and to develop the customers who will become Profit Peaks in the transformed industry.

Train Sales Associates to Accelerate Profit Peak Orders and Customers

The Profit Peak sales reps, especially in Profit Peak stores, provided virtually all the company's profits. Training this group to (1) increase Profit Peak product sales, and (2) convert a small fraction of Profit Drain, and especially Profit Desert, customers to Profit Peaks promised to have a huge impact on profits very quickly. After that, the training program could be spread to other reps throughout the company and adapted to provide a vehicle for introducing and growing the new customers and products that will become Profit Peaks as the industry changes.

It is important to develop a supplemental near real-time profit-monitoring system, with order-by-order profit monitoring and frequent coaching, perhaps daily. It is best to start with the Profit Peak stores, which have the highest leverage. (The highest-profit customers and stores are the easiest to grow because they have shown their ability to form productive relationships.) When their profits skyrocket, the other stores will want to follow fast.

Consolidate Vendors to Raise Profit Drain and Profit Desert Products' Profitability

The objective is to systematically build volume in the Profit Peak vendors (and those who should be or will be) by consolidating vendors in return for support and price reductions to lower the cost of goods sold (COGS) and increase profitable sales.

It is very helpful to share with each vendor the evidence of the unprofitability of the vendor's products and to challenge the vendor to enable you to carry its products profitably. Your transaction-based profit metrics and analytics are very helpful in this discussion. In our experience, vendors respond very positively to this concrete evidence.

Begin to Adjust the Store Portfolio

The company's 63 Profit Peak stores generated nearly $38 million in profits, while the worst-performing 31 stores generated $109.2 million in revenue but lost $15.2 million. The objective is to begin to shift resources from the money-losing stores to the Profit Peak stores (both current and prospective stores).

Profit-Driven Processes

A company's core business processes—ranging from account selection to pricing to supplier management—are the prime drivers of day-to-day profitability. Today, most companies' business processes are disconnected from direct profit maximization.

For example, sales—choosing your customer—is the front-wheel drive that moves the company through its industry. Yet, virtually all sales reps are compensated on revenues, sometimes on gross margin or other factors like new product introductions. As we have seen, neither revenue nor gross margin maximization produces maximum profits, and some revenues are vulnerable to impending competition from digital giants with arm's-length customer relationships, low costs, and network effects.

Instead, managers can insert net profit information directly into their sales-targeting and product mix development processes, directly increasing net profits. The same is true for operating-cost reduction. Managers can supplement this profit information with transition initiative inputs that steer the company toward its defensible strategic high ground, and away from destructive competition. Moreover, several very important business processes like demand management (managing order frequency and volatility) are nearly always unseen and unmanaged; profit information strongly impacts these processes as well.

Profit-driven processes utilize transaction-based profit information to directly maximize the profitability of each of these core business processes in three vital areas: customer, product, and supply chain management. This includes *descriptive information*—showing the current profitability, profit-generating efficiency (current profitability relative to potential total profit opportunity—that is, projected profitability if the process were operating at company demonstrated best practice), and existing profit opportunity (remaining potential profit upside); and *prescriptive information*—identifying and prioritizing profit opportunities across the relevant processes, including the changes that need to be developed to adapt to the currents of change.

Moreover, it is important to separate each set of profit-driven processes—customer, product, and supply chain—into the three profit segments: Profit Peaks, Profit Drains, and Profit Deserts. Each profit segment has a very different population, and each is reasonably homogeneous, but the three are very different from one another. For very granular analysis, it is best to use a nine-node customer-versus-product profit contour. This clustering is especially important when applying machine learning to the processes because each node has different customer behavior and profitability patterns.

For a company starting to develop its profit-driven processes, it is helpful to cluster them into *near-term opportunities* (mostly adding the right profit information to existing processes); *midterm opportunities* (mostly completing adding the right profit information to existing processes, plus starting to modify existing processes and developing processes that do not exist); and *longer-term opportunities* (completing the development of profit-generating processes).

Customer Profit-Driven Processes

Seven profit-driven processes are important determinants of customer profitability: the right customers, prices, contracts, product mix (by customer), sales process and channels, customer relationships, and customer promotions.

Product Profit-Driven Processes

Seven profit-driven processes are key determinants of product profitability: the right products, prices, customer mix (by product), suppliers and product cost, product promotions, returns process, and manufacturing process.

Supply Chain Profit-Driven Processes

Six profit-driven processes are crucial determinants of supply chain profitability: the right order pattern, supply chain product flow (for example, drop ship from main warehouse, ship from local DC), facility network, inventory (overall and at each stocking point), transportation, and supplier relationship.

It is important to bear in mind that the currents of change make this a moving target. While these processes will maximize a company's ongoing profitability, it is crucial to overlay a set of repositioning goals (for example, develop a set of new accounts or products that are increasing in importance, or, conversely, reducing exposure in the accounts or products that are becoming vulnerable to new competitors). Transaction-based profit metrics and analytics enable managers both to identify these emerging needs and to manage the transition through transition initiatives.

Profit Crossroads

The *profit crossroads* is an information exchange forum that fulfills a critical need for coordination among operating managers who are working on profit-driven processes. While this need is very important, it is rarely systematically addressed in companies today.

In current practice, most day-to-day interfunctional communications (for example, a product manager asking a sales rep to alter the product mix in a particular customer) are done largely through ad hoc emails or other means. The profit crossroads provides a systematic and effective solution to this important unmet need.

As operating managers and sales reps work to bring every process of the company to best practice, they need detailed information, and they require coordinated responses from their counterpart managers for tasks that they cannot alone achieve. For example, if a sales rep sees that a customer's order pattern is much too frequent and is driving the customer into unprofitability, the rep should ask his or her supply chain counterpart to discuss changing the order pattern with the customer's inventory replenishment manager.

The number of information and action requests increases exponentially as granular profitability management through a company's profit-driven processes ramps up. This is a natural consequence of moving from the isolated all-the-same functional management of the mass market world to the current diverse markets era with its multiplicity of tightly coordinated teams of managers responding to diverse customer needs.

The profit crossroads has two functions: information sharing and action coordination. Both are critical success factors.

Information Sharing

The company's profit landscape contains important profit information, including current profit stack information for literally every transaction. This information is available to the company's managers through simple profit crossroads queries. Managers can aggregate and explore it in any way the company's data will allow. The profit crossroads also shows a side-by-side comparison of any particular company element, like customer or product, to the company's best practice.

A second set of information available through the profit crossroads is the agenda of profit improvement tasks that managers have committed to accomplish, along with the expected and actual gain to date. This is a valuable reference for other managers working on particular customers, products, operating plans, and the like.

A third set of information provided by the profit crossroads is a capability to "follow" particular customers, products, or other company elements, as events unfold. This is provided in the form of "profit notices" sent to managers who "subscribe," and it is updated as new tasks are undertaken or completed or as new information becomes available.

Action Coordination

As managers consider committing to profit tasks in the context of their profit-driven processes, they need to coordinate with their counterpart managers both to request coordinated action and to find out whether the counterpart can agree. The profit crossroads provides this capability.

For example, a manager might post a request to another manager. The request would remain open until the other manager responds. If the request were agreed to, it would be posted to the manager's notes, as well as to the relevant customer's and/or product's (or other element's) notes. The profit crossroads would keep a set of these notes, including if and when the requested action was completed so others could see the ongoing profit improvement activities by customer, product, or other element, as well as open requests.

Inevitably, some requests are a high priority to the requestor and low priority to the responder. The profit crossroads accommodates this by keeping a list of denied requests. If the requestor still wants action, he or she can appeal to a supervising manager, who will decide what to do.

Transforming the Profit Landscape

The four cornerstone business processes—strategic positioning and risk management, profit river management, transition initiative management, and profit-driven process management—are critical building blocks for success both in accelerating the profits of your ongoing business, and in repositioning your company for sustained profitability in the transforming profit landscape of the Age of Diverse Markets.

These processes cover the three success imperatives: **choosing** your customer, **aligning** your functions, and **managing** your organization.

Managers who creatively and systematically drive these powerful processes will pilot their companies through today's turbulent business conditions, while competitors focused on tuning up their traditional business practices are left wondering why they are falling further and further behind.

THINGS TO THINK ABOUT

1. Have you created a defensible strategic positioning against the digital giants for your Profit Peak customers? For the customers who will be your Profit Peaks in three to five years?

2. Have you quantitatively evaluated the risks of this positioning against the upcoming changes in your competitive environment?

3. Have you aligned your organization's functional departments to create and manage your profit rivers?

4. What are your priorities in transforming your organization to align with your Profit Peaks?

4

MANAGE TO THRIVE IN A PERIOD OF CRISIS

The economic news, as we write this, headlines descriptions of our stalled economy, punctuated by concerns that we are slipping into a recession. Most managers have not had direct experience with managing in a crisis-level deflationary economy. This economic environment creates extraordinary challenges and requires a completely different way of managing—generating lessons for managing not only in today's pandemic crisis but also in the other crises, such as trade disruptions, that arise from time to time.

A LETTER FROM MALAYSIA

Tenglum Low is a top Malaysian executive (and former MIT executive student), who has successfully managed major Malaysian companies through a series of severe deflationary episodes that accompanied the Southeast Asian economic crises of the 1990s.

In 1999, Tenglum wrote a letter about managing in a severe economic crisis that Jonathan reads to his MIT graduate class every year. We reproduce the letter below (with some minor editing). Tenglum wrote:

It has been a while since we last met and corresponded. The Asian crisis has been going on for almost two years. The initial stage was a lot of arguments between IMF medicine (that is, International Monetary Fund mandated belt-tightening) and Keynesian theory (that is, increased government spending).

Under the IMF package, we saw the recovery of Korea. Until the restructuring of our bankruptcy law, we have yet to see a major shakeout. Indonesia is still going through chaos because the tightening affects the poor more. One school of thought is that unless there is military power, peace would be a long way off because of the breakdown in law and order.

Malaysia is already near the bottom and has not shown signs of further decline. Meanwhile, the banking sector is undergoing major restructuring, and major M&A is just beginning. However, we think foreign direct investment will still be slow until investors see stability in long-term government policy.

Meanwhile, we are beginning to feel a breakdown in the international trade system due to more protectionism everywhere—like don't export your problem away.

As for me, this is the second recession I have gone through in Malaysia during the past ten years. The last one was milder because it did not hit all of Asia. This round is much tougher because it is a combination of financial and economic crises. Further, I was made responsible for what used to be a US$200 million company, which has plummeted to US$80 million.

Probably, I have learned my lesson well. There are many things we needed to do which can now be summarized into newly conventional wisdom (which seemed to be lacking at the beginning of the crisis, or perhaps we could not swallow our pride and face reality or overcome denial):

1. The first step is to clear all inventories because selling prices will drop very fast, and demand will shrink even faster. Two months stock will turn into nine months stock.

2. Next, go on just-in-time to reduce financial risk, and focus on making only the manufacturing margin (variable cost); otherwise you will be too rigid to sell at all.

3. When you are in a difficult time, still allocate time and money for new products.

4. Strengthen your strategic alliances with your best customers, and be prepared to drop your fringe customers because you cannot count on everyone to be able to make it.

5. Further, it helps to see clearly beyond the current distortions to determine whether you can be an ultimate world player with sound competitive advantages.

6. The weak foreign exchange rate will help you to export, but the bigger question is whether you can create productivity improvements over the next few years that will enable you to sustain business growth when economic order returns.

Tenglum's letter closes with these six points of essential management advice. It is clear that a severe economic crisis removes all the safety nets and requires a completely different way of managing.

Nevertheless, Tenglum's advice reflects the three success imperatives that form the core of this book, focused on his essential survival agenda:

Choose Your Customer

- "Strengthen your strategic alliances with your best customers, and be prepared to drop your fringe customers because you cannot count on everyone to be able to make it."

- "It helps to see clearly beyond the current distortions to determine whether you can be an ultimate world player with sound competitive advantages."

Align Your Functions

- "The weak foreign exchange rate will help you to export, but the bigger question is whether you can create productivity improvements over the next few years that will enable you to sustain business growth when economic order returns."

- "When you are in a difficult time, still allocate time and money for new products."

Manage Your Organization

- "The first step is to clear all inventories, because selling prices will drop very fast, and demand will shrink even faster. Two months stock will turn into nine months stock."

- "Next, go on just-in-time to reduce financial risk, and focus on making only the manufacturing margin (variable cost), otherwise you will be too rigid to sell at all."

MANAGING IN THE CORONAVIRUS CRISIS

The coronavirus pandemic and sky-high unemployment raging at the time of this writing is causing a terrible human toll and producing an economic crisis greater than any in almost everyone's lifetime. As this is being written, in the United States, hundreds of thousands of people have died and tens of millions of people are unemployed.

The peak crisis is likely to extend for several months, and the readjustment period may last for a year or more after that. More concerning, we may have an extended multiyear period of severe deflation, in which consumption may not rise beyond a portion of its former level. Most of those currently unemployed had little or no savings, and they may have what used to be called a "depression baby" mentality, in which they are loathe to spend more than is absolutely necessary.

This means that there probably will be a prolonged period of consolidation in most industries, even after the pandemic passes, with only a fraction of the preexisting firms surviving. The purpose of this chapter is to provide managers with a guide to hands-on managing in this prolonged crisis and in the extended deflationary period that's likely to follow.

The good news is that the steps that you must take to survive, and even prosper, in this difficult period are the same ones you will need to thrive and win in your transformed industry in the years after that.

The three management imperatives that we highlighted above are central to succeeding in this period: **choose** your customer by growing your customer loyalty, **align** your functions by focusing your downsizing program, and **manage** your organization by mitigating your supply chain shock waves. These initiatives are closely interrelated and can be accomplished in a few months.

GROW YOUR CUSTOMER LOYALTY

The looming supply disruption caused by the pandemic presents historical opportunities for companies to build long-term customer goodwill, in the process claiming the industry's current and evolving strategic high ground and generating high sustained profitability. However, if executives do not manage this as well as their competitors do, they are in danger of destroying customer goodwill, creating years of problematic performance.

A Tale of Two Companies

Consider the fate of two companies: Company A and Company B. Both companies are relatively successful, and both are faced with an extended supply disruption.

Company A responds to the shortage by trying to maintain its traditional customer management processes with diminishing product availability. The VP of sales is careful to be transparent, informing the customers of the company's supply shortages and assuring them that it is doing everything possible to secure increasingly scarce supplier allocations.

The company's sales reps try to prioritize each of their customers. Soon the company is overwhelmed with conflicting priorities, with each sales rep trying to hold inventory for his or her customers, leading the company to adopt the default option—first-come, first-served—as its response to the shortage. This is essentially no customer management strategy at all, and it is a recipe for a long-lasting pool of customer ill will.

Company B, on the other hand, has a prioritized strategic plan for supply shortages, which it developed as an essential part of its risk management process. When shortages materialize and increase, the whole management team becomes a crisis management steering committee, systematically and strategically guiding the company through the crisis.

The company emerges from the crisis period with profits preserved and customer loyalty increased. In fact, the management team used the supply disruption to *build* long-term customer loyalty, and with it, sustained profit growth and market positioning advantages.

Five Rules for Growing Customer Loyalty

Much is being written about how to manage the supply chain crisis caused by the pandemic. The problem is that virtually all of this focuses on disruption threats to inbound supply chains from suppliers. The equally important, longer-lasting challenge is managing your customers through the crisis period to maximize their long-term loyalty and profitability.

If you get this right, the upside is enormous. If you get this wrong, you will suffer the consequences for years to come.

Five rules form the cornerstone of an effective customer management program in a time of supply disruption:

1. Prioritize your customers by profitability.

2. Incorporate your emerging channel strategies.

3. Align sales compensation with your priorities.

4. Develop product substitution groups.

5. Prevent overordering.

Together, they will ensure that your company will emerge from this difficult period in a much better position than when it commenced, hurtling past your scrambling competitors.

Prioritize Your Customers by Profitability

The key to customer prioritization is profit segmentation: focusing your resources on accelerating your relationships with your Profit Peak customers; using the shortage of products to renegotiate your relationships with your Profit Drain customers; and moving strongly to reduce your cost to serve your Profit Desert customers.

Profit Peak Customers

The single most important initiative a company can make is to give priority to its Profit Peak customers. These critical customers warrant your working aggressively to make products available, even if it costs more to support them. Also, this may be an opportunity to lock in longer-term contracts, if possible.

As we have seen in prior chapters, these customers may represent only 10 to 20 percent of your customers, but they provide the majority of your profits. Moreover, they generally are less price sensitive, more loyal, and eager to try innovative products and services.

In all times—especially in difficult times—you should dedicate a set of multicapability teams to these valuable customers, and not serve them through a general sales force. These dedicated teams can focus on building extended contracts with supply chain integration and other operating ties that ensure steady, long-term profit growth for both your customers and for you.

At the same time, your strategic planning process, which we explained in the prior chapter, may show that your current Profit Peak customers are very vulnerable to the currents of change and that shifting to another set of customers is necessary. If so, you need to develop a set of transition initiatives to purposefully shift the composition of this segment, while protecting your needed cash flow.

Profit Drain Customers

The second priority is counterintuitive. A time of supply shortage presents a perfect time to use the disruption as an opportunity to change the nature of your relationship with your Profit Drain customers by approaching them with proposals to increase the profits they generate for you in return for full allocations of scarce products. It is essential to use dedicated multicapability teams skilled in focused cost reduction to work with this set of problematic customers.

The *wrong way* to do this is to gouge them with large price increases, generating lasting bad feelings. It is much more effective to increase the profitability of their business by working with them to *decrease your (and their) operating costs*. In our experience, most Profit Drain customers can be turned around through smart, targeted supply chain and category management measures that create joint efficiencies, like increasing order size by reducing order frequency or developing proactive substitute product policies.

While this requires clarity of purpose, it does not cost much, and it has a huge *permanent*, positive impact on both companies. Doing this requires very capable multifunctional teams dedicated solely to this customer segment. If a Profit Drain customer refuses to work with you, it makes sense to reduce your supply to it.

Profit Desert Customers

The third priority is to carefully manage your Profit Desert customers by understanding their potential and carefully curating their product availability. Importantly, some of these customers are large companies for whom you are a minor supplier. You may be able to award these customers with secure supply access in return for a contract for a bigger share of wallet. The objective is to convert these customers into Profit Peak customers. Digital marketing probes are particularly effective tools to accomplish this.

Many other Profit Desert customers, however, are simply small companies that do not have the ability to grow significantly. These customers typically generate the majority of your operating costs because they issue a large number of very small orders (for example, it generally takes the same time and cost to pick an order line with a small number of items as it takes for an order line with a much larger number of items). This is where your cost reductions (for example, automating your customer ordering and service interfaces, and restricting your menu of services) and aggressive constraints on product availability should be placed. This is also the time to enforce limits on free services that have been neglected (for example, minimum order sizes for free shipping).

It is important, however, to be very transparent and to work with these customers to ease their difficulties as much as possible. For example, many customers may be willing to accept substitutes that are more readily available.

The essence of customer service is always to keep your promises to customers—but you do not have to make the same promises to all customers. If you have to allocate product availability to Profit Desert customers and you deliver on your promised allocation 100 percent of the time, they will be very loyal.

Incorporate Your Emerging Channel Strategies

The current era is characterized by the emergence of critical digital channels and omnichannel management, as we discussed in Chapter 2. The digital giants are gaining prodigious market share in industry after industry through their web-based capabilities. Most companies are sprinting to catch up, by developing competing capabilities or by repositioning into other strategic groups, at the risk of their very survival.

It is critical, therefore, to incorporate your developing channel or repositioning strategy into your customer supply prioritization. This will ensure that your crucial new strategic capabilities will continue to develop and grow, even if they produce modest losses. This must be systematically integrated into your customer management strategy to ensure your long-run viability.

Align Sales Compensation with Your Priorities

There is an old adage that a sales rep might understand your priorities and buy into your priorities, but he or she will (and should) do what you pay him or her to do. Another way to put it is that the fundamental rule of sales is, "Work your pay plan." If the pay plan is wrong, it is not the salesperson's fault.

This means that sales compensation (commissions, quotas, and so on) must be adjusted to reflect your profit segment plans and priorities. The root problem is that all too many companies, like Company A above, fail to develop realistic priorities. This leads to the counterproductive scramble for product and the first-come, first-served processes that are so harmful to short-run profitability and longer-run customer loyalty.

Develop Product Substitution Groups

Substitution groups are sets of products that perform the same function. These are important in the normal course of business both to enable sales reps to move customers to a higher-profit product mix and to ensure high fill rates when a product stocks out (and the customer has agreed to a specific substitute).

These groups are essential in times of supply disruptions because they can ensure steady supplies and eliminate costly back orders, even if the disruptions are intermittent. However, this needs to be agreed upon with customers in advance.

Prevent Overordering

Overordering is a characteristic difficulty in times of product shortage. It has two main sources: customer hoarding and unadjusted EDI replenishment algorithms.

Inventory hoarding is a natural response to supply shortages. Purchasing departments try to grab product whenever it is available as a protection against later shortfalls. This causes extreme problems for suppliers because they cannot forecast actual customer demand. Instead, sales reps scramble to grab tight supplies to meet their customers' accelerating requests, leading suppliers to short other customers—especially their Profit Peak customers with whom they typically have vendor-managed inventory or other operating ties that ensure the correct order flow.

The second cause of overordering is unadjusted EDI replenishment algorithms. If products are allocated to customers, most replenishment systems will simply recognize the shortfall in product availability and endlessly order more. We have seen cases where replenishment systems order the same product multiple times per day. The problem is that the supplier's systems interpret this as incremental demand and award more scarce stock to the overordering customer.

The solution is to develop a set of agreements with customers to allocate products relative to historical demand, unless the customer notifies the supplier that its product demand has actually changed. For example, Profit Peak customers could be supplied at their historical demand; Profit Drain customers at 75 to 80 percent of their historical demand; and Profit Desert customers at 60 percent of their historical demand (unless they contract for a larger share of wallet). It is very important to develop explicit agreements with customers on this so they can make similar agreements with *their* customers.

Manage Your Customers Strategically

Times of product scarcity are the most important times to choose your most important customers and grow your customer loyalty with them. Done well, you will preserve short-term profits and lock in long-term sustained profit growth. Done poorly, you will generate years of damaging customer ill will.

The key to success is to focus your top management team on relentlessly driving a strategic customer management plan based on the five rules for growing customer loyalty. This provides the basis for turning despair into lasting victory in a period of supply disruption.

FOCUS YOUR DOWNSIZING PROGRAM

The current crisis era of the coronavirus pandemic and crashing economic demand present top managers with a truly historic challenge: they face both enormous financial and operating difficulties, and at the same time, they have a historic opportunity to reshape their companies to produce vast benefits for years to come.

Downsizing is one of the most important factors that is instrumental in aligning your functions, and it can either weaken or strengthen your company—both during the crisis and for years after—depending on how you do it.

Downsizing has become rampant almost overnight. Major layoffs and furloughs are nearly everywhere, and managers must develop and implement effective responses in real time. Prior management practices are completely inadequate for this historic challenge.

Managers must use different rules to make these decisions—rules that enable them to align their company and succeed in the waves of economic disruption that are flowing throughout our economy, and for the prolonged adjustment period that follows.

Managers who get this right will own the best customers and leave their competitors in the dust. Those who get this wrong will face years of struggle trying to catch up.

• • •

Virtually without warning, many businesses are being forced to deal with unprecedented sales declines without nearly enough time to align expenses with available revenues. This is placing survival-threatening burdens on cash flow and financial reserves.

The greatest danger lies in the inability to focus and align your reduced resources on targets that offer the greatest potential for success. Weakly focused or unfocused broad-brush responses are certain to fail or produce inadequate results.

Poorly targeted downsizing programs in which each department takes the same percent force reduction will be counterproductive. Companies that use the right metrics and make surgical decisions about resource deployment and focused downsizing will survive today's crisis and lead in the postcoronavirus markets.

Creative new approaches are essential. What worked in the past will not work now. Three key principles provide the foundation for success:

1. Focus on your profit core.

2. Emphasize people and relationships.

3. Concentrate on practicality and rapid implementation.

Figure 4.1 (illustrated with Edison Furniture's numbers) shows the management imperatives for each profit segment.

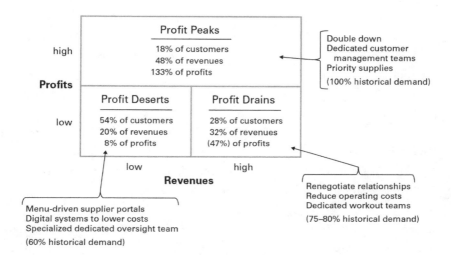

Figure 4.1 Profit Map with Imperatives

Focus on Your Profit Core

The most important thing you can do is to focus your resources on your Profit Peaks by locking this business into place and growing it aggressively. The next priority is converting Profit Drains into Profit Peaks, to the extent possible. Matching the cost to serve Profit Deserts with their profit potential is the third priority. You can do this even with a reduced workforce and shrinking revenues by managing your profit core using both transaction-based profit metrics and sharply focused efforts.

Powerful metrics are the essential starting point. Transaction-based profit metrics give you the granular profit information needed for profit segmentation, as we have explained before. Higher-level aggregations typically available today hide vital information about cost drivers and their interrelationships.

Emphasize People and Relationships

Crisis times require a renewed emphasis on people and relationships to supplement the recent trend toward impersonal systems and related digital transformations. Systems are more cost-effective in certain high-volume applications, but a crisis requires capable people to deal with the human concerns, questions, and complex intercompany coordination challenges that dominate our economy.

This can be seen clearly in three key areas: customers, suppliers, and supply chains.

Customers

Effective customer management requires fundamentally different programs for Profit Peak, Profit Drain, and Profit Desert customers.

Profit Peak Customers

Your objectives for Profit Peak customers are twofold: (1) Build the efficiency of your day-to-day coordination, while (2) taking steps to develop a more integrated operating relationship featuring win-win mechanisms like joint forecasting, focused vendor-managed inventory, and coordinated category management.

This requires a set of highly skilled, dedicated multicapability customer management teams composed of managers from sales, supply chain, finance, and IT, who can link with their Profit Peak customer counterparts. You must staff the teams with skilled managers who can work together to manage change in the customer. Supporting systems are a secondary need. Reducing costs by downsizing these teams would be enormously counterproductive; in fact, adding selected resources is a great investment.

These customer management teams should meet weekly (over the phone or the internet or in person) with their customer counterparts to review critical product forecasts in light of changing needs and to develop substitutions where necessary, take measures to generate cash, and coordinate on other immediate concerns.

In monthly meetings, they need to join with their customer counterparts to manage near-term issues like reviewing forecasts, adapting product mix to rapidly changing supply and demand trends, ensuring that replenishment systems are working properly, and installing interim coordinative mechanisms like partial vendor-managed inventory for volatile key products.

This is where you should invest people and resources, especially in tight times. You cannot do this everywhere, and bonding with your Profit Peak customers is a life-or-death issue.

Profit Drain Customers

Your objective for Profit Drain customers is to plug their profit and cash drains by developing mutual operating-cost reductions that increase your profits from these customers, ideally by converting them into Profit Peaks. Offering access to secure supplies of scarce products provides a strong incentive for these customers to renegotiate their relationships with you.

This process requires a different set of highly skilled dedicated multifunctional teams to focus on reducing the joint operating costs in order to reduce the immediate cash drains while creating Profit Peak profitability levels. Weekly coordination and monthly planning meetings enable you to leverage your relevant capabilities to manage both cash and inventory.

Your Profit Drain customer management teams need to establish weekly coordination meetings with their customer counterparts to address rapidly changing supply and demand mismatches and other immediate concerns.

In monthly coordination meetings, these teams should focus on fixing the underlying problems that are causing the profit and cash drains. The customer's profit stack, built from its transaction P&Ls, is the critical metric.

As in the case of the Profit Peak customer teams, downsizing this group would be disastrous.

Profit Desert Customers

Your prime objectives for Profit Desert customers are (1) to reduce your cost to serve to match their profit potential by moving them to more efficient engagement modes and (2) to lower their priority for allocated product. This is where you should downsize by replacing people with systems. It is important to understand the actual cost to serve these customers in order to charge correctly for the services you offer.

You should use digital marketing to manage these customers, creating a "menu-based" set of service offerings and enforcing your "rules of engagement" carefully. This is where your most productive downsizing should occur.

However, a few Profit Desert customers may be large companies for whom you are a minor supplier. You can offer to fully meet their needs in return for a larger share of wallet and long-term contracts. These are prime prospects to be developed into Profit Peaks.

Suppliers

The most effective program for transforming your suppliers is analogous to that which is best for your customers.

Your Profit Peak *suppliers* provide your most profitable products. These suppliers warrant dedicated teams of managers who are skilled at developing and growing productive relationships featuring both weekly coordination meetings and monthly forecasting and planning meetings (along with selected early steps to build integrated processes in supply chain management, category management, and product development). The systems required are relatively standard.

Profit Drain suppliers have large enough revenues to warrant dedicated teams of managers who can partner with their supplier counterparts to reduce joint operating costs. This is a good opportunity to improve your relationships and drive them toward Profit Peak behavior. Your supplier-specific profit stack will show you exactly where the drains are occurring and which actions will plug the cash and profit depletion. Reducing joint operating costs is a surprisingly effective, often hidden, profit lever.

Downsizing either of these sets of supplier management teams would be very counterproductive.

Profit Desert suppliers are the "long tail" of your supplier revenue distribution. A small team should manage these suppliers using supplier portals with standard terms and low human resource requirements. This is where systems are particularly effective in lowering your costs, and this is where downsizing will be most productive.

Supply Chains

In crisis times, as we discuss below, most automated supply chain systems are unable to handle the highly volatile, unpredictable supply and demand.

Highly skilled managers and well-designed processes with selective manual intervention are critical.

In tight supply situations, you must make customer product allocation decisions in advance and communicate them broadly. All too often, companies do this in real time in response to ad hoc sales rep requests, leading to a scramble for inventory and a default to the non-policy of first-come, first-served.

During crisis, most important supply chain decisions cannot be made by supply chain managers alone. These decisions are strategic and must be made by the multifunctional teams differentially managing the company's key profit segments.

Managing allocations—both those you receive from your suppliers and those you give to your customers—is particularly difficult. Your Profit Peak *suppliers* probably will give you some preference, especially if you have taken measures to reduce your joint operating costs, making you a Profit Peak customer *to them*. Looking downstream, your Profit Peak *customers* warrant full allocations of product, while your Profit Drain customers may only get 75 to 80 percent of needs, and your Profit Desert customers may get a mere 60 percent.

In manufacturing companies, high-level interfunctional coordination is especially critical. Component shortages may block the production of certain sets of products. The all-important decisions on which products to produce and market require both supply chain and marketing expertise.

Losing these capabilities to downsizing would be extremely problematic.

Concentrate on Practicality and Rapid Implementation

Profit segmentation must form the core of your financial planning and analysis process. This process has three essential components: (1) **choosing**—identifying and prioritizing your Profit Peaks, Profit Drains, and Profit Deserts; (2) **aligning**—creating an integrated set of programs for each segment; and (3) **managing**—organizing around your profit segments to maximize the performance and minimize the risk of each segment. This will guide you in building your human resource capabilities, and downsizing where it will provide an actual net benefit.

Managing through dedicated teams focused on each key profit segment—at both the upper management and operational management levels—will enable you to deploy your resources wisely and maximize both your company's near-term survival and its long-term profitable growth.

Managers have no choice but to act quickly in today's crisis. The time frame for effective action is very short. Those who act decisively before the situation takes over and the range of options closes will create life-preserving cash flow and lock in the best customers for years to come.

MANAGE YOUR SUPPLY CHAIN SHOCK WAVES

In the pandemic crisis and for a long time afterward, supply chains throughout our economy will experience volatile shock waves of product supply and demand. Most companies' automated supply chain systems are incapable of handling this level of volatility. This creates chaos in both customer fulfillment and supplier replenishment unless managers adopt a completely different way of managing their supply chains.

Huge Disruption

Supply chain shock waves reflect the wide variety of companies and consumers throughout each industry. Because each company and individual have a unique demand and supply pattern, and each entity is shutting down and ramping up in a different way, the net effect is chaotic.

This will be further exacerbated by the nature of consumption after the economy restarts. In the past months, millions of people have become unemployed. In the Great Depression, a generation of formerly unemployed workers became "depression babies," focused on saving and afraid to spend money. The same effect may influence our economy to some extent for years to come, creating even more volatility and uncertainty.

The net effect of this economic situation is to create extremely volatile and unpredictable patterns of supply and demand in supply chains throughout our economy. Most of these supply chains have been designed over the past decade to be extremely "lean"—with just-in-time and other innovations aimed at compressing cycle time, reducing safety stock inventories, and boosting intercompany coordination to lower costs.

These lean supply chains require that the information exchanged between customers and suppliers be highly accurate and that the product flow remain within a relatively small range of variance, often 5 to 10 percent. Without rapid, accurate forecasts and controlled product flow, a just-in-time supply chain quickly becomes a "just-in-case" supply chain, often with three times the safety stock needed to meet uncertain demand.

This situation has created a perfect storm in which radically increased supply and demand volatility has generated constant streams of shock waves in supply chains throughout our economy. Our existing supply chain systems and processes simply cannot handle this level of unpredictability and disruption.

Supply Chain Shock Waves

Chaotic supply chains have been making headlines in our daily newspapers. This situation reflects the interaction of propagating shock waves and supply chain system limitations.

Propagating Shock Waves

Consider the example of a company facing rapidly declining demand. In order to save cash, management draws down its inventories, especially for slow-moving products. After weeks of drawing down these inventories, the company is forced to replenish its stock. Its automated replenishment system requisitions double its normal order so it can rebuild its safety stock while meeting current demand.

The company's distributor sees several weeks of no demand for these products, followed by a more than double amount of demand. The distributor is unable to infer the actual demand, so it ships all its stock to this customer. Its replenishment system interprets this as a major spike in demand, so it raises its internal demand forecast and safety stock, and then sends the resulting increased order to its supplier, a manufacturer.

The manufacturer's system interprets this greatly increased demand as a trend so it changes the factory's production schedule to urgently make much more of these slow-moving products. This reduces its capacity for making its faster-moving products, creating stockouts throughout the downstream supply chain.

The distributors and their customers grow concerned because these fast-moving products generate most of their remaining cash flow, so they give urgent reorders to their suppliers, who in turn, are unable to fulfill them. This lack of available fast-moving products causes their systems to double their reorders, eventually creating a pileup of products throughout the supply chain with companies hoarding all available stock.

The result of this vicious cycle is that the companies throughout the supply chain wind up with warehouses full of the wrong products and little cash to rectify their situations. Because the ultimate demand does not stabilize, the imbalance gets worse and worse, sending larger and larger shock waves throughout the supply chain.

Supply Chain System Limitations

Most automated supply chain replenishment and order acceptance systems are unable to handle the supply chain shock waves that are roiling the economy because they are designed to operate with relatively small demand variance.

In times of crisis, data throughout supply chains fail to reflect actual underlying demand. Moreover, to the extent that end consumers are hoarding scarce goods, their purchasing patterns fail to reflect their actual consumption, making the problem worse.

For companies with thousands of customers and products, demand pattern and replenishment calculations are extremely complex. Supply chain managers, no matter how experienced, are unable to make effective ad hoc manual adjustments to enable the systems to operate acceptably. This leads them to fall back on failed old rules of thumb like first-come, first-served, resulting in customers perceiving that getting fulfilled orders is a random event, leading them, in turn, to chronically overorder and hoard products.

This chaotic situation has become the "new normal" in industry after industry, and it will stay that way for a long time.

Managing Your Shock Waves

Companies can manage their supply chain shock waves and avoid being overwhelmed by them by adopting a three-step process:

1. Plan for paradigmatic supply chain change.

2. Prioritize your customers and suppliers.

3. Adjust your current systems.

Managers can deploy this practical process rapidly, but all parts of their companies' organizations must become involved.

Plan for Paradigmatic Supply Chain Change

In order to effectively manage a company's supply chain shock waves, its top management team must understand the strategic nature of the problem—how supply chain shock waves are generated and the concrete steps needed to master them. This is extremely urgent today, when demand volatility is accelerating rapidly. Without this understanding, events will simply overwhelm managers throughout the economy, freezing their ability to respond effectively.

In a nutshell, managers must supplement their automated systems with a process that (1) prioritizes customer and supplier segments, (2) focuses manual interventions only on selected priority customer segments, and, (3) sets customer order allocations to reflect segment priority. This requires both organizational and system changes.

The most effective mechanism for creating and overseeing this process is a top-level team composed of the heads of sales, supply chain, supplier and product-supplier management, and finance. Together, they will be able to manage and coordinate the actions that will enable their company to successfully mitigate its supply chain shock waves and position itself for success both in the immediate crisis and in the prolonged recovery period that follows.

Prioritize Your Customers and Suppliers

The starting point in prioritization is to segment your customers by profitability using transaction-based profit metrics and analytics, as we have explained in prior chapters.

Profit Peak customers warrant allocations of 100 percent of historical demand. However, their replenishment systems probably are overordering, so company managers need to meet with them weekly (by phone or internet) to review the situation, agree on orders, and ensure that they adjust their EDI replenishment systems.

Profit Drain customers are prime candidates for cost reduction, often through costless operational adjustments, so company managers should also meet with them weekly to review and agree on orders (and EDI system adjustments)—with allocations of perhaps 75 to 80 percent of historical demand if costs are not reduced, but full historical demand if they become Profit Peaks.

Profit Desert customers should be served through automated systems, with menu offerings, and they should get perhaps 60 percent of historical demand.

This prioritization aligns your fulfillment allocation commitments with each profit-based customer segment's importance, while it systematizes and minimizes the need for manual system interventions.

Adjust Your Current Systems

Some existing supply chain systems can specify order fulfillment gates, such as limiting fulfillment of orders from specific customers if they are above a certain percent of the customer's historical demand (without manual override). Similarly, some systems have the capability for specifying replenishment requisition gates such as preventing requisitions to certain suppliers of amounts exceeding a particular percentage of historical supply requests from these suppliers (again, without manual override).

Most supply chain managers are not familiar with these system capabilities, as they are rarely used in the normal course of business. It is imperative that a company's systems experts be urgently assigned to investigate whether the company's order fulfillment and replenishment requisition systems have this capability and, if so, to actively manage these settings.

Companies with systems that do not have this gating capability need to urgently assign their best systems experts and operating managers to develop a set of ad hoc procedures that will accomplish the same gating capability, with the ability to change the settings as events unfold.

In crisis, supply chain managers quickly encounter a dilemma: their automated supply chain systems cannot operate without extensive manual interventions, but the business is too complex for managers to constantly intervene on an ad hoc basis in every order from every customer for every product. Instead, they need to organize and prioritize this process.

With this prioritization and agreed-upon weekly orders, the customers can submit orders at the agreed amounts, and the company's automated systems should accept these orders. By getting ahead of the key customers' order development process, a company's supply chain managers will be able to regain control over the situation.

Here is what the EVP and chief supply chain officer of a New York Stock Exchange company said in response to his experience with this program:

> Much of what you described has played out. In times like this, you need to take the yoke and fly by feel. You can't let the systems run on autopilot. We have made a number of dial turns to adjust our demand patterns manually. I look forward to the day when we can turn the autopilot back on. I think that is going to be a while.

Managing the Process

Implementing this management process is complex. It affects nearly every part of a company's organization and has many moving parts: teams choosing and working with Profit Peak customers, other teams working with Profit Drain customers, and yet others working with Profit Desert customers. A set of parallel teams have to work with the three analogous sets of suppliers. This interaction must occur on both a weekly and a longer-term basis—tracking and managing both individual customer and supplier situations, as well as following and reacting to longer-term secular trends.

This process is very practical and manageable, and it can be developed relatively quickly. The key to success is to train your focus and resources on your three success imperatives: **choose** your customer by growing your customer loyalty, **align** your functions by focusing your downsizing program, and **manage** your organization by mitigating your supply chain shock waves.

Managers who accomplish this will ensure their company's success and their customers' loyalty both in today's period of crisis and in the years beyond.

THINGS TO THINK ABOUT

1. What are you doing to increase customer loyalty with your Profit Peak customers?

2. What are you doing to convert your Profit Desert customers into Profit Peaks?

3. Have you evaluated your systems' responses to disrupted demand patterns and uneven product availability?

4. Have you planned and prioritized the investment you need to automate your relationship with your Profit Deserts?

PART III

ALIGN YOUR COMPANY

5

CREATE A WINNING CUSTOMER VALUE FOOTPRINT

Several years ago, SKF had a problem.* For years, the company had been a major producer in the world bearing market, with manufacturing facilities, dealers, distributors, and direct sales. With the rise of competition from Asian suppliers, along with automobile companies and digital competitors selling into the aftermarkets, sales and profits had become flat.

The company had three primary market segments: vehicle original equipment manufacturers (OEMs), machinery OEMs, and the vehicle and industrial aftermarkets. The OEM segments composed about 60 percent of the company's revenues, with relatively low profitability, while the aftermarket segments contributed about 40 percent of SKF's revenues, with higher profitability.

---

* Sandra Vandermerwe and Marika Taishoff, SKF Bearings: *Market Orientation Through Services* (Lausanne, Switzerland: IMD, 1990).

The top management team felt that the aftermarket customers had high potential but were underserved because the factories, which had dominated the company throughout its Age of Mass Markets history, favored the large OEM customers. In response, management split off the aftermarket business into a separate division, reasoning that it had a lot of unrealized potential and it was very different from the relatively monolithic, stable, high-volume, low-profit OEM business.

When the new aftermarket management team analyzed its markets, it saw that the aftermarket had two very different sets of customers. The industrial aftermarket, such as machine shops, constituted about two-thirds of this business; its customers' most important need was to minimize machine downtime. The vehicle aftermarket, including auto repairers, on the other hand, contributed about one-third of the revenues; its customers' most important need was to identify, locate, and install the right part.

This realization led the new team to develop two very different programs with different value footprints for these two very different customer sets.

DIFFERENTIATING BEARINGS

The industrial aftermarket customers were primarily concerned with keeping their equipment running and minimizing costly downtime. This meant that it was very important to maximize the lifetime of the bearing, which depended on bearing product quality, installation quality, protection from environmental contamination, and maintenance quality. Note that the latter three factors were controlled by the customers.

The team decided to focus on ensuring that the industrial aftermarket customers' complete set of needs were met, which meant that the company either had to perform all of these services itself or train the customers to perform the services expertly on their own.

Based on this understanding, they developed a set of planned maintenance programs to minimize downtime. The program consisted of providing a comprehensive range of specialty bearings, specialized lubricants, automatic lubricating devices, cleanliness programs and products, sealing products, shaft aligning systems, monitoring systems, and installation services, products, and tools to speed the repair process.

The vehicle aftermarket customers had a very different set of issues: (1) to identify and locate the correct bearing for the vehicle, application, and year; (2) to understand how to mount and install it; and (3) to obtain the necessary accessories.

In order to address this customer need, the team developed literally hundreds of kits to sell to customers, each of which contained the right bearing, the right accessories, and the right installation instructions. They even included competitor bearings if SKF did not make the correct part. In order to support this program, the company developed a number of product support centers to provide technical support.

The results were stunning: the aftermarket profits rose by double digits relative to the OEM sector of the company, and the company's stock price rose by double digits as well.

Breakthrough Understanding

SKF's breakthrough was rooted in its relentless focus on its customers. This customer focus was a sharp break from the product focus that characterized most companies in the Age of Mass Markets. The company understood that the aftermarket business was diverse and that the cost of the bearing was only a very small portion of the total cost of the customer's processes in which the bearings were an essential part.

The company succeeded by focusing on the customers that were receptive to a broader value proposition and building a set of extended products that resonated with the respective needs of the customers in its two aftermarket profit rivers. SKF left the price shoppers to its low-priced competitors.

In this formulation, the "product" that SKF was selling was not bearings, per se. Rather it was "trouble-free operations." This was a very subtle but critical difference. When SKF shifted its focus and changed its offer, the company made it hard for customers to comparison shop because the company's "product" became a unique package of products and services.

SKF developed an intimate knowledge of its customers. The company understood that its new value proposition fit many customers, but not others. It had to be very thoughtful about choosing where to invest the resources to develop its extended products, and it had to be very careful in identifying its new target customers.

This is critical: building a winning customer value footprint is just as much about choosing the right customers as it is about developing a compelling extended product. This underscores the importance of **choosing** your customers, **aligning** your functions to obtain these customers and creating the extended products appropriate for your different sets of customers, and **managing** your organization to produce your product-service packages at scale.

The first critical step in the transformation process was to "walk in the customers' shoes," with SKF's product managers and sales reps actually spending significant time inside selected customers (not just interviewing them). This led them to understand their customers' real problems. It also enabled them to identify the customers in each aftermarket segment who were receptive to a more comprehensive solution and, importantly, to identify the customers who simply wanted a low-priced bearing from low-cost providers.

SKF modified its product offering by building a more comprehensive extended product, which in essence, enabled it to "draw a bigger box around the business" and extend its customer value footprint.

The second critical step was to recognize that its customer segments were very different from each other, which in turn, required it to build very different extended products for its two aftermarket profit rivers. This is really important. While the physical bearings remained the same, the extended products in which they were embedded differed greatly from segment to segment.

This produced a sort of "theme and variations" effect, in which a physical product, like a particular bearing, was like a "theme," while the various packages of services, like bearing maintenance, were like "variations" aimed at the different needs of the company's diverse customers.

This situation makes product management, which includes product redefinition and extension, particularly complex and extremely productive. It is a core management process that is strategically critical and growing rapidly in today's Age of Diverse Markets—and it is immensely important in positioning against the digital giants and other aggressive competitors, who often have only a limited ability to build extended products.

SKF's experience illustrates the principle that today a "product" is defined by the customer's use, not just by the physical product itself. By creating its portfolio of extended products, SKF was essentially creating a suite of "products" for each physical product. In the Age of Mass Markets, product management and customer management were very separate functions. In the Age of Diverse Markets, however, both customer knowledge and customer targeting are integral parts of *product management.*

Extended products almost always involve profoundly comingled sets of products and services. Deep customer understanding and transaction-based profit information are needed to productively analyze the cost to serve of these products (which usually varies from segment to segment and customer to customer). This understanding is essential for deciding which products to develop, determining where to deploy them, and managing their growth and extensions. It also is essential for pricing these extended products correctly.

Extended products are frequently a key cornerstone in a company's larger strategy. For example, when Baxter developed its stockless system, which we described in Chapter 1, it essentially created a pipeline directly into every patient care area and clinic of a hospital. This channel was so efficient and convenient that it propelled sales by over 35 percent, even in the most highly penetrated accounts in the country.

Once Baxter developed its stockless system, it bought American Hospital Supply, which had a broad portfolio of products that complemented Baxter's and which were used by the patient care areas and clinics that were serviced by Baxter's vendor-managed inventory system. This gave Baxter a dominant position with the hospitals and transformed the industry.

When a company's extended products, like those that made up Baxter's stockless system, are deeply embedded in its customers, and especially when they need a degree of customization, managers need to be especially thoughtful about choosing their customers. The prime candidates for deep extended products are Profit Peak customers, who generally are vendor loyal and relatively price insensitive and who like service innovations that bring them new value. In contrast, spending a lot of time trying to sell these products to Profit Drain customers (because they are large), who generally are price shoppers, is unproductive and dangerous because they usually will not be willing to pay for the new service.

The SKF initiative builds on the same principle as Baxter's stockless innovation: that extended products create enormous new customer value that digital giants and other narrow competitors generally cannot follow. However, the SKF case adds the important proviso that different customer segments often want and need very different extended products to fit their particular situations. Therefore, a company has to be very thoughtful about **choosing** its target sets of customers, **aligning** its functions around its respective customer segment needs, and **managing** its organization to produce its customer value. The company's managers need the courage to say no to those customers who want a different value proposition.

VIRTUOUS CYCLE OF MUTUAL VALUE CREATION

Company after company in today's economy is reducing its supplier base by 30 to 60 percent. The decision on who wins big versus who gets pushed out is almost always determined by a supplier's ability to produce more essential customer value through an innovative customer value footprint: creating enhanced profits and strategic advantage *for the customers*.

In addition to the plentiful customer value gains that flow from building an innovative customer value footprint, the supplier harvests significant value as well. For example, the stockless system that Baxter created for its hospital customers generated very important gains in every key component of Baxter's profitable growth:

- **Revenues:** Provided 30 to 40 percent revenue increases, even in highly penetrated accounts; eliminated price sensitivity; refocused sales reps on selling products, not solving service problems

- **Costs:** Enabled cost reductions of 25 to 40 percent in both sales and marketing, and in supply chain management

- **Profitability:** Identified targeted profit improvement initiatives, often with gains of 25 percent or more

- **Cash flow:** Created immediate cash flow increases, as inventory was lowered and excess costs were reduced, with no investment needed

- **Asset productivity:** Rapidly eliminated nonearning assets; put assets to more profitable and more productive uses

- **Risk management:** Built enormous switching costs in key accounts; dropped unneeded assets and expenses

This broad set of value points was created in parallel for the hospitals as well, leading to a virtuous cycle of mutual value creation and ever-deepening business relationships.

In fact, several years ago, at the height of the last financial crisis, we were invited to participate on an innovation panel, along with top executives of three Fortune 100 companies. After our presentation on the process of innovation, the three executives discussed their innovation processes.

All three companies had the same strategy and process: they were building closer operating ties with their Profit Peak customers to increase the customers' profitability. In the process, they were reducing their own costs and raising their profits. At the same time, they were investing a portion of the new profits to extend their value footprint and deepen their key customer ties, producing even more profits for the customers. This led the customers to give them an increasing share of wallet.

Even at the depth of the prior recession, their Profit Peak customer revenues and profits were growing at strong double-digit rates.

WIN THE CUSTOMER VALUE WAR

Building a compelling customer value footprint is a critical strategic imperative that is most starkly illustrated by a situation every company faces from time to time and every manager fears most: a price war. This is an especially troubling and increasingly serious problem as the digital giants and other aggressive competitors with streamlined costs and Big Data advantages move into incumbents' traditional markets.

This raises an important question: how can a company win a price war without destroying its own profitability?

Any way one looks at it, a price war is the ultimate in self-destructive, lose-lose behavior. Yet it is one of the most common of all management problems and concerns.

Paradoxically, not only is a price war devastating for a company and its competitors, but it is very bad for customers as well. When a customer forces its suppliers to focus on price competition, it loses the opportunity to work with its suppliers to increase its real long-term profits in two crucial ways: (1) by reducing the joint costs of doing business together and (2) by helping the suppliers to find creative ways to turbocharge their customer value footprint.

In short, the real win strategy—for both customers and suppliers—is to turn the price war into a customer value war.

Winning the Price War

When confronted with aggressive competitor pricing, the instinct is to respond with a price cut. After all, why lose the business? Even worse, if a company loses those customers by failing to respond, it could be in danger of losing them permanently, sacrificing the lifetime value of the relationship. This concern pushes managers to respond even more aggressively, and before long the pricing discipline of the competing companies collapses, and with it goes the companies' profitability.

What can a manager do? The best tactical answer is to attack the hidden assumptions that frame the price war.

For example, if a competitor quotes an uneconomically low price, why not suggest to the customer that it demand a five-year contract. After all, the price certainly will rise back to former levels once the incumbent is out of the picture. This demand will force the attacker to back down because the losses would be too great over a multiyear period.

Another effective tactic is to rein in the instinct to respond where the attack takes place. In most price wars, the attacker aims at the incumbent's most lucrative accounts and products—its high-profit customers. By re-sponding where it is attacked, the company effectively does the most dam-age to itself—and often the least damage to the attacker.

In fact, in most price wars, the attacker is funding the price war by maintaining a very lucrative, protected portion of its business—its Profit Peak customers—as its core source of cash flow and profitability. The an-swer, therefore, is to strike back at the competitor's source of cash flow—*the competitor's* Profit Peak customers.

A classic example comes from the airlines a few decades ago. Some car-riers, like United and American, had very lucrative east-west routes (for example, between NY and LA), while others, like Delta, had very lucrative north-south routes (for example, between NY and Miami).

When an east-west carrier tried to enter a north-south route with low prices, the incumbent's most common response was to match the price reduction, thereby losing a huge amount of money in its lucrative north-south routes—routes in which the attacker had little to lose but much to gain.

Instead, the smart response was to strike back by entering the attacker's prime east-west routes with low prices—attacking the source of cash flow that supported the price war. This very quickly ended the price war. (Re-member that it is illegal in the United States to conspire with a competitor to set prices.)

Preventing Price Wars

These tactics are effective in framing an effective response to a price war. But how can a company prevent one? We were asked this question a while ago by a writer who was working on an article about distributor branch pricing.

She asked how much "wiggle room" branches have when it comes to dif-ferentiating themselves from the competition based on price, and whether there is an argument for price matching if customers come in demanding a cheaper price they may have received down the road.

The answer is that there is a progression of three increasingly effective ways to respond to a price war: match the price, lower the customer's total cost, or increase the company's value footprint.

Match the Price

The seemingly obvious, and instinctive, way to respond is to simply match the competitor's low price.

This is an invitation to lose a company's profitability for two reasons: (1) the competitor probably will up the ante with another price cut, setting off a vicious cycle, and (2) the company is essentially training its customers to hammer it on price at every turn. After all, it is showing them that it will fold under pressure.

The more effective countertactics mentioned earlier—shift the time frame or shift the locus of attack—produce much better results than simple price matching. But it is even more effective to proactively act to *prevent* a price war. A company can do this in two ways: reducing the customer's total cost and turbocharging its customer value footprint.

Lower the Customer's Total Cost

The second—and much more effective—way to respond is to systematically find ways to reduce the cost of doing business with the most important customers. By reducing costs for both its customers and for itself, a company can create new value that will endure in the long run. Smart customers will strongly gravitate toward this process.

A company can take measures to reduce its customers' direct costs. They range from supply chain cost reductions (for example, flow-through supply chains) to product and category management (for example, product rationalization). Subsequent chapters of this book discuss these measures.

Conversely, customers can create surprisingly big cost reductions for the supplier. For example, by helping the customer smooth its order pattern, a company can reduce *its own* supply chain costs, often by 25 percent or more, even while reducing the customer's ordering and handling costs. Better forecasting offers similar gains, as does a limited but well-aimed product substitution policy. These profit measures benefit both the supplier and the customer—by much more than a simple, temporary price cut.

Smart suppliers pass a big portion of their savings back to their customers in *price reductions*. Here the customers know that the price reduction is fully warranted by real savings, and therefore it can endure over time.

Increase Your Customer Value Footprint

The third, and most effective, way to "win" a price war is to prevent it by waging and winning a customer value war. Yet all too many managers think of this last, if they consider it at all.

The example of Baxter's stockless business illustrates the enormous potential value in increasing a company's customer value footprint.

Baxter developed a way to permanently "win" the price wars that raged in its business by converting them into a one-firm race to lower the total cost of the joint supply chain, passing this saving to the hospitals. And this saving was so large that it dwarfed the pennies at stake in the price wars.

However, Baxter packed even more value into this business initiative. In the prior period, before stockless was developed, the hospitals were reluctant to operate large networks of off-site clinics and surgical centers. Many top hospital managers did not have confidence that their materials management staff could handle the complex scatter-site network of critical products.

The new partnership with Baxter enabled the hospital executives to gain confidence that the newly created supply chain, managed by a supply chain expert like Baxter, could support the evolving network of facilities. In short, Baxter created a fundamentally new value footprint *for the hospitals to offer to their customers*—enabling them to radically change the way they operated to bring huge new value to their patients.

The progression was incredibly powerful: from price matching, to total cost reduction that competitors couldn't match, to partnering with the hospitals to enable the *hospitals* to create a fundamentally new and much more effective customer value footprint for their patients, which again the competitors could not match.

Baxter did not just win the price war. It eliminated it. Baxter turned the price war into a customer value war in which Baxter was the only viable competitor.

Several highly successful companies, like Southwest Airlines, have developed extended products that transformed their respective markets so they had few effective competitors. Southwest, for example, redefined its business from competing with other airlines to competing with buses for the business of travelers with modest incomes. It did this with a cluster of extremely innovative cost-minimizing measures that included standardizing its fleet, rejecting assigned seats, and serving secondary airports in smaller cities that were underserved by air carriers. As another example, consider how Apple virtually eliminated the music CD and low-priced camera businesses by developing the iPhone, which is a convenient, multipurpose device anchored by a portable telephone, which everyone wants and needs.

The most effective competitors will not be those who win by doing better what incumbent firms have always done. Rather, they will win by doing things that have never been done before in an industry—creating a fundamentally new and much more effective customer value footprint for their Profit Peak customers. Of course, every manager has a golden opportunity to seize these all-important first-mover advantages by being the innovator.

The key imperative is very clear: once a manager has a lead, step on the gas—and the most effective way to do this is by turbocharging the company's customer value footprint.

Winning the customer value war is most often surprisingly easy because the competitors rarely think about it. All too often they focus on tactics like so-called price optimization (in essence, selective price raising), rather than accelerating their customer value proposition and lowering the customers' total costs.

This is especially critical for securing a company's Profit Peak customers. These customers are less susceptible to a competitor incursion, yet they also are the customers that are most receptive to innovations that fundamentally transform the company's customer value footprint and reduce its joint cost structure. Managers risk losing these critical customers if they reduce their efforts to push the frontier of customer value creation. In this sense, choosing your customers implies the need to push the envelope on the customer value footprint that those customers seek and embrace.

A company's Profit Drain customers, on the other hand, are usually the most price sensitive, and very often they are the ones driving the price war.

The essential question is whether a company's managers are so busy with tactical issues like price wars that they "do not have the time or resources" to systematically and relentlessly build their customer value footprints— especially for their Profit Peak customers.

Winning the customer value war is the only way to permanently prevent price wars and secure a company's future.

TWO LANDMARK INNOVATORS

The cases of General Electric and Zara further illustrate the process of developing and managing integrated packages of products and services to build winning customer value footprints, capture the strategic high ground, and create years of profitable growth.

General Electric's Power by the Hour

Several years ago, General Electric undertook a sweeping transformation to enhance its high-service customer value footprint. This program brought it a major increase in strategic advantage, profits, and market share. It innovated by creating a set of powerful extended products that provided unique combinations of physical products plus outstanding customer service and comprehensive technical support.

For example, General Electric's aircraft engine business decided to combine its products with enhanced service offerings to create a hard-to-follow strategic advantage. The business always had a variety of offerings, including engines, spare parts, and a variety of related services. It had innovated by improving and proliferating each of these offerings.

At that time, the company took a close look at its customers, figuratively "walking in the customers' shoes," and it determined that what most of the customers really wanted was working aircraft engines, and not an array of individual products and services that enabled that to happen.

Based on this insight, General Electric developed a breakthrough offering called Power by the Hour, in which it offered its customers an all-in price that reflected the customers' engine usage. In this way, it created a customer value footprint that strongly aligned with the customers' real need. This not only produced powerful sales and marketing advantages, but importantly, most of their competitors, many of whom were niche players with limited capabilities, could not follow.

In essence, General Electric redefined its industry by "drawing a bigger box around its business"—from selling products, to selling products plus services, to selling all-in results—to create a strategic positioning that implicitly defined most of its competitors out of the industry. General Electric **chose** customers who wanted an all-in service, **aligned** its functions to provide this package of products and services, and **managed** to coordinate in producing this unique extended product at scale.

Zara's Innovation

Zara is a Spanish retailer with an innovative strategy. The company focuses on customers who want the latest fashions. It developed a merchandising policy of stocking a limited amount of each product in each store. Because it had chosen its customers for their desire to be at the cutting edge of fashion, these customers rushed to the Zara stores to get the fashion merchandise before it ran out.

This policy was tremendously effective. The company developed very strong sales at the beginning of each season, and it restocked the stores with new fashion lines as the season progressed. The customers rushed to obtain garments while they were available, eliminating the need to mark down products toward the end of the season.

Zara developed a very effective supplier management policy to match its merchandising strategy. It conceptualized demand as "waves on the ocean," and sourced the "ocean" portion of demand in Eastern Europe where suppliers were low priced but inflexible, while it sourced the "waves" locally, where suppliers were higher priced but very flexible to changes in volume. Because the merchandise was fashion oriented and Zara's customers were not bargain hunters, they were willing to pay full price. Besides, if Zara ran out of a product, it had another desirable new product to replace it.

Zara was successful because it **chose** its customers carefully, **aligned** its business to serve these customers, and **managed** the company's operations to make the system work.

STRATEGIC CATEGORY MANAGEMENT

Strategic category management—positioning a company's product set (both physical products and extended products) to be essential to its target customers as its industry transforms and grows—is the management process that is at the heart of virtually every highly successful company. This is where strategy, sales, supply chain management, and channel management—**choosing** customers, **aligning** functions, and **managing** the organization—come together in a complex set of processes that largely determine your company's success or failure.

The history of how Microsoft became one of the world's most successful companies in an amazingly short period of time illustrates both the power and subtle success factors of this critical business capability.

Microsoft's story starts in 1975, when Bill Gates was a sophomore at Harvard. His high school friend, Paul Allen, showed him the January 1975 issue of *Popular Electronics* featuring a story about how the Micro Instrumentation & Telemetry Systems (MITS) company developed the Altair 8800 microcomputer. Gates and Allen focused on the microcomputer customers' emerging needs, determined that there would be a personal computer industry, and saw a need for programming languages. This spurred them to develop the programing languages that would position them at the heart of the new, emerging industry.

In his Harvard Commencement 2007 address, Bill Gates told of how he went to his dorm room and called the responsible executive at MITS, offering to provide software for the new PC. He worried that the executive would realize that he was just a student calling from a dorm room, but the executive told him to come see him in a month, which was fortunate because Gates and Allen hadn't written the software yet.

When Gates received the nod, he dropped out of Harvard, Allen left his programming job, and they moved to New Mexico to finish the software. That was how Microsoft began.

An observer at the time noted that Gates and Allen started Microsoft with the stated mission of putting a computer running Microsoft software on every desk and in every home. That is how they chose their customer.

Before long, Microsoft was the dominant provider of software to the early PC business.

Unlike many other PC and software pioneers, however, Bill Gates was first and foremost a businessman. He clearly saw the need to get an inside track on the industry's revolutionary growth by using his products to create a dominant strategy. This became the basis for aligning his company and managing its early organization.

The second major cornerstone of Microsoft's early success came about five years later. IBM had developed its PC, and Gates had agreed to provide BASIC for the new computer. He also offered to provide an operating system.

At that time, Microsoft was the dominant provider of PC software, but Digital Research's CP/M was the dominant PC operating system. IBM sent a team of managers to Digital Research and Microsoft to find out more about the companies.

First, they went to Digital Research. Unfortunately for Digital Research, and fortunately for Microsoft, Digital Research's Gary Kindall decided to skip the meeting.

Needless to say, when the IBM team arrived at Microsoft, they were greeted by Bill Gates. Gates proposed providing an operating system, and IBM was interested. The only problem was that Gates didn't have an appropriate system.

When he heard that IBM was interested, Gates contacted Seattle Computer Products, a small local company that had an early operating system called QDOS ("quick and dirty operating system"—later to become a more respectable-sounding MS-DOS). Microsoft bought the system for $50,000 even though it didn't work well. The company rewrote it and entered into its historic agreement with IBM in which MS-DOS would be provided on every IBM PC, while Microsoft was free to sell MS-DOS to every other PC maker as well.

That is how Microsoft became Microsoft. The rest is history. Bill Gates was 25 years old at the time.

This story is remarkable. What's even more amazing is that at every point, someone else had a better product. But Microsoft always had a much better strategy: **choosing** the right customers, **aligning** the company's activities to meet these customers' needs, and **managing** to produce the needed products and services.

In checkers, there's an old rule of thumb: if you're not sure what to do, move toward the middle. Bill Gates relentlessly moved toward the middle of his target market and won by constantly positioning Microsoft at the center of the entire evolving PC industry.

The moral of the story is that a great strategy always beats a great product. Or, as they say in sailboat racing: a good sailor in a bad boat will always beat a bad sailor in a good boat.

The danger is that day-to-day *operational category management* issues like pricing, promotion, and packaging are so pervasive and pressing that they often crowd out the opportunity to focus on *strategic category management*, which is much more important to a company's success.

Product Positioning Excellence

What made Bill Gates so successful was his intuitive sense of strategic category management, linked of course, with a terrific ability to manage. He was intuitively able to visualize the development of a historical new industry almost like a chessboard on which he could position his budding company.

The actual products that Gates offered were in a sense derived from his need to meet opportunities that were emerging in his customers' businesses. By moving fast to fulfill these developing customer needs, he was able to lock up market opportunities that would rapidly become huge and enormously lucrative.

Microsoft's key success factor in its early days was not product excellence, per se. It was product-positioning excellence. Once the company locked in its customer positioning, even with a marginal product, it could then work hard to improve the quality and performance of its product.

This is the power of strategic category management. The most effective category managers operate at two levels: strategic and operational.

Strategic category management—an integral part of broad-gauge category management—concerns how to create strategic dominance and sustained profitable growth by positioning a company through its product offerings to be a central factor in its target customers' business.

Category managers need to devote a significant amount of their time teaming with their sales and supply chain management colleagues to target the right customers and stay deeply involved in constantly improving their company's extended products that move the company into new realms of customer value creation. The key to accomplishing this objective is to initiate a constant series of *profit-showcase projects*, in which company managers have an opportunity to learn by doing. They "walk in the customers' shoes," through which they join with selected customers to identify and develop new customer value footprint opportunities that even the customers themselves did not initially see.

Profit-showcase projects, described in the next section, are a primary way to create new breakthroughs in customer value. Market research—both surveys and focus groups—cannot do this because while most consumers are able to differentiate among attributes of products that they know, like determining whether they probably would like mint-flavored coffee or soap in dispensers, most consumers cannot judge products that are outside their range of experience, such as flying cars today, or using Google to surf the web in the early days of personal computing.

Steve Jobs was famous for not using market research. Instead, he trusted his own vision and creativity to develop the iPod, iPhone, and iPad, along with a few less successful products. Thomas Edison was another visionary who developed the electric light, movies, record players, and a host of other world-changing inventions without market research.

Key Success Factors

Many managers of companies that make or distribute physical products lose valuable strategic and profit opportunities because they don't capitalize on the benefits of building extended products through strategic category management.

This is natural. They are very focused on managing their physical products. Consequently, they often view designing and managing related services, such as information support, vendor-managed inventory, and joint category management, as almost an afterthought, a nuisance cost to be recouped if possible. This is a big mistake.

Benefits of Extended Products

Extended products are central to strategic category management.

Today, managers have a unique historical opportunity to create decisive first-mover advantages as the Age of Diverse Markets disrupts old, established industry orders. But these will be available for only a limited time—until industries settle into new orders and the players are locked into new, permanent roles.

Selling more products can give a vendor additional presence in customers, but selling extended products can give a vendor a new strategic positioning and a host of top-level contacts deep in their target customers' organizations. This can be immensely important in reversing a vendor's slide toward commoditization and price competition.

Paradoxically, in most extended product sales, especially those that involve deeply embedded extended products, the larger the change, the easier it is to sell the new relationship. This occurs because larger, more comprehensive value footprints almost always produce new value in multiple areas of the customer's organization. The purchase decision naturally gets elevated in the customer's organization to an officer who has broad responsibility and a long-term strategic perspective, rather than a lower-level, price-oriented buyer.

Building your extended product can offer the opportunity to create compelling value in unexpected ways. For example, Nalco, a company that provides chemicals to water treatment systems, installed sensors that could be read remotely in the chemical tanks on the customers' premises. This enabled Nalco to be much more efficient at replenishment and production. But the company didn't stop there.

Nalco's managers developed a deep understanding of the customers in their target market. They had many conversations and on-site visits with their counterparts in customer organizations, which enabled them to "walk in their customers' shoes." Through this process, they realized that their innovation allowed Nalco to monitor the actual rate of chemical drawdown and compare it to the expected rate if the customer's water treatment system were operating at peak efficiency. When the Nalco engineers saw a variance, they would call the water system's managers and alert them to adjust the system. This routinely led to customer savings many times the cost of the chemicals. In a city like Chicago, for example, the cost of a poorly performing system was tens of millions of dollars, compared to the cost of hundreds of thousands of dollars of Nalco's chemicals.

This innovation created unique differentiation that even digital competitors with big data and AI could not follow because once Nalco modified a customer's chemical tank and established its information links with the customer's engineers, it had an inside track into the account. This gave Nalco compelling first-mover advantages and competitive advantage.

In the process, it made Nalco indispensable, transforming the company's positioning from commodity supplier to essential strategic partner with strong information-based barriers to entry. Nalco drew a bigger box around its business, expanding its customer value footprint—and internet-based competitors could not follow. The moral of the story is that you always have an opportunity to increase your customer value footprint, and real value always wins.

Most deeply embedded extended products enable a company's account managers and operations personnel to develop close relationships and trust with their counterparts throughout the customer's organization. Many of these managers in the customer's organization are important members of the customer's buying center who otherwise would have been inaccessible. These new relationships throughout the customer's organization are essential to identifying, creating, and selling new generations of ever more effective extended products.

Extended Product Issues

Extended products provide many valuable advantages—far beyond new fees and the ability to raise prices. However, these products, especially the deeply embedded extended products, involve some very important issues.

It is critical to choose your customers carefully and align your functions with the needs of your respective profit rivers. Many customers are not good candidates for extended products, especially for deeply embedded extended products, because of their profit potential, buyer behavior, capability to partner, or operating characteristics.

For example, Baxter soon learned that its stockless system was best suited for sophisticated large hospitals clustered in a medical area because the hospital cluster provided logistical economies, had large profit potential, and preferred longer-term contracts with demonstrated savings. This means that category managers must develop a thoughtful, practical set of account qualification criteria, as well as one or more fallback extended products in the company's relationship hierarchy.

Unfortunately, many companies' sales compensation systems reward all revenue increases. They have no choice but to do this unless they utilize the transaction-based profit analytics needed to understand actual customer net profit.

Very often, extended product costs are not incremental, and they are difficult to quantify. They usually involve facilities that are jointly used by different processes in a company. Also, well-designed extended products, like Baxter's stockless system, actually lower a supplier's costs, even while they increase its sales. Transaction-based profit analytics enable managers to define, price, and manage these complex products.

Profit-Showcase Projects

A profit-showcase project is a critically important component of strategic product management, both for exploring customer potential when you are choosing your customer and for understanding how to enhance your value footprint in your target customers. It provides a very valuable opportunity to "learn by doing" by spending time physically in a customer to understand how your company's products are selected and used in the broader context of the customer's business processes in which they are embedded. In order to successfully develop innovative extended products, it is very important to have several profit-showcase projects running at all times.

For example, Baxter developed its stockless system in a profit-showcase project in which a small team from Baxter spent a few weeks in a hospital systematically observing and measuring its supply chain processes, without an initial hypothesis on how to make them more efficient.

Several years ago, we were involved in a showcase project in which a company's CEO approached the CEO of a very innovative customer. He asked if he could place a team in the customer for a month or two. They would observe the customer and perhaps generate some measures of the customer's activities. In essence, they would be "walking in the customer's shoes."

The CEO explained the profit showcase to his customer's CEO by saying, "I have an empty bag today. After two months, my team will tell me what to put into the bag, and I'll see if you want to buy it." Of course, the customer's managers were instrumental in helping to identify what would be in the bag—codefining the customer's evolving real needs and codesigning the new extended-product offering. Needless to say, the customer's CEO bought the innovation that was "in the bag."

Only by spending time and working on-site in the customer can a supplier's team and their customer counterparts evolve a really deep understanding of the customer's needs and embody it in an innovative, compelling extended product. In the process, of course, they develop very strong relationships with each other, which are important in both selling the innovation and in implementing the new processes.

A profit-showcase project is very different from a pilot project. A pilot project is usually a proof-of-concept demonstration for a process that has already been analyzed and tentatively approved, while a profit showcase project is a "voyage of discovery" without a predetermined result.

The best locations for showcase projects are those where the conditions for innovation are most favorable. These are typically smaller, highly innovative customers.

It is important to bear in mind that the most effective profit-showcase projects develop completely new ways to structure and conduct a business (for example, Baxter's stockless vendor-managed inventory system). Thus, market acceptance is a moving target; it will rapidly increase once the early adopters have shown stellar results.

The most productive way to develop and manage profit-showcase projects is to create a formal, ongoing process that is the responsibility of a committee of upper management (directors and VPs), and not an occasional ad hoc event. In fact, this is an essential responsibility of a company's MPG Committee, which we describe in Chapter 8.

Selling Extended Products

In selling deep extended products, especially those that require some customization, it is very effective to form a team jointly with each customer. The team's objective is to "rediscover" the extended-product opportunity and to quantify the benefits. Because innovative extended products involve completely new ways to do business, it is critical for a group of customer managers to move through the process of specifying the innovation and verifying the benefits—even though the supplier already has this knowledge. The customer managers on the team will become core supporters, which is essential to selling the innovation (at least until it is accepted widely by the market).

When building a company's value footprint in its Profit Peak customers, it is important to shift from transactional to relationship selling. (We will explain this process more thoroughly in the next chapter.)

In transactional selling, the sales rep typically takes the lead until the customer relationship is well established. At that point, the supply chain manager makes contact to ensure smooth operational interactions.

Relationship selling, especially with high-profit customers and prospects, is very different. It is a joint multicapability selling process with the sales reps, supply chain managers, and other involved departments teaming closely to engage the account.

Because high-profit customers almost always should have a degree of supply chain integration inherent in their relationship, a very different dynamic naturally occurs. Supply chain managers are essential—especially in the early stages of high-profit customer engagement—because they will naturally bond with their customer counterparts to start solving joint problems and creating joint operating efficiencies. This process will drive the relationship deeper and accelerate both revenues and profits—as we saw in the Baxter case with the relationship that developed between the Baxter materials management coordinators and their counterparts, the head nurses.

It is important to put every element of a company's relationship with its high-profit customers under the microscope by "walking in your customers' shoes." For example, at Edison Furniture, which we described in Chapter 1, the delivery manager noted that about a third of the drivers had great customer service skills, while the rest simply drove trucks. In the existing system, each driver loaded his or her truck and drove through traffic to the customer who happened to be next on the list.

Instead, the delivery manager suggested that they station the "master" drivers, those with strong customer service skills, near the Profit Peak customers in the field. When an order was being delivered to a Profit Peak customer, the regular drivers would shuttle the products to the master driver located in the field; then they would change trucks so the master drivers always were the ones who interacted with the premier customers. The master drivers were trained in selling, as well as delivering, and, in time, they generated so many sales that they were given commissions.

This example underscores the importance of moving past the old functional view of a company, where sales owned the customer. Today, everyone can—and must—add value to the customers' experience and increase profitability, even those in what were traditionally considered cost centers.

Expanding the Customer Value Frontier

Successful strategic category managers create a stream of innovative extended products that meet the rapidly evolving customer needs of their target sets of customers. This is a moving target. Once a company has success and momentum in creating an innovative extended product that really expands its customer value footprint for its target customers, it is easier to build on its experience and relationships to keep *expanding* its customer value footprint.

Unfortunately, all too many managers see this as a one-time task and fail to keep innovating—essentially losing the opportunity to make their customer value innovations a permanent strategic category management capability.

The moral of the story is that once your company has the lead, step on the gas. Never give customers even the slightest reason to look around for an alternative. A company's customer value footprint tells the story of its success or decline.

MANAGING TO STAY ON TOP

The following four essential steps frame the most productive processes for systematically building a company's value footprint.

Walk in Your Customer's Shoes

Spending significant time physically in a set of customers is a great way to judge the potential of a set of prospective customers and, once chosen, to build a powerful customer value footprint. The objective is to observe the entire purchase-to-use cycle for your products. This includes everything from selecting the products, to procuring them economically, to understanding how the customer is using them.

Here, a manager is looking for opportunities to build the broadest, most powerful customer value footprint. The early development of innovations like vendor-managed inventory and category management provide examples. So do the contemporary early initiatives to create strategies based on the industrial internet, also called the *internet of things* (IoT).

Importantly, building a company's extended-product portfolio can offer the opportunity to create compelling value in unexpected ways, as illustrated by the cases of Baxter, SKF, Nalco, and Zara.

Here is our take on the ultimate truth in business: managers always have an opportunity to increase their companies' value footprint, and real value always wins.

Move Toward the Middle

A classic rookie move in chess is to go for checkmate on an early move, instead of laying out the board position. The equivalent of the board position in a supplier-customer relationship is real value and customer trust. Once a manager has worked to understand and develop a truly winning value footprint with a very creative extended product, the next essential task is to systematically align the company by putting the core pieces in place. And often, the core pieces are subtle.

For example, suppose a supplier wants to develop a highly integrated supply chain with a major customer, and the customer is not interested in this type of relationship. The core building blocks, as always, are real value and customer trust. These grow naturally out of the broader multicapability customer engagement teams that go far beyond the traditional sales rep and buyer relationship.

Even with an arm's-length relationship, the supplier can arrange for its supply chain managers to meet periodically with their counterparts in the customer in order to discuss ways to enhance customer service. Over time, the supplier's supply chain managers will develop a trusting relationship with their customer counterparts. Note that this process does not focus on selling products or solving problems; it focuses only on building trust, although some long-festering misunderstandings may have to be cleared up early in the process.

Later, once the trusting relationships have developed, the supply chain managers can bring these customer counterparts to meet operations managers in other customers that already have productive, highly integrated relationships with the vendor. These meetings will naturally gravitate toward identifying and confirming the value produced.

Through this process, the supplier can align its functions and build the essential core of real value and customer trust that will lead to a highly productive, highly differentiated relationship with the target account.

Touch the Dream

Every top manager in every company has a dream—a vision of what real success looks like. This nearly always centers on turbocharging business growth, inventing creative new business initiatives, and building a dominant strategic position.

When a company's customer value proposition enables its customers to move toward their dreams, the company will become an essential strategic partner to its customers.

This can happen in unexpected ways. For example, we're deeply familiar with the operations of a number of vendor-managed inventory systems and other integrated supplier-customer innovations. These certainly create important benefits, including customer cost reductions. But surprisingly often, the most powerful, but unexpected, benefit is that the partnership enables the customer to enter new markets or offer new services because it can draw on the supplier partner's deep, specialized capabilities—as Baxter did when its stockless system enabled hospitals to create networks of remote clinics and care centers.

By enabling the customer to grow its business in powerful new ways that the customer alone could not have done, the supplier becomes an essential part of the customer's success. The supplier wins the value war by touching the customer's dream.

Have the Discipline to Remain Focused

It is so tempting to operate close to the surface of a customer relationship, focusing primarily on the day-to-day sale of a company's products and services, searching out tactical gains. And if a manager does achieve tactical gains, it is overwhelmingly tempting to focus on celebrating these "victories."

However, the top managers who succeed in the long run have the discipline to remain focused on understanding their target customers, developing the most powerful customer value footprint, and systematically building the alignment in their company to be able to deliver results at scale. When they have created this understanding, they redouble their efforts to push the value creation envelope even further and continue to search relentlessly for new ways to create real value and customer trust.

RELENTLESS FOCUS

We're reminded of a wonderful exhibit on American ingenuity mounted several years ago by the Smithsonian Institution: *If We're So Good, Why Aren't We Better?*

The best managers in the best companies are always relentlessly focused on this question, and they are almost frantic to find an ever-better answer.

This is how they got to be market leaders, and it is why they stay in front—**choosing** their customers, **aligning** their functions, and **managing** to build their winning positions as their industries undergo revolutionary change.

THINGS TO THINK ABOUT

1. What is your customer value footprint other than low price? How is this different for each of your profit segments?

2. What is the problem that the users of your products are trying to solve? How are you organized to systematically probe and meet this need?

3. What extended products provide the best value to your Profit Peak customers? How will this change over the next three to five years?

4. Have you quantified the benefit *to your customer* of your value footprint?

6

OWN YOUR CUSTOMER HIGH GROUND

You are what you sell.

Your customers are the front-wheel drive that pulls you through your marketplace. All too many companies today implicitly assume that their objective is to maximize their sales revenue, and they make the subsidiary assumption that they can minimize their costs through ancillary processes, thus maximizing their net profits.

This set of management assumptions is completely wrong. It is an obsolete holdover from the vanishing Age of Mass Markets. Today, the core management objective is to maximize your profitable growth in your chosen market segments.

BUILDING DOMINANCE IN YOUR CHOSEN MARKET SEGMENTS

Consider Custom Research, a small but successful market research firm.*

---

* Susan Greco, "Choose or Lose," *Inc. Magazine*, 1998. Also, Susan Harmeling and William Bruns, Custom Research (A) (Boston: Harvard Business School Publishing, 9-199-001, 2001).

Custom Research had a problem. The company had grown from a relatively small startup over the course of several years into one of the larger, well-respected companies in its business.

Over time, however, the company's financial performance had eroded. After a number of years of high growth, the company's return on sales (net profit as a percent of revenues) was steadily dropping, and sales had slowed. When management looked closely at the company's situation, most clients were Profit Desert clients, with only a few small and marginally profitable projects each year, as shown in Figure 6.1.

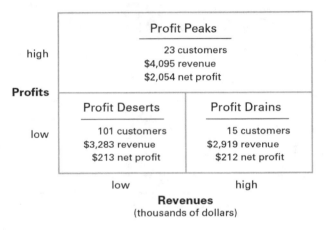

Figure 6.1 Custom Research Customer Profit Map

The company's strategy was essentially to take all clients that it could land, under the assumption that each would contribute to overhead and that the company needed a significant market share to be a "player."

The problem, however, was that the industry was consolidating, and the surviving firms were becoming relatively large and aggressive. In that context, Custom Research found its profit growth slowing substantially despite having a significant market share and lots of clients. The company was running out of resources, and it was essentially "stuck in the mud."

The action questions were these: What happened? and, What should they do? In today's Age of Diverse Markets, company after company across a wide range of industries is facing these same two essential questions.

The underlying problem was that Custom Research was so focused on growth at all costs that it neglected to build a sound account selection and management process that would *produce not just growth, but profitable growth.*

Custom Research was becoming flooded with numerous low-potential, high-maintenance customers that were taking increasing amounts of the producing partners' mindshare, time, and resources. These accounts were crowding out the partners' ability to focus on deepening their penetration of their lucrative high-potential Profit Peak clients. Worse, the firm's increasingly scattered portfolio was endangering its partners' ability to produce high-quality work for its premier clients, and it was diluting its strategic differentiation—a deadly combination.

The company's indiscriminate account selection situation almost eliminated the opportunity to create and implement an effective account management process (that is, managing the client's buying process to deepen its relationship) with the right clients.

The way out of this type of dilemma is to clarify and enforce an effective, practical set of account qualification criteria. In Custom Research's case, this included factors such as these: (1) revenue potential; (2) net profit potential; (3) strategic and operating fit; (4) willingness and ability to partner (versus transactional buyer behavior); and (5) likelihood of closing.

These account qualification criteria would bring in the most profitable business—which left the important residual problem of how to manage down the current Profit Desert client population. The way that Customer Research's managers thought about their situation was that in the past, their goal was to maximize market share, but now they needed to maximize their profit.

Your real goal is to maximize your market share of the most inherently lucrative, high-potential portion of the market—your Profit Peaks, and those that should be in this group—both in your current industry paradigm and in your transformed industry. The key to success is understanding that there is *not a trade-off between high growth and high profits*, and in fact they reinforce each other if you utilize transaction-based profit metrics and analytics, along with effective profit management processes.

After analyzing its problem, Custom Research's management team decided to end the practice of taking every client that requested a project. The firm would not work with clients with annual business of less than a set amount, and it would begin to focus on building the larger Profit Peak client relationships.

In deciding to stop taking all business that was available, Custom Research achieved two important goals. First, the business it did take was more profitable, producing more net profits per project; second, the company's staff was freed up to better manage their high-profit and high-potential accounts by providing the best possible service, building their customer value footprint.

In a second step, a few years later, management decided to double the minimum set amount and take only those clients with the potential to grow to two to three times the minimum amount within a few years.

The results: Custom Research reduced its client count by about 50 percent, sales rose by about 60 percent, profits more than tripled, and the company's return on sales rose from 9 to 20 percent.

Account selection—choosing your customer—is a critically important process that you can structure and manage in a very systematic way that maximizes your sales resource productivity. We explained the process of identifying *future* Profit Peak customers in your transforming industry in Chapter 3. In this chapter, we turn to the need to build, retain, and manage your current and prospective Profit Peak customers; to manage your Profit Drain and Profit Desert segments in order to convert as many as possible to Profit Peak customers; and to avoid diluting your resources by working to increase your business with your current and prospective customers in these low-profit segments.

Choosing your customers means two things: (1) identifying and obtaining those customers who are and will be Profit Peaks and (2) avoiding the prospects who *will not become Profit Peaks*. The second point is particularly important, and this is where most companies fail both because they do not have a clear understanding of their Profit Peak customers' profile, and because they do not have a clear set of processes (including compensation) to avoid selling to prospective customers that are unlikely to develop into Profit Peaks.

Digital giants have certain overwhelming advantages that we have been highlighting throughout this book. Few companies can match these strengths in a head-to-head contest. The bottom-line message of this book is that most companies have plenty of opportunities to stake out a very lucrative strategic high ground in the remaining segments of the markets— if they have the discipline and processes to focus their resources on this objective.

The lesson of the SKF case in the prior chapter is that the open competitive playing field often is composed of a number of diverse market segments, each of which requires a somewhat different customer value footprint, and many of which can become very lucrative profit rivers.

CURRENT PROFIT PEAK CUSTOMERS

The absolute priority for your entire account selection and management program is to increase your business with your Profit Peak accounts— current, prospective, and future. Period. Deciding to double down on your most profitable customers is your wisest account selection strategy, and it is your fastest, most productive profit opportunity.

This is somewhat counterintuitive because many managers assume that these already are your "good" customers, so you should work on landing new customers and fixing your profit drains instead. This is a big mistake.

Profit Peak customers are typically underserved. If your Profit Peak customers are providing 120 to 200 percent of your reported profits, they should get a comparable amount of your attention. In most companies, however, the Profit Drain customers, who are typically bargainers, shoppers, and complainers, get much more attention. So do the Profit Desert customers who are many times more numerous and are often inexperienced. In nearly every company, the Profit Peak customers are woefully underresourced.

Moreover, your Profit Peak customers typically are very loyal, and they are more service sensitive than price sensitive. They are usually willing to accept a price increase if it is packaged with an extension of your value footprint both small (for example, a new ordering process or better packaging) and large (for example, vendor-managed inventory, category management,

	Profit Peaks				Profit Drains			
Quartile	Customers	Revenue		Net Profit	Customers	Revenue		Net Profit
Q1	1.3%	43.5%		55.4%	0.2%	1.5%		1.4%
Q2	1.3%	10.5%		14.5%	0.2%	1.8%		0.6%
Q3	1.3%	6.9%		9.3%	0.2%	2.2%		(0.8%)
Q4	1.3%	6.0%		6.2%	0.2%	9.4%		(11.7%)
All Quartiles	5.1%	66.9%		85.4%	0.9%	14.9%		(10.6%)

	Profit Peaks					Profit Drains				
Quartile	No. Customers	Revenue	Revenue/ Customer	Net Profit	Net Profit/ Customer	No. Customers	Revenue	Revenue/ Customer	Net Profit	Net Profit/ Customer
Q1	2.3	$644.7	$276.3	$102.7	$44.0	0.4	$22.0	$56.4	$2.5	$6.5
Q2	2.3	$155.3	$66.6	$26.9	$11.5	0.4	$26.2	$67.3	$1.1	$2.8
Q3	2.3	$102.4	$43.9	$17.2	$7.4	0.4	$32.6	$83.7	($1.5)	($3.8)
Q4	2.3	$88.7	$38.0	$11.4	$4.9	0.4	$139.5	$359.3	($21.7)	($56.0)
All Quartiles	9.3	$991.1	$106.2	$158.2	$17.0	1.6	$220.3	$141.6	($19.6)	($12.6)

Figure 6.2 Customers by Customer Segment and Profit Quartiles

Note: Customers in thousands; revenue per customer and net profit (NP) per customer in thousands of dollars; and other figures in millions of dollars.

product codesign). Importantly, they often are early adopters of new products and services, are more willing to accept private-label products and substitutes, and are open to changes in their product mix.

Although some Profit Drain and Profit Desert customers are unprofitable for reasons that can be fixed in the short run (for example, overly frequent ordering, excessive expedited shipments), most of the problems are difficult, structural, and lengthy to fix (for example, changing the product mix, stopping discounting). Further, your bargain-hunting Profit Drain customers often will drop you if you try to work with them to build a more productive long-run relationship, and many of your Profit Desert customers are simply very small.

These critical factors underscore the fact that increasing your business with your current Profit Peak customers is not only by far the most lucrative

Profit Deserts				All Customer Segments			
Customers	Revenue		Net Profit	Customers	Revenue		Net Profit
23.5%	13.8%		35.1%	25.0%	58.8%		91.8%
23.5%	1.2%		1.9%	25.0%	13.5%		17.1%
23.5%	0.4%		(0.5%)	25.0%	9.5%		8.0%
23.5%	2.8%		(11.3%)	25.0%	18.2%		(16.9%)
94.0%	18.3%		25.2%	100.0%	100.0%		100.0%

Profit Deserts					All Customer Segments				
No. Customers	Revenue	Revenue/ Customer	Net Profit	Net Profit/ Customer	No. Customers	Revenue	Revenue/ Customer	Net Profit	Net Profit/ Customer
43.0	$204.9	$4.8	$64.9	$1.5	45.7	$871.5	$19.1	$170.1	$3.7
43.0	$18.4	$0.4	$3.6	$0.1	45.7	$200.0	$4.4	$31.6	$0.7
43.0	$6.0	$0.1	($0.9)	$0.0	45.7	$141.0	$3.1	$14.9	$0.3
43.0	$41.6	$1.0	($20.9)	($0.5)	45.7	$269.9	$5.9	($31.2)	($0.7)
171.9	$271.0	$1.6	$46.8	$0.3	182.8	$1,482.3	$8.1	$185.3	$1.0

thing you can do—if you double your Profit Peak business, you more than double your profits—but also, it is often the easiest and fastest thing to do. The biggest roadblocks to this are (1) complacency with the status quo in this critical segment—the natural tendency is to celebrate landing new customers, and to underemphasize further penetration of customers who are already "good customers"—and (2) failure to use transaction-based profit metrics and analytics to track their profit erosion and growth.

Your Profit Peak customers are your most important assets, but some Profit Peak customers are more profitable than others. Figure 6.2 provides an example. It shows that this company's Profit Peak customers provide over 85 percent of the company's net profits, while the Profit Drain customers erode over 10 percent of this amount, and the Profit Desert customers add a surprising 25 percent of net profits.

On closer examination, however, the picture has some important variance. The top *quartile* of the Profit Peak segment contributes a whopping

55 percent of the company's overall net profits, or about $44,000 per customer; the upper quartile provides 15 percent, or about $11,000 per customer; the lower quartile provides about 9 percent, or about $7,000 per customer; and the bottom quartile adds about 6 percent, or about $5,000 per customer.

The 4,600 customers in the top two quartiles of the Profit Peak segment provide about 70 percent of the company's profits—with the 2,300 customers in the top Profit Peak quartile alone contributing over 55 percent of the company's net profits.

In light of the intense concentration of net profits, especially in the top two Profit Peak quartiles, it is imperative that these customers be the prime focus of the company's sales program with dedicated resources.

The top Profit Desert quartile is producing a strong 35 percent of the company's profits, but it has nearly 43,000 customers. Here, the net profit contribution per customer is about $1,500. Contrast this with the $44,000 per customer, and the $11,000 per customer for the top and upper quartiles of the Profit Peak segment, respectively. This means that the payoff from having a top sales rep or team focus on a Profit Peak top or upper quartile customer is extremely strong, while the payoff for a top sales rep or team focusing on a top Profit Desert quartile customer is much weaker. Instead, managers should engage their companies' top quartile Profit Desert customers through intensive, customized social media, digital marketing, or telesales.

The bottom Profit Drain customer quartile, on the other hand, is eroding over 12 percent of the company's profits, while the bottom quartile of the Profit Desert segment also is eroding about 11 percent. Together, these two poorly performing quartiles are reducing the company's profits by nearly 25 percent. Both are candidates for remediation.

However, note the big difference in the number of customers in these two problematic customer quadrants. The bottom Profit Drain quartile is losing $56,000 per customer, so it is clearly worthwhile to give it intensive specialized attention. The bottom Profit Desert quartile is losing about $500 per customer, so the company needs to deal with these customers through other, more economical, modes of engagement.

Building Your Profit Peaks

How can you systematically build your business with your existing Profit Peak customers? Several processes will enable you to accomplish this.

First and foremost, develop transaction-based profit metrics that identify your Profit Peak customers, and train all your personnel, especially your sales and customer service reps, to give them well-designed priority service. For example, Edison Furniture, which we profiled in Chapter 1, placed icons on the sales reps' iPad screens so they could instantly recognize Profit Peak customers when they entered the stores. They could quickly scan a customer's buying history and preferences, and they could steer the customer toward his or her preferred sales reps and products.

In essence, this created "mass customization" of customer service, while it informed the sales rep of the customer's willingness to accept high-margin add-ons like product protection and warrantees. Importantly, at the end of each day, the sales managers reviewed the Profit Peak customer engagements with the sales reps, evaluating and coaching the reps in near real time. The company coupled this with a set of related services, including customer concierge services and delivery by master drivers.

It is also imperative to understand your Profit Peak customers' potential and build relationships with their entire buying center. This is almost common wisdom in sales circles, but the problem is that it takes valuable time.

What is important here is that it is also common—but flawed—wisdom to target all big customers. While all customers must be treated well, the sales process should focus primarily on the high-payoff Profit Peak customers, devoting the time and dedicated resources it takes to fully develop these all-important accounts. This will ensure that you have a steady increase in high-profit business, while you cement your long-term profitable growth and accomplish any repositioning that you need to do. This process will enable you to build tight ties and competitive differentiation with your true strategic accounts—those who will become or remain Profit Peaks in your transformed industry.

Your Profit Peak customers are much more open to innovative services that deepen your relationship, as we saw in Chapter 5. These will reinforce the incredibly productive virtuous cycle in which you lower your customers' costs, drive up your sales as a result, and lower your own costs in the process, thus enabling you to invest in renewing and broadening the cycle.

When building your value footprint in Profit Peak customers, it is important to shift from transactional to relationship selling.

In transactional selling, the sales rep typically takes the lead until the customer relationship is well established. At that point, the supply chain manager makes contact to ensure smooth operational interactions.

Relationship selling, especially with Profit Peak customers and prospects, is very different. It is a joint multicapability selling process with the sales reps, supply chain managers, and other involved departments teaming closely to engage the account. Because your Profit Peak customers are very important and different from your Profit Drain and Profit Desert customers, it is essential to recruit, develop, and manage them with dedicated multifunctional teams that are specialized in creating deep productive relationships with these customers.

Profit Peak customers almost always have a degree of supply chain integration inherent in their relationship, so a very different dynamic naturally occurs: after the initial contact, the increasingly coordinated and integrated supply chain relationship itself drives deeper and deeper sales penetration, as we saw in the Baxter case in Chapter 1. Thus, even from the early customer contacts, supply chain managers are essential to building and furthering your relationships with this very important set of accounts.

Today, everyone can add value to the customers' experience and increase profitability, even those in what were traditionally considered cost centers. The example of Pacific Financial Services, a disguised company, illustrates the importance of moving past the old functional view of a company.

Pacific, like most financial services companies, had a very sophisticated risk management process, in which they evaluated new loans very carefully. The problem was that this evaluation process took a lot of time, especially at busy times of the year, and some key customers were pursuing deals with a very short time frame.

Pacific's innovation was to create a "fast lane" for Profit Peak customers (who were repeat customers) in which their risk profile was refreshed frequently, and not just when they requested a loan. This minimized the company's response time to a loan request. It turned out that this was so important to these key customers that they happily accepted an incrementally higher interest rate on the loan.

PROFIT-FOCUSED SELLING

Over the past 40 years, multitiered selling emerged as one of the prime tools for account management. In essence, *multitiered selling* is the process of matching sales resources to account revenues.

Some huge national customers might have had a dedicated national sales rep at headquarters, but this rep was essentially seeking a "hunting license" within contract pricing guidelines for the local sales reps who were calling on the local facilities that actually did the buying. In this period, most sales reps focused on honing their closing skills, and they called on accounts largely according to their purchases—in a simplified version: a sales call every week for a high-revenue A account, every two weeks for a medium-revenue B account, and every month for a low-revenue C account.

Multitiered selling was developed in response to the growth of centralized purchasing in major companies. In this process, a highly skilled national account manager called on the major customers' headquarters and was the "traffic cop" into the account—directing product managers and other specialists where needed and coordinating with local reps calling on the customer's local facilities.

The domain of territory reps continued to be midlevel accounts, along with major customers' local facilities. Telesales increasingly sold to smaller accounts, although the line between territory reps and telesales reps was often blurred. At the same time, companies were deploying customer service reps to take orders and answer questions, freeing up sales rep time.

As some large companies started to integrate their supply chains with some of their major customers, supply chain managers began to develop relationships with their customer counterparts. Leading companies, like Baxter and P&G, formed integrated multicapability customer teams, but most often the internal supplier coordination was ad hoc and not systematic.

Today, the world has completely changed, creating very important new profit opportunities. More and more suppliers are seeking closer operating ties with their Profit Peak customers, and many of these customers are seeking them as well.

Fortunately, the advent of transaction-based profit metrics and analytics enables leading companies to move from multitiered selling to the ultimate level of sales effectiveness, which we call *profit-focused selling*. Instead of assuming that revenue maximization is the objective of the account management process, leading managers now understand that directly maximizing all-in customer net profitability is the right objective.

Profit Peak customers are very profitable, large, and usually very supplier loyal. They generally want more integrated relationships and continuous value footprint innovations. This account relationship requires joint planning, joint management, and joint value creation.

Accomplishing this requires that the supplier deploy an experienced, highly integrated multicapability team, often largely dedicated to one or a few accounts. This is especially important for customers in the top two quartiles of the Profit Peak segment. Today, this approach is appropriate, effective, economically justified, and, in fact, necessary.

In the past, major account penetration was largely a one-size-fits-all process. Many companies trained their sales reps to be "trusted advisors," who could work with a company to deepen the relationship. Their goal was to understand the customer's business goals—really the respective objectives of the various members of the buying center—and to bring to bear products and programs that would help their customers' managers to meet their various objectives.

The trusted advisor role is certainly a worthy objective. However, today a major account sales process needs a completely different set of capabilities. These include the ability to identify and offer tightly aligned sets of profit-maximizing products and related services to meet each customer's specific needs; the assembly of a tightly integrated multicapability team that can devise and manage positive change within each customer; an understanding of which relationship each customer should have; and the ability to sell each relationship.

In today's Age of Diverse Markets, the trusted advisor needs to become a tightly integrated multicapability team that is a *trusted profit partner* that can work with the Profit Peak customers on a cross-functional basis to generate *for the customer* sustained profitable growth and strategic differentiation. In the process, this will create strong sustained profitable growth and strategic dominance *for the supplier*.

By transforming from a trusted advisor to trusted profit partner, your company will be able to provide significantly more value, building barriers to entry into your Profit Peak accounts based on customer knowledge and trust—and the ability to manage change within the customers—consequently accelerating your sustained profitable growth.

The final imperative is to keep your Profit Peak customers. This means systematically monitoring when a Profit Peak customer leaves or when purchases diminish. It is especially helpful to have an Early Alert monitoring system that keeps track of this, notifying the trusted profit partner team when a Profit Peak customer's sales or profits start to erode.

When you lose a Profit Peak customer, conduct an *exit interview* to understand what problem arose, and change your processes to ensure that this does not happen again. Most customers will be impressed that you cared enough to investigate how to get better, and, in our experience, many will give you another chance.

CURRENT PROFIT DRAIN CUSTOMERS

Your Profit Drain customers are very important, primarily because in most companies they consume a large amount of sales and operations resources, and they chronically underperform. Two elements are particularly important in managing your Profit Drain customers.

First, *avoid* potential Profit Drain customers when targeting and selecting customers. When evaluating prospective accounts, especially those with the potential to be large accounts, understand your current Profit Drain customers' characteristics, and be very cautious about pursuing and accepting prospects with these problematic attributes. You can separately survey your Profit Peak customers and your Profit Drain customers to profile each group as we described in the Edison Furniture case in Chapter 1.

There is a very strong temptation to take a small amount of business in prospects that fit the Profit Drain profile simply because they are large companies (and most sales reps are compensated on revenue increases). Most major companies want to have at least a weak relationship with a number of suppliers in case their main suppliers have a stockout, and many try to cherry-pick for bargains. Preventing your sales reps from deepening your relationship with large, money-losing customers is a very productive but counterintuitive profit lever.

Second, although Profit Drain customers are costly, some have activities that are reasonable to fix. Some of these may even be the supplier's fault.

In Chapter 2, we described a company that pushed its sales reps to install vending machines in customers' facilities. The sales reps responded by arguing to the customers that they could set the machines' inventory at very low levels in order to "save money on inventory" by ordering very frequently because it was "costless."

This practice generated large, unnecessary costs for both the customer and supplier, but the sales reps only saw high revenues and gross margins—and the sales compensation system rewarded them for this. The customers, on the other hand, did not see their excessive costs of ordering, receiving, putting away, and paying invoices because they did not have transaction-based profit metrics that exposed and tracked these costs. After all, you cannot manage what you do not measure. In most customers, this frequent ordering issue is "hidden," but it is fairly easy to fix (although it is best to address this issue in the contracting phase early in the relationship).

Reducing these unnecessary costs will enable you to convert some of your Profit Drain customers to Profit Peaks. However, bear in mind that most operational costs are much harder to reduce, and many Profit Drain customers, who are essentially transactional bargain hunters, have buyer behavior that is extremely difficult to reverse.

There is a strong temptation to place your primary focus on stemming your profit drains. This is a major error because the real payoff comes from growing your Profit Peaks, which is usually a much faster strategy than changing Profit Drain customer behavior.

A company's relationship with its Profit Drain customers requires tightly integrated, multicapability supplier teams, but ones with a very different set of objectives, capabilities, and processes than that of the Profit Peak supplier teams. It is important to manage these problematic customers with specialized, dedicated teams that are experienced in reversing large, money-losing or marginal relationships (analogous to a bank problem loan "workout group").

It is important to keep your Profit Drain account teams separate from your Profit Peak teams to the extent practical. Each has a very different, highly specialized mission and set of customer relationship processes. This is a complete shift from the multitiered selling of the past, which comingled all large accounts because companies did not have the transaction-based profit metrics and analytics needed to identify their Profit Peak and Profit Drain customers.

CURRENT PROFIT DESERT CUSTOMERS

Profit Desert customers present several thorny, but solvable, problems because they are small and numerous. In the past, traditional mass market metrics made it extremely difficult to profile and target this segment with precise programs for improvement. As we explained earlier, transaction-based profit metrics and analytics remedy this because they can assign all costs and display the net profit components of every product in every customer.

First and foremost, in most companies, a small but important portion of the Profit Desert customers has the potential to be developed into Profit Peaks. The difficulty is that most companies have a very large number of Profit Desert customers, so it is very hard to identify and engage those with the potential to develop into Profit Peaks customers. Today, this has changed.

The first step in this process is to profile your Profit Peak customers—separately from your Profit Drain customers—as we explained earlier. Typically, when you identify Profit Desert customers that are Profit Peak prospects, you can create a few effective *account development pathways* into which you can slot customers. For example, one company slotted its prospects into groups by buyer behavior: customers who wanted product variety versus those who wanted low prices versus those who wanted fast service versus those who wanted technical support, and so on. Each customer group had its own account development plan and account development team.

In order to profile your Profit Desert customers, you can send a simple survey, designed to reveal each customer's size, potential, and buyer behavior. You can match the results to your Profit Peak customer profile to harvest a set of likely prospects. You can then intensively mine this set of prospects by slotting them into your predefined development pathways that match their buyer behavior.

It is particularly productive to use digital marketing and social media to probe these customers and track their responses, as we explained earlier. This sophisticated B2C capability is a prime application for artificial intelligence and machine learning.

Among the remaining Profit Deserts, typically there is a set of four or five "maladies" that drive down profitability, many of which can be rectified. For example, we often see some customers that order very sporadically, with periods of overly frequent orders, coupled with lapses; other companies can be recognized as cherry pickers or bargain shoppers; yet others demand custom services that cannot be justified.

Each of these Profit Drain customers produces low profits or losses, but these can add up to big numbers because companies generally have a lot of small customers. This segment also requires a tightly integrated customer management team, but one with yet another set of objectives, capabilities, and processes.

This team needs a strong analytical capability to sort through the accounts—much of which is facilitated by transaction-based profit metrics and analytics—and a strong ability to work with numerous small customers to diagnose their issues and change their behavior, often through telesales and internet communications.

The companion objective is to dramatically lower their cost to serve, as we described in Chapter 4, in order to bring it into alignment with their profit potential. Focusing your digital transformation on reducing the cost to serve these customers through menu offerings and automated customer service is a very high payoff activity.

PAST PROFIT PEAK CUSTOMERS

This is a very important and often neglected set of customers. For example, we remember meeting with the top Honda car sales rep in the United States. He said that his sales strategy was very simple: "I want to sell you this car; I want to sell you every car you will buy in the future; I want to sell your family and friends their next cars; and I want to sell your family and friends every car they will buy in the future."

There are a variety of reasons why a Profit Peak customer lapses. Sometimes, the company moves or goes out of business; sometimes it changes its product lines or simply has fulfilled an occasional need for product. But more often, the customer elects to change suppliers because of supplier complacency.

A surprising number of these relationships can be renewed. In our experience, the best approach is to be very straightforward. Tell the customer that you want to be its supplier again, ask the customer what happened, and ask what you can do to start to rebuild the relationship.

Transaction-based profit metrics, applied to the historical situation, are especially helpful in this situation because often pricing or other cost issues caused the original problem. These metrics will provide a grounded explanation of why (or whether) your past actions were reasonable. They also will enable you to show that your current policies are reasonable as you rebuild the relationship.

PAST PROFIT DRAIN AND PROFIT DESERT CUSTOMERS

These past customers are important as well. In some cases, the customer was a Profit Drain for reasons that would have been fixable if you had had the right information to identify and remedy the profit drains or to establish the right relationship. In other cases, the customer may have changed purchasing and/or operating personnel in the interim, and a new buying center has developed. Past Profit Drain customers almost always are large enough to warrant an investigation, especially with internet information and sophisticated telesales probing.

Past Profit Desert customers present a more difficult account selection opportunity. Your priority is to probe for those who have the potential to be developed into future Profit Peak customers. For this, you can use the approach and tools that you have created to identify and develop your current high-potential Profit Desert customers.

BROWSERS

Browsers are potential customers who have visited your store, website, or other channel and have declined to buy. Sometimes, you have information on the products that interested them, while other times you may not even know their identity.

The prime objective with browsers is to determine whether they are likely to have the potential to become Profit Peak customers. Again, the starting point is to have a clear profile of your high-profit customers.

The next step is to gather enough information to see who might fit the profile. In some situations, the company may have enough information to make this assessment early. In other situations, it may be possible to develop information by probing through social media and digital marketing; while in others it would be costly and difficult to gather enough information to make the assessment.

Where you do not have sufficient information to follow up with customers who are browsers, you can develop a sample, perhaps by surveying a random selection of browsing customers over a month or two. This information will enable you to estimate the likely payoff from developing a program to more systematically identify these prospective customers.

Some very advanced companies, like Amazon, are developing technologies in which customers register automatically as they enter a store, and the store tracks them, even if they do not purchase anything. Most leading B2C companies do this with visitors to their websites.

This process relies on a benefit-cost assessment with rough likelihoods. Today, social media and digital marketing are very scalable with little or no incremental cost, which makes the process increasingly feasible. Narrowing your hunt to prospective Profit Peak customers based on a tight profile gives you a laser focus and clear objective that increases the process's economic viability.

Other Prospects with the Potential to Be Profit Peak Customers

This group requires a broader outreach process, but as always, it starts with a clear profile of your Profit Peak customers—both those who are Profit Peaks in your current industry paradigm and those who will become Profit Peaks in your transformed industry. The key to success is to develop a very tight focus on hunting for prospective Profit Peak customers so you do not catch a lot of prospective Profit Drain and Profit Desert customers with your efforts.

With your Profit Peak customer profile clearly in mind, you can narrow in on various segment characteristics: buyer behavior, key product purchases, zip-code locations, and a host of other factors depending on the business. This clear objective will enable you to productively and economically extend your resources.

MANAGE YOUR ACCOUNTS SYSTEMATICALLY

Today, account management is undergoing a powerful transformation, which is creating a very important new set of profit opportunities. Leading managers are managing their accounts to systematically maximize their profitable growth—accelerating their profits as they accelerate their revenues—rather than just trying to increase revenues with the assumption that profits will increase as well.

In this section, we explain how to implement four powerful account management profit opportunities that transaction-based profit metrics and analytics create in your company: profit-based price optimization and contracting, product mix management, customer service and substitute management, and returns management.

Profit-Based Price Optimization and Contracting

Raising your prices seems like the most obvious profit opportunity in the world: it looks like "free money"—revenues without costs.

The problem is that you invite a similar response from your customers—after all, they can get "free money" by forcing you to lower your prices to them. Arm wrestling with your customers over price is a classic lose-lose situation, as we saw in Chapter 5.

Over the past several years, price optimization software has been introduced to the market. In essence, most price optimization software is based on a demand curve, which charts price-volume relationships. The under-lying logic is that if your prices are below the curve, you probably can raise them to the "market" price, which is on the curve. There are a number of variations, which can reflect factors like inventory availability, past buyer behavior, and customer segmentation.

This approach has three problems: (1) the objective is to increase revenues, sometimes taking a few cost factors like inventory into account, rather than being designed to increase all-in net profits; (2) the definition of "products" does not systematically differentiate among extended products, which are profoundly comingled products and services and are particularly important to your Profit Peak customers; and (3) customer segmentation is not based on transaction-based profit metrics and analytics.

Profit-based price optimization, our term, is much more effective because it incorporates transaction-based profit metrics and analytics, along with the best practices of profit-driven process management.

The core objective of profit-based price optimization is to maximize your bottom-line net profits, not revenues. It is absolutely possible to accomplish both strong revenue growth and strong sustained profit growth using transaction-based profit metrics and analytics. However, this requires the completely different and more effective approach to pricing, which profit-based price optimization offers.

Conditional pricing is the starting point in profit-based price optimi-zation. This is the process of using your transaction-based profit metrics and analytics to identify the strongest profit-increasing factors—sometimes price, but more often reduction of cost to serve. In fact, it is often feasible to offer *price reductions* in return for larger decreases in operating cost.

Here's an example. We have worked with several beer distributors, and in our work, we have seen a characteristic pattern of profitability.

The anchor brands, like Miller and Budweiser, typically constitute about two-thirds of the companies' revenues. Of these revenues, about three-quarters are profitable, while one-quarter are unprofitable. The unprof-itable revenues' losses in the anchor brand segment erode about 20 percent of the profits earned by the profitable business in this segment.

The craft beer brands, which represent a major strategic initiative in the beer business today, contribute about one-third of the companies' revenues, and of these revenues, only 30 percent are profitable. In the craft beer segment, the unprofitable 70 percent generates losses amounting to three times the profits generated by this segment's profitable business.

Managers who saw these results were shocked because the craft beers had much higher prices and gross margins than the anchor brands. Fortunately, however, transaction-based profit metrics and analytics showed the underlying problem, and once the problem was clear, the solution was obvious.

Initially, management thought that the problem was their policy of delivering daily to large retailers. In fact, this segment was very profitable on an all-in net profit basis. The real problem stemmed from the large number of small, Profit Desert customers, neighborhood grocery stores, which ordered several times a week. While each anchor brand order from this set of small customers had enough gross margin dollars to cover its selling, picking, and delivery costs, the craft beer brands, with much lower volumes per order, could not generate enough gross margin dollars to cover these costs.

When we looked into why the Profit Desert customers ordered so frequently, we found that most of the time they ordered when a sales rep called or visited to prompt an order. When we asked the sales reps what determined how often they called for an order, they were puzzled by the question and said that they had never thought about it. After thinking about it, they replied that their managers told them that more orders were better because the company tracked daily sales. In some cases, the sales reps actually had a daily quota of orders to fill.

The bottom line: the Profit Desert customers' (small neighborhood grocery stores) ordering process was the primary profit determinant in this important segment, and it is, in fact, almost always unseen, unmeasured, and unmanaged. Since the company controlled the order-taking process, it was relatively easy to change these customers' order patterns, which transformed the entire segment from losses to profits, even without an incentive.

Moreover, the transaction-based profit metrics showed the precise monetary value of changing the order frequency. With this knowledge, we understood the value of less frequent ordering, so we could have negotiated a price reduction, if necessary, to induce a change in customer behavior and still increased our net profits.

As another example, we are familiar with a major national trucking company that used transaction-based profit metrics and analytics to uncover a huge hidden source of profitability. This company traditionally gauged its performance by the profits it earned on its primary hauls (that is, the outbound "headhaul" movements) that its customers booked. It did not look systematically at the backhaul or triangulation movement it needed to reposition a truck for the next primary load.

When the company looked at the full cost of each movement, including both the primary haul and the necessary backhaul or repositioning movement, a completely different profit picture emerged. It turned out that the profit contribution of the backhaul actually was the most important determinant of profitability—and the profit contribution of the backhaul depended on whether the company had a lead time of several days to book the backhaul load, or whether it was forced to quickly find a load on the spot market.

In fact, the value of booking a backhaul load a week in advance versus on the spot market was equivalent to a 20 percent price reduction on the primary haul. For example, the company would make a fortune if it gave customers a 5 percent discount for booking loads a week in advance. The company's pricing VP even joked that his job changed from arm wrestling customers for price increases to convincing them to *take lower prices* (in return for booking early). Fortunately, many customers were willing to do this as a courtesy, once the trucking company broached the subject.

Hidden discounting is another important profit determinant that is generally hidden from traditional profit metrics. Consider the case of a retailer of consumer durable products.

This retailer's sales reps were compensated primarily on revenues, and to a lesser extent on gross margin. The company delivered most of its products to its customers, and the delivery costs were blended into the supply chain department's budget and costs.

When the company's managers looked at the discounting on deliveries shown in their transaction-based profit metrics, they saw a big problem. Because the delivery charges were assigned to the supply chain department, the sales reps were using this category to hide their product discounting. In this company, delivery charges net of discounting were a $39 million revenue item. However, of the over $8 million in discounting, nearly $6 million in delivery discounts were given to unprofitable orders. With this knowledge, the store managers quickly remedied this profit drain.

In many companies, loss leaders are common. These products are discounted, assuming that they are "traffic drivers" that will attract customers who will also buy high-margin products. In auto parts stores, for example, fluids like oil are considered traffic drivers. Transaction-based profit metrics and analytics enable managers to analyze this assumption, and in many cases, this process can be tuned so the discount is given only to Profit Peak customers and prospects.

In contemporary pricing, it is important to redefine your "products" to incorporate your extended products, which are profoundly comingled products and services. Increasingly, products are being combined with services, especially in your Profit Peak customers. This makes the "product" and cost to serve very different from customer to customer. The information needed to really understand full all-in net profitability is only available to companies that use transaction-based profit metrics and analytics. Price optimizations that disaggregate the "product" from the service portion of the extended product give incorrect recommendations.

Strategic price testing is a very powerful, but little-used method to constantly probe the market. A big problem with pricing is that it changes only occasionally in many companies, and it is usually based on false assumptions and inadequate information. You can remedy this problem by probing the market and letting the customers *tell you what they will pay*. Many online sales channels do this constantly, but with transaction-based profit metrics and analytics, it is possible to accomplish this in bricks-and-mortar and sales rep channels as well.

For example, we worked with a retailer that had several hundred stores. The company developed a policy of strategic price testing. *At all times*, each product was "in play," with a slightly higher price, in a few stores. The company tracked this carefully. If the volume fell, it lowered the price and tried to raise it in a few other stores. If the volume remained the same or rose, the company increased the product's price in several more stores, and if volume was constant or rose, it again increased the price across the whole company.

The company was able to track customer willingness to accept price increases by customer profit segment. For example, if the Profit Peak customers were willing to accept a higher price, but the Profit Drain customers were not, the company raised its prices. Transaction-based profit metrics were essential in discovering and managing this critical profit generator.

Strategic price probing sets a profit-maximizing price that reflects the market in each locality at all times. Conditional pricing, discounting management, and extended-product pricing can modify this base. In this way, profit-focused price optimization offers a set of powerful profit improvement processes that are instrumental in maximizing a company's profitable growth.

Product Mix Management

Product mix is another account management profit determinant that is undergoing enormous transformation. In the past, sales reps were primarily compensated on revenues, and sometimes on gross margin. Because most companies could not measure the all-in net profitability of their products on a consistent basis, they simply and incorrectly assumed that gross margin was correlated with net profits.

Transaction-based profit metrics and analytics completely changed all this. Now, leading managers can see the true all-in net profit on every product in every customer, based on the latest cost figures. This includes the ability to project likely all-in profits for prospective products in prospective customers, based on the company's actual best practice, average practice, or anything in between.

This much more granular, accurate information enables sales reps to understand how to construct and sell specific packages of products and services to particular customers that will maximize profitable growth. The difficulty is that many companies have large numbers of products, and many sales reps have difficulty working with this much complex information.

The answer is for category managers to develop what we call *product mix development pathways* that reflect the company's best practice in assembling and selling packages of products and services that are purchased by similar accounts, which we call *customer peer groups* (for example, midsized machine shops).

Companies can determine their product mix development pathways in a three-step process: (1) cluster your customers into customer peer groups;

(2) divide each customer peer group into three or four segments by stage of development (for example, new accounts versus growing accounts versus mature accounts); (3) identify the most profitable product mix profiles of the top profitability quartile customers in each group (not necessarily Profit Peaks because some groups of customers are in the new account and growing stages). This will produce a profile of the company's best practice product mix for customers by customer peer group and stage of development.

Customer Service and Substitute Management

The customer service paradigm also has completely shifted, and it will not shift back. This has created a very important set of profit opportunities.

In the Age of Mass Markets, the objectives of customer service were to ensure that the supplier was "easy to do business with" and to minimize operational errors. Company managers focused on the operational measures we mentioned earlier, like call response time and order fulfillment rate.

More recently, customer service measures broadened to include metrics like waiting time for repairs, spare parts availability, product usage guidance, and returns management. Leading B2C companies, and some leading B2B companies, have included customer reviews and Q&A information on their websites.

Today, customer service has become a very different and more comprehensive profit determinant. Consider the example of Dell.

Dell in its heyday was the poster child for stellar customer service. It offered just-in-time shipment of products that customers ordered—all with virtually no inventory. The results, over a four-year period were breathtaking:

- The compound annual growth rate was 50 percent.

- Revenue increased from $2 billion to $16 billion.

- The stock price rose 62 percent per year.

- The stock increased 17,000 percent.

- The return on invested capital was 217 percent.

How did Dell do this—especially since it was committed to fulfilling customer orders overnight, while it had a time lag of 45 days to get components? The company developed three key profit management processes: account selection, demand and substitute management, and supplier management.

Account selection—choosing its customer—was a core profit lever in Dell's success. The company studied the market carefully and assembled an extensive database on its buyers' behavior. Based on this, it laser targeted the customers with predictable demand—primarily corporate accounts that could schedule their purchases and higher-end customers who would upgrade to the next-generation PC at a predictable time interval (for example, six months after the introduction of a new model). That way, it could align its major blocks of incoming demand with its component purchases.

Demand management, which Dell called "sell what you have," was the company's second major profit management process. It worked in two ways.

First, since most of Dell's customers had predictable demand, the company could fine-tune the purchase time by offering targeted discounts and special packages.

Second, when a customer called a Dell customer service representative (CSR) to order a PC, the CSR had on his or her screen the set of PCs that could be made that day, given the production schedule and components on hand. If the customer wanted a configuration that was not available, the CSR had the authority to offer a discount on an upgrade that was makeable that day. Most customers would gladly take the upgrade, and the discount was less than the cost of expediting components, or it reflected the diminished value of components that were nearing the end of their life cycle (relative to even a discounted price).

Supplier management was the company's third key profit lever. Most companies simply focus on negotiating a supplier's prices down. Instead, Dell selected and managed its suppliers based only 30 percent on cost, but 70 percent on quality, service, and flexibility to change order sizes on short notice.

Dell had a very deep understanding of its all-in net profits, and with this, it provided stellar customer service with maximum sustained profitable growth. The key to accomplishing this high customer service level was to construct a business model and cost-to-serve system that shaped and managed its supply and demand to align them with minimum cost and maximum profit.

Did Dell have a classic service-to-cost trade-off curve? No. It managed the system to provide stellar customer service with maximum profitable growth by choosing its customer and drawing a bigger box around its service provision system.

In an important sense, Dell's "sell what you have" system and the customer service paradigm that it built around it were a very creative and effective substitute management system.

Substitutes are a very important determinant of profitability, especially when they are clustered into sets of similar products (for example, safety glasses), which we call *substitution groups*. Transaction-based profit metrics provide the relative profitability of each product in a substitute group.

First and foremost, sales reps gain ready knowledge of product profitability, and they can steer customers' purchases toward higher net profit products, unless a customer has a strong need or preference for a specific product.

Substitution groups also reduce supply chain costs. Most customers will agree in advance that if a particular preferred product is temporarily out of stock, they will accept a specified substitute product—providing this happens a maximum of, say, 5 percent of the time. This will virtually eliminate back orders, which are extremely expensive, while maintaining a very high level of customer satisfaction.

Returns Management

What do a typical hospital and a typical retailer have in common? Surprisingly, they both have a problem managing returns.

A few years ago, we spent a day with the President's Cabinet of a major medical center. This is one of the most prominent institutions in the country, with a very talented and dedicated management team. During the day, we reviewed and discussed a number of important topics, ranging from prospective healthcare legislation to growth plans.

One comment in particular caught our attention. A senior physician noted that the hospital did not systematically monitor readmissions—patients who are discharged and soon return to the hospital for additional care.

We thought about a friend who had started a company to oversee the care of patients who had a particularly difficult chronic illness. He had done studies of patient care, and he found that a surprisingly large portion of hospital readmissions occurred because of simple logistical errors. For example, when many patients were discharged, the oxygen or other medical supplies were not delivered to their homes in time, which resulted in very costly readmissions.

Over the years, we have worked with a number of retail and distribution companies. We have found that most companies viewed returns as a logistical hassle to be managed primarily to minimize the handling cost and maximize the residual product value.

When we dug into the companies' performance, using transaction-based metrics and analytics, however, we saw something very interesting. When we compared retailers in the same industry, their rate of product returns varied significantly. Not only that, but even within the same retailer, different sales reps had very different returns rates—even for the same product.

Our conclusion: the returns rate was really a measure of the *quality of the sales process and the supporting extended products* that the company was providing to its customers. The retailers and sales reps who had low returns rates were very good at diagnosing a customer's real needs and had a good understanding of what supplemental instructions and ancillary products a customer typically needed. The others did not.

The traditional way of "managing returns" turned out to be just *handling* them efficiently. This is not the right way to *manage* returns. Instead, the right way to manage returns is to view them as a quality feedback loop that enables a manager to pinpoint the places where the sales and product management processes break down, and to formulate sharply targeted provisions to improve these processes.

In an important sense, the hospital readmissions rate was very much like the retail returns rate. Some patients legitimately needed additional care, but many simply came back because they experienced avoidable errors—most of which did not result from problematic patient care. Moreover, in most institutions, this critical measure is not monitored or analyzed systematically.

Hospitals, retailers, and distributors all have the potential to monitor their "returns," not just for handling efficiency but more importantly to improve the quality and drive down the cost of their core organizational processes.

The big profit gain that comes from managing returns—not just handling them efficiently—is that the returns rate offers a very important window into how well the institution or business provides service to its customers.

In both business and not-for-profit management, there are a number of "hidden" profit opportunities, like those that remedy the hidden problems that cause high returns rates. While most companies track their returns rate, very few systematically relate this back to the problematic selling, product, and customer service deficiencies that cause it.

BUILDING YOUR CUSTOMER HIGH GROUND

The top priority for every manager is to own his or her customer high ground. This starts with a clear understanding of your Profit Peak customers—both those in your current business and those who will be your Profit Peaks in your transformed industry. Transaction-based profit metrics and analytics provide this understanding.

The second step is to make sure that your account management teams are spending enough time with your Profit Peak customers to drive their sales and net profit higher and that they are converting your appropriate Profit Drain and Profit Desert customers into Profit Peaks. It is especially important to closely monitor your Profit Peak customers for early signs of profit erosion.

Once you have put effective processes into place to manage your current customers, you can turn to prospecting for Profit Peak customers from among your past customers and potential prospects. The key to success is to have a clear profile of Profit Peak customers, both present and in your transformed industry.

In managing your customers, four processes are particularly important: profit-based price optimization and contracting, product mix management, customer service and substitute management, and returns management.

With these in place, you can grow your Profit Peak customer profits, while matching the cost to serve your Profit Drains and Profit Deserts with their profit potential.

THINGS TO THINK ABOUT

1. Do you have the detailed profit metrics necessary to profile your Profit Peak customers?

2. Who are your Profit Drain customers? Profit Desert customers?

3. Do you have different sales processes, teams, and metrics for your Profit Peaks, Profit Drains, and Profit Deserts?

4. Are you systematically evaluating your Profit Peak and Profit Drain customers for conditional pricing opportunities?

7

DEVELOP THE RIGHT CUSTOMER RELATIONSHIPS

What is customer service?

A few years ago, our group at MIT held a workshop on customer service for executives of our affiliated companies—companies that support our activities and host thesis research. About 40 top managers gathered in Cambridge for a full-day session.

We shared our latest research findings, and we invited top managers from the Ritz-Carlton Hotels, Disney, and a few other customer service leaders to share their insights. At the end of the day, we led a session in which the executives discussed their thoughts and experiences in turbocharging customer service.

We started the session by asking, "What is customer service?"

This straightforward question drew a variety of more-or-less expected responses: line fill, case fill, answering the phone in 30 seconds, no telephone tag, fast order cycles, and others. The thread that linked these responses was that they all were operating measures.

More importantly, they all were internal operating measures. After all, what good does it do to have high fill rates if the customer has too much of the wrong inventory? Or if the customer is ordering twice as often as is economical? Or if the customer has a quickly answered phone call about a very disruptive service problem that should not have arisen?

(Note that the customer service measures that really count are those that reflect what the customer is actually experiencing, not what you are experiencing in your operations. It is a very common false assumption to simply equate the two.)

After the executives in the MIT workshop had developed a long list of internal operational measures, we asked a very different question: "What could your competitor do to revolutionize customer service that would be your worst nightmare?"

At first the group was silent. After a few minutes, the discussion gathered steam and moved in a very different direction. The answers varied in form and content, but they all had the same underlying message:

> If my competitor could coordinate internally to really improve my customers' profitability, business processes, and strategic positioning, I would be in deep trouble. If my competitor really could do this, my customers would abandon our relationship and run to the competition without looking back.

This was the customer service prospect that really worried everyone in the group.

So we asked the logical next question: "If this is the ultimate win strategy, and we now know the secret to competitive success, why don't we do it first? It seems we have a golden opportunity to secure our best customers and take away our competitors' prime business."

The answer to this query still echoes in our minds. In essence, everyone in the group said in so many words, "We won't. We just won't."

Why not?

"Because," the conversation continued in essence, "we can't get our functional departments to coordinate around really innovative customer initiatives. They are too focused on their own functional department objectives and metrics"—like the internal operational measures the group focused on initially. Certainly, managers can get limited cooperation, but all too often this is overwhelmed by the momentum of the mainstream business.

In most cases, the counterpart managers in other silos were appropriately focusing on the objectives they were given by top management. They were responding to the measures top management had told them were most important, and for which they were being held responsible.

The profit management processes we described in Chapter 3 are the key success factors that will ensure that all of the managers in your company are aligned and working together in laserlike synchronization to maximize your profitable growth and to build a dominant competitive position in your evolving industry in this Age of Diverse Markets. Customer relationships are at the heart of this process.

This story sums up one of the biggest problems in companies today. In the prior Age of Mass Markets, managers had a clear responsibility to look after their respective departments' interests first. Strategy was set at the top, and top management issued periodic marching orders that were the basis for coordination to the organization. No one wanted a maverick department to distract other departments with ad hoc initiatives.

Today, the situation is completely different. Companies are forming highly integrated relationships with their target high-profit, strategically important customers. These relationships require tightly coordinated multi-capability teams that can devise and meet the rapidly changing needs of diverse target market segments.

At the same time, for nontarget customers, companies need very different relationships that match the cost to serve with customer profit potential. These should be managed by specialized multicapability teams deeply experienced in transaction-based profit metrics and analytics. The definition of customer service has changed dramatically, and the locus of customer service management and coordination has moved much lower in the organization.

In May 2020, Jonathan delivered a keynote address to the Chief Executive Group's Disruptive Tech Summit. At the end we asked the participants, about 200 major company chief executives and directors: "Think about your worst nightmare with regard to what your main competitor could do using profit analytics. Now rate the degree of damage that would result to your organization." The majority responded that the damage would indeed be high.

Customer relationships, determined by transaction-based profit metrics and analytics, are central to a company's success. They are the mechanism for both a company's internal alignment and its alignment with its customer segments. They reflect increasingly differentiated profit segments and form the basis for the company's profit rivers—which have to be lucrative and defensible both in a company's current environment and in its transformed industry. They are central to the process of managing and organizing the company.

Customer relationships must be managed thoughtfully and systematically. Yet in all too many companies today, they simply evolve without strong, proactive management.

SUPPLY CHAIN PROFITABILITY

As business has entered a new era, transitioning from the Age of Mass Markets to the Age of Diverse Markets, supply chain management has changed in fundamental ways. This is critical because supply chain management, along with channel management, is one of the most important elements underpinning successful customer relationships.

The Age of Mass Markets was the era of logistics. The objective of logistics was to minimize the cost of the physical distribution and materials management activities that took place within the boundaries of a company.

A few decades ago, logistics became supply chain management. The primary difference was that supply chain management also was concerned with linking a company with its vendors and customers through a variety of mechanisms, such as vendor-managed inventory, which we described earlier.

Today, supply chain management is undergoing another fundamental transition, shifting to what we call *supply chain profitability*. The objective of supply chain profitability is to maximize the earning power—the profitability—of your supply chain assets and processes, including demand management, inventory, facilities, customer and supplier operating ties, and customer service. In short, the objective of supply chain management has transitioned from managing capabilities and cost reductions in the context of homogeneous markets and arm's-length customer relationships to managing product flow and profitability in today's world of fragmenting, heterogeneous markets and highly differentiated customer relationships.

This change is parallel and complementary to the fundamental changes in product management and account management that we described in the prior two chapters, and it forms the basis for aligning these three cornerstone go-to-market functions. In the past, account managers and product managers were responsible for increasing revenue, while supply chain managers were responsible for managing their capabilities and controlling their supply chain costs. In leading companies today, all three sets of managers are jointly and directly responsible for aligning and coordinating to maximize profitable growth.

Because a company's profit rivers cross all functional areas, each function must understand the value, and process, of maximizing each profit river's performance in an appropriate way as it flows through that part of the organization.

In today's Age of Diverse Markets, companies no longer can survive with monolithic functional departments that only coordinate with each other at the highest levels. Instead, winning companies today increasingly need to form tightly integrated multicapability teams that work with increasingly heterogeneous profit rivers and profit streams. In this context, a company's account, product, and supply chain managers need to be expert at jointly assessing and meeting diverse customer needs through integrated profit action strategies.

Customer relationship strategy is the process of matching each customer's cost to serve with its profit potential, both in the current business environment and in its transformed industry. It is one of the most important company processes, although most companies develop and manage it in an ad hoc way.

Relatively few companies develop and implement this critical process systematically, which opens up a very important opportunity to create first-mover advantages. It has three building blocks: relationship hierarchy, market mapping, and service differentiation. These are supported by four important capabilities: demand management, order cycles and multiple parallel supply chains, delivery service strategy, and channel strategy.

RELATIONSHIP HIERARCHY

A *relationship hierarchy* is simply a well-defined, well-understood set of perhaps four or five standard ways in which a company can engage its customers. It enables managers to match their cost to serve with their customers' profit potential in a standardized way.

Customer relationships range from an occasional arm's-length account, to a steady arm's-length account, to light integration (for example, a standing-order arrangement for fast-moving products, which we describe later in this chapter), to full deep integration (like Baxter's stockless system and other forms of vendor-managed inventory). Various industries have different bases for their respective relationship hierarchies.

By keeping the set of allowed relationships limited, the company can create a set of tailored operating and supply chain processes—and a distinct set of management processes—for each relationship. We call this *service differentiation*. These processes include a standardized set of planning and coordination procedures, a standardized product flow with clearly defined order cycles, a clear to-do list for each side of the relationship, and clear measurable reported value for each side.

We remember visiting a million-square-foot DC in the southern United States. When we spoke with the DC management team, they were justifiably proud of their performance and safety record. However, when we looked over their financial reports, we were surprised to see á very large set of unexpectedly high expenses.

We learned that the problem was that over 70 percent of their costs were caused by one-off service requirements promised by sales reps to Profit Desert customers (for example, shrink-wrapping certain pallets, putting labels in unusual places, off-hour deliveries). The Profit Peak customers generally had uniform, high-volume, low-cost flow-through supply chains, but the Profit Desert customers, and most Profit Drain customers, were dominating the DC's cost structure—and the company was not charging for these services, instead simply adding their cost to the overall order cost, which they then averaged across all of their orders.

A clear relationship hierarchy coupled with concise service differentiation solves this all-too-common problem. It is essential that this process be headed by a high-level manager who has the responsibility to design the permitted set of relationships, to monitor compliance, and to continuously push the limits to search for new relationship configurations that will build the company's value footprint, especially for its Profit Peak customers—those who are most amenable and anxious for new forms of customer value.

Some sales reps might argue that having an effective relationship hierarchy might hinder sales because customers have unique needs and "the customer is always right." Certainly, the manager overseeing the relationship hierarchy could make an exception for a limited set of common issues, and then standardize the procedures for handling each. But generally, these are one-off requests for exceptions that are not economically justified, and they merely deepen the company's profit drains.

There are, however, very important, compelling sales benefits stemming from a well-defined, well-managed relationship hierarchy. For example, it gives the sales rep a clear ladder to move an account from relationship to relationship, with evidence that the customer value will increase in clear, measurable ways as the customer moves up the ladder.

If a customer pushes for services that are not justified by the economics, the rep can reply that the customer should sign up for the relationship option that provides the required services, with the understanding that the customer must meet the qualification standards requisite for the relationship.

The sales group's job is to move each customer from the relationship it initially wants to that which it should have. The key to doing this effectively is to define a set of relationship migration paths, and to deploy tightly integrated teams with sales and supply chain managers to sell and build the right relationship. Market mapping is the key to determining the right relationship for each customer.

MARKET MAPPING

Market mapping is the process of matching accounts to relationships. The most important point is that this process must match each customer to the relationship the account *should have*, not necessarily the one that the account initially *wants to have*.

The factors that determine what relationship an account should have include potential profits, operating fit, willingness and ability to partner, buyer behavior, and other salient factors. This diverse set of factors means that the market mapping process must be a joint venture of all involved departments—generally, sales, marketing, and supply chain management, and depending on the nature of the relationship, perhaps category management and R&D.

As we have seen in earlier chapters, account selection today is a moving target. As the currents of change sweep through an industry, some Profit Peak customers may become vulnerable to competitor incursion, while others remain solid profit generators. Conversely, some Profit Desert and Profit Drain customers may well become prime Profit Peak prospects. It is very important that the market mapping process fully take this into consideration.

If an account wants a more intensive relationship than it should have, the sales rep's job (in conjunction with the other members of the multicapability account team) is to reshape the customer's perception by explaining that the value produced by the right relationship is appropriate. Alternatively, in some cases, the rep can explain how the customer can increase its share of wallet purchases, change its product mix, or do other things that will enable it to qualify for the more intensive relationship that it seeks.

Not only is the market mapping process necessarily a joint venture of sales, marketing, and supply chain management, the relationship development and relationship building process at all stages is a joint venture as well. As the relationship moves from arm's length to more integrated, the relationship between the supplier's supply chain managers and the customer's supply chain managers becomes more and more critical to driving sales growth, increasing profitability, and extending the value footprint.

This raises a very important question: when should you bring in your supply chain managers?

In the Age of Mass Markets, the standard progression was for the sales rep to land the account, then focus on ramping up the sales volume, with a courtesy call from the company's local supply chain manager only when the account was "safe." Today, for your Profit Peak customers and prospects, this is the wrong answer. The big problem is that all too often supply chain managers are not systematically involved in creating and managing these relationships for Profit Peak customers and those with the potential to grow into Profit Peaks.

In a well-managed Profit Peak customer relationship, your supply chain managers can dramatically lower both your customers' costs and your own costs by influencing your customers' inventory levels, order patterns, and other key factors. When you increase your premier customers' profitability, it almost always drives sales increases of 30 percent or more, even in highly penetrated accounts.

A top executive of Proctor & Gamble, discussing how his company's innovations had lowered Walmart's inventory, once noted at MIT, "Our customer is Walmart's CFO. We sell more products by increasing Walmart's ROI on our products."

Importantly, while Proctor & Gamble was developing its well-known highly coordinated relationship with Walmart, it was reducing its direct relationships with its smaller customers. If a customer could not take a threshold amount of product (for example, a truckload per week), Proctor & Gamble required that it be served instead by a master distributor, with whom Proctor & Gamble had a highly integrated relationship. This is a striking example of a relationship hierarchy in action.

SERVICE DIFFERENTIATION

The objective of the relationship hierarchy, supported by the process of market mapping, is to align the company by matching relationships with accounts. The objective of *service differentiation* is to specify a set of coordinated management, operating, and supply chain processes that enable a company to meet its relationship objectives, cementing in place the right relationships with the right accounts, and maximizing the profitability of each one.

Profit Peak Customers

The objective of relationship development with these high-profit accounts is simple: secure the relationship, grow the relationship, and invest in growing your value footprint. If you can double the revenues with these customers, you will dramatically increase your profits. This is your highest priority. You certainly can search for efficiency-based cost reductions, but not at the expense of the high service that these accounts warrant.

The appropriate management process for Profit Peak accounts is aligned, long-term life cycle management. This encompasses (1) tailored customer centricity—fitting generic programs to a customer's unique needs (remember, if you do this with Profit Drain customers because they have high revenues, you could easily lose a fortune from increasing their cost to serve without an increase in profit potential); (2) innovative, responsive programs; (3) ongoing strategic and operational dialogue to develop a shared vision of the relationship and its possible future directions; and (4) careful monitoring of the value created for each partner from each element of the relationship.

Profit Peak customer relationships are characterized by integrated processes and systems. They should be managed by dedicated multicapability teams that are expert in building deep, integrated customer relationships. The managers on your teams should be trained to approach opportunities through the eyes of the customer, always looking for new ways to create customer value rather than primarily responding to customer requests.

In many highly productive relationships, the customers naturally evolve a counterpart multicapability team, so both the vendor and customer managers develop a close, innovative relationship that drives ever-increasing profit improvements for both organizations.

Profit Drain Customers

These are customers with low profit but high revenue. They are important but not strategic. Some have the potential to convert to Profit Peaks with some targeted changes in their cost structure, product mix, or other factors, but many are primarily looking for the next deal.

These customers warrant some investments to enhance the relationship, especially if you have identified a pathway to higher profitability in a specific customer (for example, by lowering operating costs). The key to success for these customers is to create an aligned strategy and scorecard based on transaction-based profit metrics and analytics, with collaborative, trustworthy actions, which will induce the partners' interests to converge over time.

The management processes that best fit these accounts involve process-driven alignment through coordinated processes and dedicated resources when the business case warrants.

The most productive way to engage and manage your Profit Drain customers is with a set of dedicated multicapability teams that are experts in identifying customer cost drivers (often problematic operating issues like overly frequent ordering), and managing change within the customers to convert the Profit Drain customers into Profit Peaks. These teams function in a way that is analogous to the problem loan workout groups in financial services companies.

Profit Desert Customers

These customers are low-profit, low-revenue accounts. The objective is to develop a low cost-to-serve business model that will turn these accounts into at least moderate profitability and to invest in maintaining a profitable relationship. As mentioned earlier, the Profit Desert customers with the potential to grow into Profit Peak accounts warrant carefully monitored investments in account development.

You can develop a low cost-to-serve model by offering consistent, cost-efficient reliable service with a menu approach to product and service offerings, which is carefully confined to the space between well-defined guardrails.

For these customers, the company's objective is to lower the cost to serve by standardizing product and service offerings and automating all processes as much as possible. This requires a dedicated multicapability team, with a strong IT component. This should be a priority in a company's digital transformation program.

DEMAND MANAGEMENT

Demand management, shaping a customer's order frequency and order pattern, is one of the most important determinants of both your cost to serve and your customer's cost of doing business with you. *Order frequency* reflects how often a customer places orders, while *order pattern* reflects the volatility in the size of the orders.

The reason why this has such high profit potential is that the cost of processing and fulfilling an order line is largely a fixed dollar increment, while the gross margin dollars (and net profit dollars) increase as the units per line rise. These are hidden in traditional metrics, but they are clearly identified in transaction-based metrics and analytics.

In the paragraphs below, we present an actual disguised case of a major hospital supply company, which we call Ashby Med, which worked with its customers to smooth their order patterns by instituting a carefully crafted standing-order system that created major profit gains. The set of figures shows how transaction-based profit metrics and analytics enabled the company to systematically expose, gauge, and develop this important hidden profit opportunity.

Ashby Med is a major provider of consumable supplies like IV solutions under multiyear contracts with a number of hospitals. The company manufactures products and distributes its own and other manufacturers' products.

Figure 7.1 shows the pattern of shipments of Product A to hospitals from the local DC in Region 1. Product A was a critical high-volume product, like an IV solution, which Ashby Med itself manufactured. It was essential to the hospitals' daily operations. Region 1 was the third-largest region in the country. It was distant from the central warehouse, and it had large rural areas punctuated by several large and moderate-sized urban areas.

The figure shows 26 weekly shipments to hospitals from the DC. The 10 black bars are singled out for more detailed analysis in the figures that follow. Note that this 10-week period is reasonably representative of the whole 26-week period.

Cases

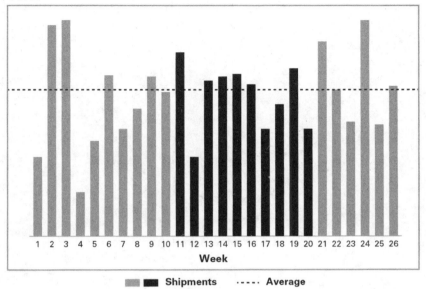

Figure 7.1 Ashby Med–Manufactured Product
Customer Shipments (Product A, Region 1)

Meetings with the customers showed that this product was used absolutely steadily at the points of consumption by hospital patients. The critical questions were these: Why did the shipment pattern have so much variance when the actual end-point consumption was completely steady? How could the company smooth it out? And what costs could be reduced?

Figure 7.2 shows the number of cases shipped in each of the 10 weeks to the 23 large hospitals versus the much more numerous small hospitals. This graph shows that most of the variance was coming from the large customers, so the subsequent analysis focused on these customers.

Figure 7.3 displays the company's overall national shipments for this period of time. The strong variance indicates that the law of large numbers (which indicates that the more observations, the lower is the variance) was not sufficient for the variance in each region to balance the variance in the other regions.

Cases

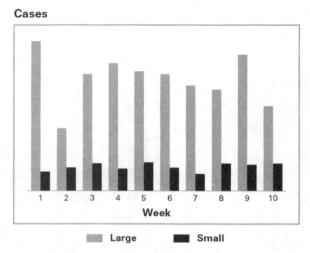

Figure 7.2 Ashby Med Large-Use (23) Versus Small-Use Hospitals (Product A, Region 1)

Cases

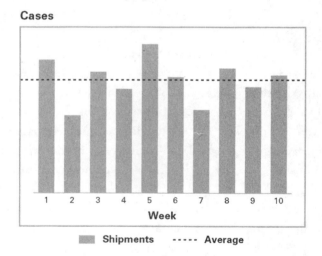

Figure 7.3 Ashby Med National Customer Shipments (Product A)

Figure 7.4 is very important. Product A was the highest-volume product the company sold, and it was critical to the hospitals' operations, so the company could not simply stock out. And because of the very erratic national shipment pattern, it was not possible for the factory to hold a steady production schedule.

Cases

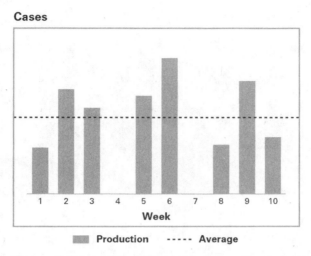

Figure 7.4 Ashby Med Production Output (Product A)

The company was constantly breaking its production schedule to make new batches of this critical product, causing the factory to lose its scheduling discipline. This was an extremely costly issue because the factory managers could not keep costs disciplined when they knew that whatever they did might have to change without notice. This critical measure is not tracked by traditional mass market metrics, but it is highlighted in transaction-based profit metrics and analytics.

Figure 7.5 displays the total inventory in the system needed to support Region 1 operations each week during this period. It is composed of the central warehouse inventory, in-transit stock (moving from the central warehouse to the regional DC), and regional DC inventory. Observe the high inventory levels needed to support high service levels due to the strong variance in customer demand.

When Ashby Med's managers saw the pattern, they developed a very effective, relatively straightforward solution: a simple standing-order system for major products purchased by major hospitals (a customer ordering a quantity of each product greater than a few cases per week). The system featured weekly standing orders based on the hospital's *actual end-use consumption*, with contingency backups if actual demand varied.

Weeks of Supply

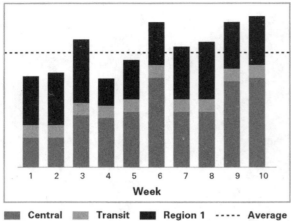

Figure 7.5 Ashby Med Region 1
Total System (Product A)

Because the standing orders would be the same from week to week, the company could work with the hospitals to create customized pallet packs, similar to the *rainbow pallets* in retail (that is, one pallet for each store aisle, with products packed in put-away order). The hospitals could institute statistical receiving (that is, checking a sample of products), with no need to count every product. This was extremely important and economical.

The managers looked at the manageability of selling the new system, and they saw that although the region had 120 hospitals, and 23 were large, only 12 hospitals were "problems," and 4 were key problems. They concluded that it would not be difficult to implement the new system.

Figure 7.6 displays the DC shipments in Region 1. While there still was some variance, it was substantially reduced, and significantly, the high-volume weeks quickly returned to the average.

Figure 7.6 Ashby Med Before and After
Views (Product A to Region 1)

Figure 7.7 shows that the national variance was significantly reduced.

Figure 7.7 Ashby Med Before and After
Views (Product A, National)

Figure 7.8 shows the remarkable change in the production output. With the new reduction in variance, the factory was able to regain its discipline. This provided a critical, hidden source of substantial cost savings.

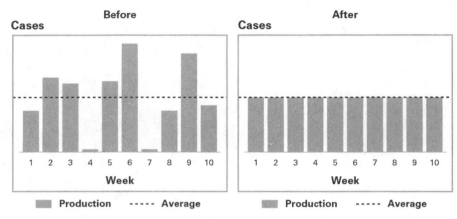

Figure 7.8 Ashby Med Before and After
Views (Product A, Production Output)

Figure 7.9 shows the inventory reductions that the new system made possible. Inventory dropped radically in both the central warehouse and in the regional DC, while in-transit inventories remained the same, as expected.

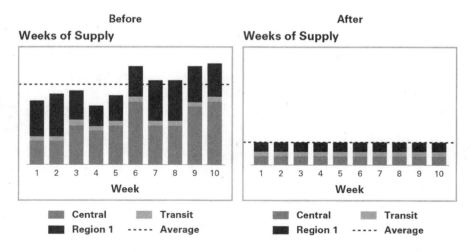

Figure 7.9 Ashby Med Before and After
Views (Product A, Region 1)

The standing-order system reduced the cost of Region 1's supply chain by about 50 percent. The next step was to verify the findings in other regions and with other major products. This research was fast and positive.

The new standing-order system created a number of other important benefits: (1) no stockouts or backorders; (2) a major capital program avoided as the DCs regained capacity; (3) customized pallet packs for customers; (4) enhanced relationships between the customers' materials manager and the company's supply chain managers; (5) stable manufacturing; (6) stable raw material commitments; and (7) significant increase in sales force productivity as most customer problem solving and expediting disappeared, which in turn, led to a major market share increase.

Demand management is one of the most productive ways to turn around an unprofitable customer, yet it is unseen, unmeasured, and unmanaged in most companies.

ORDER CYCLES AND MULTIPLE PARALLEL SUPPLY CHAINS

Merloni Elettrodomestici is a major Italian appliance manufacturer.* Merloni had two types of customers: builders and retailers. The retailers clustered into two groups: urban and rural. In the urban retailer group, some customers were relatively large and maintained their own appliance inventory both in one or more DCs and in the stores, while the other retailers were relatively small and had only a very limited store inventory.

Merloni, like most companies, maintained a network of DCs scattered throughout the country, generally reflecting the geographic pattern of demand. It also had a central warehouse that replenished the local DCs as needed. When a customer order arrived at a local DC, it was delivered to the customer on a first-come, first-served basis. The company had customer service standards that specified, among other things, that all orders received by a set time were shipped the next day.

---

* Janice H. Hammond and Maura G. Kelly, *Merloni Elettrodomestici SpA: The Transit Point Experiment* (Boston: Harvard Business School Case 9-690-003, February 1990).

In structuring a company's supply chain, the starting point is to understand the nature of demand. Merloni had several very different sources of demand.

Builders typically work on a schedule that is specified weeks or months in advance. The supply chain into this segment should be keyed to their schedules, with product flowing from the factory or central warehouse to the local DC or even directly to the building site, with *cross-docking* (that is, unloading directly into an outbound delivery lane) at every point. There is no need for inventory since the demand and forecast date are fixed.

Large urban retailers have their own inventory, often in two echelons: store and central DC. They are typically ordering to replenish their inventory, and generally they can easily tolerate a longer *order cycle time* (that is, time between ordering and product receipt) if they can rely on the vendor to fulfill the order when promised, and to expedite occasional emergency orders.

The supply chain for this segment essentially has two components. If you picture demand variance as waves on an ocean, like the Zara case in Chapter 5, the stable part (the ocean) should flow through the system from factory or central warehouse to the customer, either nonstop or with only a cross-dock at the local DC.

The variable portion of demand (the waves), on the other hand, should be fulfilled from stock in the local DC. The two segments of each order should be married up at the local DC for a joint delivery. This minimizes both handling costs and inventory, without sacrificing customer service.

Moreover, in this situation, it may well be possible to work with the customer to set specific order and delivery days each week. This will enable the company to smooth its workload and schedule the product flows from the factory or central warehouse to the local DC, generating more savings.

Small urban retailers typically have minimal inventory in their stores.

It is important to supply these customers quickly from the inventory in the company's local DC. If a small urban retailer does not have product available, it is in danger of losing the sale since there are other retailers nearby.

Rural retailers also typically have minimal inventory in their stores.

This raises a question of whether the product is an impulse or emergency buy (and it is needed quickly), or whether it is a planned buy (and the customer would be willing to wait).

If the product was an impulse buy or an emergency buy, the retailer, and Merloni, could lose the sale if it was not available quickly from local inventory. If the purchase was a planned buy, say, for an upcoming anniversary present, the customer typically would be willing to wait a few days for the product to be sent from the factory or central warehouse to the local DC.

In this analysis, we are essentially creating multiple parallel supply chains (that is, product flow patterns), with some product going directly to the customer, sometimes through a local cross-dock with minimal handling and inventory. In other situations, the product is being sourced from local DC inventory, but with thoughtfully set order cycles that reflect the nature of the product and the customer's situation.

This is a very important profit opportunity: supply chains with this service-differentiated structure can produce very large savings, often 30 to 50 percent or more.

In Merloni's case, there was no need for parallel facilities. The multiple parallel supply chains represented alternative patterns of product flow from factory to customer, often through the same facilities. The difference between this system and an Age of Mass Markets, one-size-fits-all system is the need to identify the source of demand and to specify the right product flow pathway.

Let's look at another case of multiple parallel supply chains. Figure 7.10 shows a hypothetical matrix with customer segments on one axis and product segments on the other. The customer and product axes are divided into Profit Peaks, Profit Drains, and Profit Deserts.

Order Cycle

	Products		
	Profit Deserts	Profit Drains	Profit Peaks
Profit Peaks	3 days	1 day	1 day
Profit Drains	5 days	3 days	3 days
Profit Deserts	5 days	4 days	3 days

(Customers)

Figure 7.10 Service Differentiation Matrix

Each node has an appropriate, but often different order cycle time. The example order cycle times are generally maximum intervals. In many cases, the vendor may choose to deliver the products sooner if they are available. In certain situations, however, the customer may specify a delivery window.

Setting order cycle times is an important process that will vary from company to company. In most companies, the Age of Mass Markets all-the-same process simply is carried over into the current Age of Diverse Markets, despite the huge, unmeasured opportunity cost. The intervals given below are examples.

The important underlying principle is that excellent customer service is not defined by giving everyone the same fast service. It is reasonable, and even desirable, to have your order cycle promises vary by type of customer and product—*as long as you always keep your promises.*

A few carefully selected products that are critical items or impulse buys should be managed as you manage your Profit Peak products. The Profit Desert customers that you have identified as prospective Profit Peak customers should be grouped with your Profit Peak customers. Also, some customers, like the builders in the Merloni case, may be amenable to specific product delivery dates determined well in advance.

Profit Peak Customers Buying Profit Peak Products

These customers should have a one-day order cycle time. These are your best customers buying your most lucrative, high-volume products.

Profit Peak Customers Buying Profit Drain Products

These customers also should have a one-day order cycle time. These are high-volume products that the customer needs, but they are low-profit products. These premier customers give you high profits, and in any event, it is important to bend a little to meet their needs.

Note that Profit Drain products usually have a significant portion of high-profit transactions. These transactions generally are purchases by your Profit Peak customers, so for this customer segment, these may well be, in essence, Profit Peak products, even though the overall products are Profit Drains. The profit contours in Chapter 3 illustrate this.

Profit Peak Customers Buying Profit Desert Products

These products are not needed urgently, and they can tolerate a three-day order cycle time, which enables you to bring them up from a central warehouse if you need to.

Profit Drain Customers Buying Profit Peak Products

These are large but low-profit customers. The order cycle time is set at three days, which enables you to bring them up from a central warehouse if you need to.

Profit Drain Customers Buying Profit Drain Products

These are large low-profit customers buying high-volume, low-profit products. Here, the order cycle time is set at three days, as well. This will give you enough time to source the product from a central warehouse, without the need to keep a large safety stock in your local DCs.

Profit Drain Customers Buying Profit Desert Products

These are large low-profit customers buying low-volume products. Here, the order cycle time is set at five days, which will give you enough time to bring the product up from a central warehouse, even if the central warehouse stock needs to be replenished.

Profit Desert Customers Buying Profit Peak Products

These are small customers buying important products. The order cycle time is set for three days, which will give you enough time to bring the products up from a central warehouse. On some occasions, you may choose to source the product from local stock and give the customer one-day service if doing so does not endanger your service to your premier customers, but we suggest that you reserve this for genuine emergencies.

Profit Desert Customers Buying Profit Drain Products

These are small customers buying high-volume, low-profit products. The order cycle time is set at four days. This will allow you to bring the products up from a central warehouse, but with a lower priority than you give to your large Profit Drain customers.

Profit Desert Customers Buying Profit Desert Products

These are small customers buying low-profit, low-volume products. The order cycle time is set to five days, which will allow you to source the product from a central warehouse, even if a warehouse replenishment is needed.

In this way, you can dramatically reduce your DC inventories, and consequently, your cost to serve, by aligning your order cycle times with each customer's and product's profit potential.

DELIVERY SERVICE STRATEGY

A major distribution company, which we will call Taggart Brothers, had a problem. When its managers looked at its transaction-based profit metrics, they were shocked. Their Profit Peak customers were a leaky bucket. They were making good progress landing new Profit Peak customers, but the erosion rate (that is, Profit Peak customers leaving or reducing their purchases) was shockingly high.

The managers quickly surveyed the eroding customers to find the problem. They learned that these customers were upset by the company's poor delivery service. The company's distribution manager was puzzled because the company routinely surveyed its customers, and the reported service level was very high.

When the distribution manager called the eroding Profit Peak customers, he saw that most of these unhappy premier customers were located at a distance from the local DCs. The delivery routes were designed to minimize delivery costs. The problem was that the vast majority of the company's customers were located near the DCs, but they were almost all Profit Deserts—and, in fact, the reason that the DCs were located where they were was to minimize delivery costs, not maximize profitability.

The managers quickly changed the delivery routes to give fast, reliable service to all the Profit Peak customers, even though it entailed higher delivery costs. The company's transaction-based profit metrics and analytics had shown the path to significantly increased profitability by quickly stemming the Profit Peak customer erosion.

A theme that emerges from these case examples is that in all too many companies, supply chain policies have simply carried over from the Age of Mass Markets, in which all-the-same processes were appropriate, without review or examination.

Here's another example. We recently worked with a company that prided itself on its fast, but costly, overnight service. In an experiment, the company's customer service reps asked the customers, when they ordered, when they would like the product delivered (that is, when it would be most convenient for the customer to receive the product). To their surprise, a large portion of the customers said that they would actually prefer the new system that allowed them to schedule deliveries when they were needed—as long as the company always delivered when promised. This information then allowed the company to eliminate a big expense for costly overnight delivery.

The important underlying point is that if a customer does not trust the vendor to keep its promises, it asks for faster and faster service in order to build in a cushion of time against the likelihood that the vendor will be late. If you are reliable, you can avoid a huge, unneeded expense for fast deliveries that are not only costly but also inconvenient for the customer.

CHANNEL STRATEGY

Channels are the forums through which you engage your customers and suppliers. These include selling direct to the customer and selling through dealers, distributors, and stores.

Two major changes are dramatically transforming channel strategy in today's Age of Diverse Markets: (1) the rise of the internet and (2) the power of transaction-based profit metrics and analytics.

The rise of the internet has enabled companies to bypass channel intermediaries in order to communicate, sell, and support their customers directly. The power of transaction-based profit metrics and analytics has given companies the ability to maximize their profitable growth through an understanding of how to most profitably engage, sell, and support each customer and each product each time.

These two currents of change are completely disrupting traditional business practices and relationships in industry after industry, creating historical new opportunities for companies that adapt to the new environment and endangering those that do not.

Channel Selection

In the past, manufacturers had a very limited ability to sell directly to their customers, as we discussed in Chapter 2. They needed intermediaries— dealers, distributors, and stores—to build local demand, sell their products, move the products to customers, and support the products during and after the sale.

Today, this business model is breaking down. There is a fundamental contest between manufacturers and intermediaries, and among intermediaries, to create the most value for each customer segment in order to capture more business. The internet and transaction-based profit metrics and analytics are at the heart of this struggle for realignment.

The starting point in understanding how this conflict will resolve is profit-based customer segmentation. Let's examine each segment of a manufacturer's or distributor's customer profit landscape to find the critically important profit opportunities.

Profit Peak Customers

These customers are large and highly profitable. They are relationship buyers who form a trusting bond with a relatively small number of suppliers, and they are very receptive to innovations in the supplier's value footprint.

These customers are strong candidates for relatively integrated relationships with their suppliers. Generally, they are looking for deeper relationships with fewer suppliers.

It certainly is possible for a very large manufacturer to develop a highly integrated relationship with a very large customer. For example, the major medical imaging companies, like Philips, have very close direct relationships with their major hospital customers—although some blend this with distributor service on the related consumable supplies.

In general, however, intermediaries who are willing and able to develop and build innovative value footprints and integrated relationships are well positioned to capture many of these customers. At the same time, intermediaries that are unwilling or unable to step up these more sophisticated integrated relationships are in danger of losing their best customers.

Profit Drain Customers

These customers are large but low profit. They typically are price shoppers and are not looking for innovative value footprints. Nevertheless, they will form good working relationships with suppliers if the price is right.

These customers are willing to take the best offer. If a manufacturer can ship to the customer in economical quantities and the customer does not need much support, the manufacturer can capture this business. However, because the prices are relatively low, the customer would have to have very large purchases to offset the cost to serve.

This positions intermediaries as best to serve most of these customers that do not order in economical quantities. However, these customers tend to be demanding price shoppers, so it is unlikely that the intermediaries would make much money on them without very careful attention to their cost to serve.

Profit Desert Customers

These customers are numerous, small, and low profit. A few are large companies buying small purchases, others are cherry-picking for prices, but most are simply small companies. Their buyer behavior is quite varied.

Some of these customers, who know what they want and do not need support, may well order directly from manufacturers. However, manufacturers would need to have relatively sophisticated internet capabilities for these purchases to be profitable, and they should have a separate division that can handle many diverse, largely unsophisticated customers at scale.

Intermediaries have important advantages with a segment of these customers. Profit Desert customers who have a range of product needs may well find it convenient and economical to have consolidated ordering, customer service, and delivery, especially for orders that include products from multiple manufacturers.

In this case, the intermediary needs to have a customer service group and DC operation that can handle many small orders efficiently. The intermediary also must have customer support in forms that can be scaled economically. These customers are low profit, so the intermediary has to be set up to handle them efficiently with an appropriately low cost to serve.

Amazon, for example, is a specialist in this segment. It has very sophisticated, scalable systems both for customer support (for example, product and service reviews and Q&A pages) and for order taking and fulfillment (for example, strong IT systems and highly automated DCs). It would be very difficult to compete directly with Amazon's strong, focused capability. Letting go of this segment may be a difficult, but critical, part of choosing your customer wisely—unless you are specifically set up to specialize at high volumes (or specialize in technical support) in this customer segment.

Channel Management

Stores remain an important channel to engage customers, both on a stand-alone basis and increasingly in combination with internet sales through what is called *omnichannel management*.

Store Management

Manufacturers and distributors have sales forces, so they can select and manage their customers. Store-based retailers, on the other hand, put products on their shelves and seem to have little control over who comes in the store and what they buy. Nevertheless, store managers have a significant array of ways to increase their profitability by differentially engaging their customers, and there are large opportunities for profitability improvement even in well-run retailers.

A few years ago, we held a strategy session for the CIOs of major grocery chains. Afterward, one top executive wrote, "I suppose that if supermarket executives sat down, they would agree that probably 25 percent of the customers that walk in the door cost them money. All the profit comes from the 25 percent with the largest baskets—not necessarily the largest revenue. . . . Well over half of that profit comes from 10 percent or less of the base."

In many retail chains today, stores are grouped geographically for management purposes, a practice that was cost efficient years ago when regional managers had to drive from store to store but that combines many dissimilar stores. The flexibility that profit mapping provides—letting you select a store grouping—enables you to create meaningful profit rivers by clustering stores that are similar in size, profitability, demographics, competitive situation, or other key factors, and analyzing their relative performance in key cost items. In Chapter 3, we provided an illustration.

Within a peer group of similar stores, managers can observe best practices and spread them quickly. The store managers and the store operations group can systematically move the peer group of stores to its best-practice standards. Internal best-practice benchmarking, based on transaction-based profit metrics and analytics, is one of the fastest and most productive profit levers to improve performance.

One of the most effective profit levers to create sustained high levels of profitability is to build a culture of profitability within your company. This is true for retailers, as well as for all other companies.

The merchants must understand the end-to-end net profitability, from vendor to shelf, for all of their products in every store.

The supply chain managers must know their supply chain profitability, not just operational efficiency.

The store operations managers must see the net profitability of all the products in all of their stores, as well as a comparison of their respective stores' performance to the best practice of their peer group of stores.

Omnichannel Management

The objective of omnichannel management is to engage your customers in a variety of ways that combine to form one blended entity. This is very different from the multichannel management that many companies offer.

The essential difference is that a company with a multichannel strategy, like a manufacturer that relies on its sales reps but adds a website with ordering capability, typically runs each sales channel as a stand-alone entity. A company with an omnichannel strategy, on the other hand, manages its channels as one interrelated entity in which customers are moving from channel to channel in a way that can be tracked and managed to increase the customers' profitability and loyalty.

In essence, multichannel management is an early step toward the enormously effective profit lever, omnichannel management. It is a major error to regard multichannel management as an end point.

The hallmark of omnichannel account management, as we mentioned earlier, is to "follow the money," by using a variety of means to identify a customer's buyer behavior, to probe the customer for ways to increase profitable purchases, and to shape the buyer behavior toward the ultimate objective of growing more Profit Peak business.

There are several effective means to probe for ways to increase the customer's profitable business. These include sharply targeted advertising and promotions; offers of enhanced customer services including customized web views featuring the styles and products that the customer seems to like; and events like technical webinars and workshops for machinists.

The objective of these offers is not only to increase sales but also to track and to shape the customer's buyer behavior in order to *maximize profitability*. For example, the system might track whether the customer was willing to make small standard purchases on the web but was willing to make larger purchases only in the store. It also might observe whether this pattern changed over time as the customer became more accustomed to the retailer's merchandise.

As we mentioned in Chapter 2, artificial intelligence and machine learning are very effective in developing these profiles and in guiding the offers and activities that shape the customer's behavior. Transaction-based profit metrics and analytics, which are essential in evaluating the customer's all-in profitability, need to be incorporated in the calculations so you are maximizing profits, and not just revenues.

Service differentiation is also very important. For example, many internet websites have free shipping for orders of a minimum size. This appears to be a sensible way to align order cost to order profitability. However, it is not the right frame of analysis. Instead, you should extend enhanced services, like free shipping, to your current and prospective Profit Peak customers, in order to strengthen their loyalty and ties.

For example, Amazon's Prime program charges customers an annual fee, and it offers free shipping on numerous products, even if the order size is quite small. This policy is customer oriented, not order oriented.

The fixed annual membership fee with free order shipping creates a strong incentive for repeat customers to focus their purchases on Amazon. In fact, statistics show that Prime customers have much higher annual purchases than non-Prime customers, and many of these purchases are for higher-price, higher-profit products.

The objective of crafting an appropriate product mix in omnichannel management is to match the product mix (both in aggregate and by channel) to the evolving customer buying patterns. This is difficult because these patterns are constantly shifting as customers explore and become accustomed to new channels, and as companies in turn shape their behavior.

It is important to align each channel's product mix with its customer base. All too many companies simply assume that their overall best sellers will be the right products to feature in all channels.

For example, some customers will prefer to buy simple, standard products on the internet and other more complex products direct in stores or from sales reps. Over time, this buyer behavior can shift. The product mix and the products featured need to reflect appropriately the demand in the channel. Artificial intelligence and machine learning are very important tools in this process.

Recently a friend, who is the editor of a leading business publication, sent this note:

"Another question for you. How valuable do you think segmentation is for omnichannel retailers? Should every retailer do this type of analysis before deciding whether it should engage in same-day fulfillment and delivery?"

The same-day deliveries issue, posed by the editor, really is a question of whether a company's supply chain resources should be spread across all customers, or whether they should be concentrated on the Profit Peak customers where they provide the highest returns.

Certainly, websites are open to all potential and actual customers. However, effective omnichannel retailing entails much more than that—including enhanced services ranging from recognizing who is coming to the website, to offering select customers custom views and online chat, to following up by email and phone, to enabling the customer to receive expedited shipping or priority on local store inventory.

The decision of how much to invest in enhanced services like same-day deliveries should be determined by profit-based market segmentation: it is not a question of *whether* to offer these services but rather *to whom* to offer them. And if the answer is effectively *everyone*, your best customers will wind up getting very thin gruel, indeed.

Hyperlocal Supply Chains

In many retail and distribution situations, it is necessary to tailor a store's or branch's inventory to the local customer base and to manage inventory replenishment differentially by sales volume. Here, the buyer behavior of a store's or branch's distinct mix of customer segments, especially its Profit Peak customers, should shape both the product assortment and the inventory and replenishment policy for each product.

For example, one fashion garment retailer has set up an expedited supply chain from Asia. At the height of the selling season, its supplier in Asia receives a real-time feed of the company's sales file. The supplier has arranged to keep sufficient raw materials to dye, cut, and sew any product with a spike in demand. When this occurs, the supplier immediately loads the new products onto a dedicated, chartered 747 freighter.

The products are flown to the United States, where they clear dedicated customs and are team driven to the stores—all within a 48-hour period—to replenish the stock. The cost of this expedited supply chain is about 50 cents per garment, while the net profit per garment (including this charge) is about $7.

As another example, a major national retailer recently created a hyper-local supply chain. When its managers used transaction-based profit metrics to analyze the company's profit landscape, it became clear that the company was making a lot of money in the growth and maturity phases of its product life cycles but losing nearly two-thirds of this in the end-of-life-cycle period.

When the company looked closely at the stores involved in this profit drain, it saw that most of the losses stemmed from the smallest-volume stores (about one-quarter of the total stores) during the last quarter of the product life cycle.

While the seemingly obvious explanation was that the product prices had to be marked down at the end of the life cycle, this was not the actual issue. Instead, a close examination of the store profit stacks revealed this situation: if a *high-volume* store had too much end-of-season inventory on the shelves, it had enough customers to quickly clear the shelves; the *low-volume* stores, on the other hand, could not clear their shelves at the end of the life cycle. Their managers strongly resisted taking the markdowns, so they delayed clearing their shelves. This made them miss the all-important strong-sales introductory period for the new products that should have populated their shelves.

The company's transaction-based profit metrics and analytics showed both the underlying cause of this problem and the solution. The warehouse policy was to restock the stores based on historical demand, shipping to all stores in volumes proportionate to their sales until the warehouse ran out of product. At that point, it stopped replenishing all of the stores. The high-volume stores could sell down the product, while the low-volume stores delayed writing it off and lost their prime selling period for the new products.

The answer was simple: divide the stores into quartiles according to their sales volume, and curtail replenishment shipments to the low-volume stores early, to the middle-volume stores later, and to the high-volume stores quite late in the product life cycle. This change generated an enormous amount of profit, and it was relatively easy to implement. Without the company's transaction-based profit metrics and analytics, this huge source of profits would have remained hidden.

THE RIGHT CUSTOMER RELATIONSHIPS

Developing the right relationships with your customers is the primary way to differentiate your customer service and set clear customer expectations. They enable you to match your cost to serve with your customers' profit potential and to create custom-tailored metrics that fit your service promises.

Once you have chosen your target customers, both in today's business and in your transformed industry, your customer relationships provide a core organizing principle for aligning your functions and activities and managing your company's customer support structure and processes.

Several of the core supply chain processes, like order pattern and order cycle management, have all-the-same performance standards that have simply been carried over from the Age of Mass Markets. These offer important, costless opportunities to convert Profit Drain customers to Profit Peaks, benefiting both your customers and your own company.

THINGS TO THINK ABOUT

1. Do you have a customer relationship hierarchy? Have you clearly set different customer service expectations for each type of customer?

2. Have you performed the market mapping exercise against your customer base?

3. How are you using your channels to effectively deliver your value footprint? Are you using omnichannel management? Hyperlocal inventory?

4. Are you measuring your customer order patterns and differentially setting appropriate order cycles?

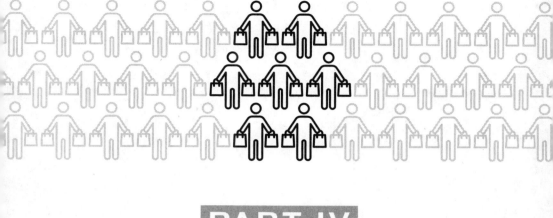

PART IV

MANAGE TO WIN

8

MANAGE AT THE RIGHT LEVEL

Big Data is a top news story in the IT world. Here's the vision. Sometime soon company managers will have an enormous amount of information at their fingertips. They will be able to see everything and optimize everything.

Recently, two very senior, astute individuals contacted us about this—one a senior IT industry analyst and the other a senior editor of a major business publication. They both had the same question: if Big Data actually becomes available, what will be the consequences?

BIG DATA: POTENTIAL PROBLEMS

This is an especially important question in the context of today's availability of transaction-based profit metrics and analytics, which provide a comprehensive, detailed view of the profitability of every nook and cranny of a company.

Our answer: Big Data offers big opportunities. However, it carries the very strong likelihood of creating really big problems in three areas: (1) paving the cowpaths, (2) driving without a road map, and (3) managing at the wrong level.

Paving the Cowpaths

A few years ago, radio frequency identification (RFID) was all the rage. The idea was that it was becoming technically and economically possible to affix an RFID tag to every item moving through a supply chain. (An RFID tag is a small passive label that essentially emits a precise identifier or other information when it is hit by an electromagnetic field.)

Armed with this capability, managers could know the identification and location of every item in their company and even those items flowing into and out of their companies. A variant of this has recently reemerged as the internet of things (IoT).

We remember discussing this with a former student who is presently the CEO of one of the largest, most successful companies in the country. His reaction was similar to ours: "What ever would you do with all that information?"

In fact, several years ago we coauthored a column, "Are You Aiming Too Low with RFID?" in Harvard Business School's *Working Knowledge*.* In this piece, we argued that one of the biggest dangers with the flood of RFID information was the almost-irresistible temptation to focus on "paving the cowpaths." Here's how we put it:

> One of the most exquisite challenges of living in Boston is navigating the labyrinthine maze of streets in the downtown area. This part of town is the oldest part, and the streets follow the original paths formed by settlers driving their cows to pasture. Traffic flows poorly because the city fathers simply paved the cowpaths, making the ineffective more efficient. It's much easier to navigate Back Bay, a part of Boson with gridlike streets, built on landfill centuries later.

In the article, we outlined a number of highly focused, high-value analytical uses for the Big Data that RFID could produce, and we counseled

---

* Jonathan Byrnes, Sanjay Sarma, and John Wass, "Are You Aiming Too Low with RFID?" *Harvard Business School Working Knowledge*, May 3, 2004.

readers to avoid the large-scale applications that simply automated routine activities.

Transaction-based profit metrics and analytics carry the same danger. The four cornerstone business processes we described in Chapter 3—strategic positioning and risk management, profit river management, transition initiative management, and profit-driven process management—together enable managers to maximize their companies' performance in the near term, in the long term, and in the transition period in between.

In the absence of this disciplined, strategic approach, managers are in grave danger of utilizing this powerful information to pave the cowpaths, further entrenching existing practices and rendering the possibility of developing sweeping paradigm-changing initiatives more and more difficult.

This will almost inevitably occur because in the capital budgeting process, the tactical payoffs from paving the cowpaths will be clear and easy to measure, while the payoffs from far-reaching strategic changes in the business will be hazy and more difficult to measure.

Driving Without a Road Map

One might ask: Won't Big Data let a company's managers optimize everything? After all, every manager theoretically will have the information needed to get everything right. And if a company's managers optimize everything, won't the company be great?

This question embodies one of the biggest false assumptions in thinking about Big Data.

When we think of Big Data, an analogy comes to mind. Imagine that you were living decades ago, at the time of the invention of the automobile. Assume further that all of a sudden, all the dirt roads and tracks were paved. What would you do? Where would you go?

The obvious answer is that either you would stay local, or you would be paralyzed in the face of the enormous number of opportunities. In fact, you would need a road map, so you could see how to get to different places. Beyond that, you would need to understand the nature of the destinations so you could decide where to go, since you couldn't get everywhere in one lifetime.

Further, if you had a number of different drivers, it is likely that each would head in a different direction because each would go after the goal that he or she thought best. If these drivers had to coordinate, the way the managers in a company have to do, what would happen? The result would be chaos.

The problem is twofold. First, a company can't do everything because it takes significant time and resources to manage the change required to harvest any major initiative. And second, the initiatives have to be coordinated and focused on the right long-term strategic goals to be effective. If the availability of Big Data encourages a massive flock of independent tactical initiatives, it will do more harm than good.

This raises an important related problem. Managers have an almost overwhelming tendency to focus first on opportunities that are near to hand and that have a quick, visible payoff. Often these are called "low-hanging fruit."

The problem is that these relatively small, parochial projects will absorb the organization's resources and capability to change, even while they give the illusion of progress. The huge opportunity cost is losing the opportunity and ability to focus on the really important initiatives with the really big long-term payoffs.

The analogy breaks down because the big money is not in harvesting fruit more efficiently, but rather in changing the location of the orchard and the type of trees you plant.

This dissipation of effort, with its focus on a large number of small, incremental projects—rather than on the smallest number of game-changing, high-payoff initiatives—is the ultimate danger of Big Data. It is especially critical today in light of the powerful currents of change that we described in Chapter 2.

Managing at the Wrong Level

Recently, we were reminded of the Big Data question when we read *Wired for War*, a terrific book by P. W. Singer, which traces the robotics revolution and the use of robots in twenty-first-century conflict.*

---

* P. W. Singer, *Wired for War* (New York: Penguin, 2009).

In a particularly telling chapter, Singer describes how the real-time video feeds from drone aircraft—Big Data—led to the systematic leadership problems that we call *managing at the wrong level.*

Over many years, improved communications technology has enabled commanders to direct their troops increasingly at a distance from the actual battles. This has led to a very effective management structure in which top commanders focus on strategy and personnel, midlevel commanders on operational initiatives, and local officers on tactical issues. This parallels the leadership structure of most effective companies.

However, the widespread availability of drone aircraft information feeds has led to serious and systematic command and leadership problems. The ability of top commanders to see battlefield video feeds in real time has rapidly increased the centralization of command, which in turn has led to an explosion of micromanagement.

Singer relates, "Too frequently, generals at a distance are now using information technology to interpose themselves into matters that used to be handled by those on the scene and at ranks far below them. One battalion commander in Iraq told how he had twelve stars worth of generals (a four-star general, two three-star lieutenant generals, and a two-star major general) tell him where to position his units during a battle."

Singer continues, "An army special operations forces captain even had a brigadier general (four levels of command up) radio him while his team was in the midst of hunting down an Iraqi insurgent who had escaped during a raid. The general, watching a live Predator video back at the command center . . . ordered the captain where to deploy not merely his units, but his individual soldiers. 'It's like crack for generals,' says Chuck Kamps, a professor at the Air Command and Staff College. 'It gives them unprecedented ability to meddle in mission commanders' jobs.'"

This direct meddling by military leaders has led to the rise of what Singer calls the "tactical general," as the line between timely supervision and micromanagement has blurred. Officers in the field lament what they call the "Mother may I?" syndrome, which has come with these new technologies.

Moreover, power struggles are common when the feeds are available to multiple command groups. Singer notes, "At its worst, this pattern can lead to the battlefield versions of too many cooks spoiling the meal. A marine officer recalls, for example, that during an operation in Afghanistan, he was sent wildly diverging orders by three different senior commanders. One told him to seize a town 50 miles away. Another told him to seize the roadway just outside of town. And the third told him, 'Don't do anything beyond patrol five miles around the base.'"

But the biggest problem with top-level micromanagement in the military—just as it is in business—is the huge hidden opportunity cost of failing to manage at the right level: a leader ignoring the critical issues of high-level strategy and organizational capability because he or she is so caught up in real-time micromanagement. This causes two very big, related problems.

First, the top leaders fail to plan for the future. For example, in business, vice presidents should primarily be focused on defining and developing the company as it should be in three to five years, since that is the time it takes to develop a new set of capabilities. Their other critical responsibility: coaching and developing the next generation of leaders.

In the absence of this hierarchical discipline, the company is in grave danger of getting mired in the present and falling further and further behind.

Second, when top managers—or generals—take over tactical decisions, the lower-level leaders cannot develop their skills. Instead, they must be empowered to act with initiative, even if it means making a few mistakes along the way—*especially* since it means making a few mistakes along the way because false starts and errors are a natural and necessary part of doing anything significant and new.

The answer is what Singer calls "enlightened control," a concept he credits to the great Prussian generals of the nineteenth century, whose ideal was that the best general gave his officers the objective and left it to them to figure out how best to achieve it. He cites the commanding general who so trusted his officers that the only order he supposedly issued on the eve of the Prussian invasion of the Danish province of Schleswig was, "On February 1st, I want to sleep in Schleswig."

The action imperative for managers is ensuring that Big Data—transaction-based profit metrics and analytics—will not be "crack" for your C-suite executives and, instead, making sure that they have the insight and discipline to double down on enlightened control.

The true promise of transaction-based profit metrics and analytics is to make your company better, not just to make parts of it more efficient. To accomplish this, you need one part technology to nine parts vision and great management. The objective of this chapter is to explain how to structure your organization to accomplish this.

MANAGE AT THE RIGHT LEVEL

Consider the case of Li & Fung, a very successful, fast-growing, Hong Kong–based intermediary in the apparel, toy, and other consumer products businesses.* The company sourced its products from large Asian manufacturers and sold to large Western retailers.

Li & Fung was in danger of disintermediation. In response to this threat, it created a very innovative system that it called "dispersed manufacturing."

The essence of this new system was to break up the supply chain and do the right thing in the right place. The company worked closely with its retail customers to plan an upcoming season's product assortment. When the assortment began to coalesce, the company issued firm commitments to the raw material suppliers, and it booked factory capacity to ensure that production was rapid and seamless. Li & Fung used its strong knowledge of supplier capability to source the right components from the right suppliers, sourcing zippers, for example, in Japan, and marrying them with assembly in Vietnam.

Li & Fung maintained close relationships with numerous suppliers and manufacturers in Asia. Because the company had large purchase volumes and could commit in advance, it gained priority in supply and capacity. This was good for the suppliers because they could better plan their capacity and make material commitments far in advance. Li & Fung provided very valuable repeat business that was essential in ensuring the suppliers' long-run economic viability and in removing the suppliers' risk of making

---

* Joan Magretta, "Fast, Global, and Entrepreneurial: Supply Chain Management Hong Kong Style: An Interview with Victor Fung," *Harvard Business Review*, September-October 1998 (#98507).

investments in quality and capacity. This made Li & Fung a very desirable Profit Peak customer to its manufacturers and suppliers.

The retailers gained as well. Because Li & Fung's supplier relationships were strong, they could adjust production quickly in response to changes in market demand. In fact, Li & Fung had direct access to many retailers' daily sales numbers by product. This dramatically reduced the retailers' inventory cost and markdowns, and it enabled the retailers to ramp up production to meet emerging surges in sales.

The system also enabled the retailers to create more, shorter "seasons," each with a new assortment. This was enormously lucrative, which made Li & Fung a Profit Peak supplier to its customers.

Both the retailers and suppliers were much better off partnering with Li & Fung. How did Li & Fung gain this terrific position at the center of this important channel? They were, and still are, relentless in understanding their downstream and upstream channel partners and in managing to innovate their value footprint in both directions.

The Li & Fung story is much more complex, however. They developed very sophisticated IT systems and management processes that enabled them to produce value for their channel partners. The company's ability to translate this opportunity into consistent results stemmed from its deep understanding of its channel partners' businesses (their real needs and dreams, not just their requests), its willingness and ability to develop innovations in its value footprint that met their customers' and suppliers' real needs, and its capability to create the information and management processes necessary for flawless implementation for its diverse clients.

Li & Fung's results were striking: it achieved compound annual growth rates in excess of 20 percent in both revenues and profits for over 10 years. The company's organization and management processes were the underlying key to its success.

The company's organization was particularly well structured to meet its complex needs:

- The top managers focused on building the company's strategic positioning, organizational processes, management team, and major customer and supplier relationships.

- The upper managers (that is, VPs and managing directors) had dual responsibilities. Each manager was responsible and accountable for a key set of profit rivers such as a major client relationship or the suppliers in a region or country. These managers were chosen for their entrepreneurial ability to build a business and develop a network of suppliers, and they regularly met as a group to ensure that the company was operating profitably.

- The operating managers within each client or regional group were selected for their ability to operate as part of a tight-knit team charged with deeply understanding and developing integrated ways to meet diverse, evolving customer and supplier needs. The CEO of Li & Fung said that the company wanted them to be "little John Waynes"—trooping through their business environment with a pith helmet and a laptop.

In this way, Li & Fung clearly specified and differentiated the objectives of its managers at each of the three essential management levels. This ensured that they could work independently or in coordination to build its ever-expanding value footprint, focusing on meeting the integrated needs of the company's diverse customers and suppliers, and of the company itself. We call this *value entrepreneurship*.

MANAGEMENT EFFECTIVENESS

Today, more than ever, managing at the right level is one of the key success factors for management effectiveness. This can be a very thorny issue because managers are promoted for being very good at their jobs as evidenced by their past performance. It is very natural, therefore, for a manager to overmanage a new subordinate who is learning the manager's prior position, instead of focusing on his or her new responsibilities.

This is an especially important issue for companies making the transition from the prior Age of Mass Markets to today's Age of Diverse Markets. This transition changes the basic nature of management's task from managing in a stable environment with a centrally determined strategy, to managing in a rapidly changing environment with a complex strategy driven by multicapability teams tasked with identifying and responding to a variety of locally driven needs.

This important difference affects all of a company's managers, but it most strongly affects a company's VPs and directors (that is, upper-level managers). In the prior era, these managers were the functional department heads, primarily charged with tuning up their departments' functional efficiency. In the Age of Diverse Markets, they must coordinate with their functional counterparts to manage sets of tightly coordinated multi-capability teams identifying and responding to increasingly diverse profit river needs.

It is useful to think about this management transition as occurring at three levels: executive managers, VPs and directors, and sales and operating managers, understanding that this is a somewhat idealized but helpful view.

Executive Managers

In today's Age of Diverse Markets, executive managers have two essential profitability management responsibilities (in addition to their traditional responsibilities relating to ethics, compliance, personnel, and other core areas).

First, these top managers need to understand, plan, and build the company's capabilities and the market position that it will need in three to five years, since this is the time frame for major change and repositioning at its fastest. Creating and overseeing the four cornerstone business processes we described in Chapter 3—strategic positioning and risk management, profit river management, transition initiative management, and profit-driven process management—are the most certain ways to achieve this objective, and they must be top management's most important priority. This is the management system that will drive the company to accelerating profit growth and strategic dominance as the currents of change transform its industry.

This means that they are responsible for ensuring that each component is set up fully and correctly, that each is functioning efficiently and effectively, and that each is updated regularly. This *does not mean* that the top management team has to perform all of the components of the process. However, it *does mean* that they are ultimately responsible for ensuring that the process produces the right results, not just initially but on an ongoing basis.

As a system, every component process is essential to the success of the whole enterprise. To be successful, each component process has to have a home and owner—an individual or group that is explicitly responsible for setting it up, managing it, and monitoring specific success metrics. The executive management team is responsible for ensuring that this happens.

Importantly, executive managers have primary responsibility for driving the strategy and risk management process. The VPs and directors, through their MPG Committee, are centrally involved in providing analysis and recommendations, but the decisions must reside at the top level.

In the preceding chapters, we explained the vital importance of the strategy and risk management process, and we described how it provides the bedrock foundation for success through the three principles of strategy that we described in Chapter 1—customer value (value footprint), customer fit (what you say no to), and competitive differentiation (being best at something).

As we explained in Chapter 3, strategy and risk management should no longer be a largely qualitative exercise. Instead, managers can use their profit contours in what-if mode to model and explore the precise quantitative consequences of the opportunities and threats ushered in by the currents of change.

Transaction-based profit metrics and analytics produce the current profit stacks for a company's customer segments, product categories, and all other aspects of the business. Managers can alter the assumptions of their profit contours to simulate the currents of change, or any other competitive or environmental factors, and they can then observe the specific impact on any segment of the company. Then they can simulate various responses and growth initiatives—and then view the net impact.

In the strategy development process, this enhanced, granular analytical capability will enable managers to be much more effective in creating both their extensive and intensive strategies. A company's *extensive strategy* enables it to position and differentiate itself in its evolving industry context (for example, Apple's moves to build on its computer platform to enter the phone, music, and camera industries). Its *intensive strategy*, on the other hand, enables it to position effectively within its industry (for example, selecting and growing Profit Peak customers, and matching its cost to serve with its customers' profit potential).

Not only will this enhanced precision make a company's strategy development much more effective, but also it will give it the ability to plan specific strategic initiatives and track progress literally profit river by profit river, customer by customer, product by product, and channel by channel.

As we explained in Chapter 3, in most companies today, risk assessment and management is a largely qualitative process. The core analytical tool is a heat map, in which managers identify the main operating elements of their companies and then assess whether each element is likely to be affected by an identified risk factor. The important point is that a risk heat map is very qualitative and vague.

Transaction-based profit metrics and analytics enable managers to develop, analyze, and monitor a very precise set of risk indexes based on the microeconomics, market characteristics, and buyer behavior of specific segments of their profit landscape. Through a process analogous to the strategy-creating process described above, managers can gauge the impact of various risk factors on their profit contours. They can identify and quantify their exact sources of risk as the currents of change transform their prospects, and they can devise and quantify measures to reduce or eliminate each risk source.

This analytical process is particularly critical as the currents of change sweep through every industry, creating new opportunities and risks and forcing managers to reposition their companies. Moreover, this quantification is especially needed in public companies, which are required to report their risk to investors in SEC filings.

The executive managers are also responsible for defining and overseeing the performance of the company's profit river management process, although the Managing Profitable Growth (MPG) Committee, which we describe below, has the prime responsibility for day-to-day management of these profit-based small sets of natural strategic business units (SBUs).

This process is somewhat problematic in many companies because a number of their executive managers grew up in the earlier Age of Mass

Markets, when markets were relatively stable and homogeneous. In this former era, top managers did not need to spend a lot of time planning big changes for the future—or developing their middle managers' abilities to plan and coordinate with each other to meet diverse, rapidly changing customer needs. This means that today's executive managers must consciously change their management mode.

The second very important executive manager responsibility is to coach the VPs and directors in their evolving positions. Most importantly, this means making sure that the VPs and directors focus on building their capability to coordinate with each other, especially in structuring and managing both internal change and change in their customers. They cannot be consumed with managing a level too low, spending most of their time doing the jobs of their functional managers.

The structure and responsibilities of the MPG Committee are designed to ensure that a company's VPs and directors make this transition. Executive managers have a critical role in coaching them in this process. Recall how the telephone company's prior EVP, described in Chapter 3, defined his job, compared to how his replacement defined his.

VPs and Directors

Today, this is an especially important position. The primary job of a VP or director has two parts, with each part taking about half the person's time.

The first and most important part of a VP's or director's job is relatively new. Each VP or director must be capable and experienced in coordinating with his or her counterparts in order to determine how to maximize the company's profitable growth and accomplish it across a diverse set of profit rivers as the currents of change transform their industry. The VPs and directors achieve this by working through their MPG Committee (composed of a subset of these managers), which is the company's locus for its profit-generating activities.

The MPG Committee must have a core capability in using the company's transaction-based profit metrics and analytics to analyze its profit landscape. This forms the basis for their assessments and recommendations in defining and managing the company's strategy and risk management process.

It is very important that all of the members of the MPG Committee be fully fluent with the details of the company's profit landscape analysis. Every committee member must be intuitively familiar with both the analysis and the underlying profit landscape. This is the foundation knowledge upon which all other committee activities are built.

The MPG Committee also has primary responsibility for defining and managing the company's profit rivers and for overseeing the sales and operating managers' identification and management of the profit streams within each profit river. The company's metrics must be aligned with this need.

The objective of profit river management is to enable top management to align the company's functions with its profit rivers and also to monitor and direct these natural business segments that are critical to the company's success. It is likely that members of the MPG Committee will become key members of various profit river management teams. These teams will rely heavily on the transaction-based profit metrics and analytics that the MPG Committee develops.

As we have seen in prior chapters, successful companies today focus on engaging and managing their Profit Peak customers in fundamentally new ways that are very different from the ways that they engage their Profit Drain and Profit Desert customers. As we have seen illustrated in Chapter 3, these segments provide an important basis for defining the company's profit rivers.

The MPG Committee's profit analysis also forms the basis for it to identify the company's transition initiatives, which are managed by teams with combinations of VPs and directors and sales and operating managers. In addition, the committee oversees the company's profit-driven processes, ensuring that the sales and operating managers manage them capably.

When managers analyze their profit landscape using transaction-based profit metrics and analytics, several major potential initiatives will jump off the page because they will be seeing the company as they have never seen it before. Once the MPG Committee has a list of about five or six major potential profit initiatives, the next step is to prioritize them in light of the company's strategic needs and organizational readiness to change.

In our experience, it is most effective to select two or three profit initiatives for focused work. The priority is always increasing a company's current and future Profit Peak business because that is the fastest and surest way to increase profits. The transition initiative teams should include, but not be limited to, members of the MPG Committee.

It is important for a company to systematically review and analyze its current and potential transition initiatives every quarter because this provides enough time for teams to make measurable progress. When a transition initiative is mature and becomes part of the company's business, the MPG Committee can select another initiative to take its place. That way, the company always will have two or three major transition initiatives in process, creating relentless forward progress.

In addition to identifying and managing the company's transition initiatives, the MPG Committee should oversee the ongoing process of developing *profit-showcase projects*. These projects, which we described in Chapter 5, feature small teams that spend a few weeks in a customer (or supplier) in order to observe how the customer is selecting and using the company's products and/or services, identifying innovative ways to extend the company's value footprint, and estimating the likely gain (both for the customer and for the company). Baxter's development of its stockless system, which we described in Chapter 1, exemplifies this process.

The second main element of a VP's or director's job is to coach his or her sales and operating managers, giving them guidance and ample opportunities to learn by doing. In the past era, supervising lower-level managers on executing their functional responsibilities was the most important element of a director's job. This responsibility is still important, but today a vital part of a director's job is to ensure that the lower-level managers can capably coordinate with their counterparts in multicapability profit stream teams meeting diverse customer needs.

Sales and Operating Managers

The primary job of the sales and operating managers is to coordinate with their counterpart managers to execute the day-to-day activities of the company under the guidance and direction of their directors. They run the company at the grassroots level by directly managing the company's profit streams and profit-driven processes. As the members of this group progress, they increasingly get involved in developing and managing the company's profit rivers and transition initiatives.

In this process, a question often arises whether profit river management replaces functional department management or complements and informs it. The answer depends on the customer and market segment.

Profit Peak customers usually warrant a dedicated or shared team, specialized in this segment's profit streams, which takes the lead. Profit Drain customers also warrant a dedicated or shared team, specialized in the very different needs of this segment's profit streams, which takes the lead for these customers.

The Profit Desert segment has a large number of customers. Some subsegments may be specialized enough to warrant profit stream teams, but most primarily need functional department management through the company's profit-driven processes, which we described in Chapter 3.

A company's sales and operating managers, the hands-on managers of its profit-driven processes, bear primary responsibility for these core profit-generating company activities, which are essential for its success across all of its business segments.

In these management processes, the *profit crossroads*, which we described in Chapter 3, is essential to internal management coordination.

THREE KEY PRINCIPLES

Three key principles are very helpful to managers at all three organizational levels in unlocking their company's profit potential and building a transition path into their company's new strategic paradigm.

Focus on Your Strengths

Identify and grow your current and future Profit Peaks. Your most important priority is to protect and grow this vital segment of your business. This is a moving target: as the currents of change sweep through your industry, the composition of this group may change, and these premier customers may need an evolving customer value footprint. The core objective of strategy and risk management is to choose your customer—the strategic group and the participants who will evolve into your future Profit Peaks.

The process of focusing on your strengths creates an important virtuous cycle. As your sales to your Profit Peak customers increase and your profits accelerate, more and more of your resources will naturally be drawn to this highly lucrative business. This will naturally lead your sales reps away from your Profit Drain and Profit Desert customers unless those customers have the potential to develop into Profit Peaks.

Create Pounds per Square Inch

In our experience, the essence of business greatness is to create *pounds per square inch of market power*. In many companies, increasing the fraction of Profit Peak customers by 20 percent, shifting 20 percent of the Profit Drain customers to become Profit Peaks, and shifting a mere 10 percent of your Profit Desert customers to grow into Profit Peaks—a total of perhaps 20 percent of your total customer count—will double the company's net profits.

Willy Sutton, the legendary bank robber, was once asked why he robbed banks. He replied, "Because that's where the money is." Aim your resources, your "pounds per square inch," by **choosing** your customer where you will get the biggest payoff, **aligning** your functions to accomplish this goal, and **managing** your organization to consistently produce the strongest results. That is the ultimate value of transaction-based profit metrics and analytics.

Utilize the Right Metrics with Accountability

Many traditional key performance indicators are inappropriate because they are focused on functional departmental efficiency, and not on maximizing your profit rivers and overall company net profits.

In business, you get what you pay for: "work your pay plan" is the watchword of every sales rep and manager. Transaction-based profit metrics and analytics enable you to measure and motivate your managers to maximize your company's profitability in every one of the company's core processes.

FINANCIAL PLANNING AND BUDGETING

In Chapter 3, we related the story of how the incoming EVP of a major telecommunications company reorganized the company to succeed in its deregulating era. Competitors were entering the market on a geographic basis, picking off the company's Profit Peak customers and districts. The EVP divided the company into five regional profit rivers, each with a multi-functional management team. Each team partitioned its region into a set of 20 or so profit streams, which they called *business blocks*.

The regional management teams used transaction-based profit metrics and analytics to profile each business block and assess the likely trajectories of competitors. The teams could then evaluate the company's possible market development responses, select their strategies for each business block—choosing their customers—and project the financial outcomes.

The company's top financial managers built a financial planning and budgeting process based on the bottom-up profit stream (business block) analysis and planning system. The new regional organization enabled them to create a new set of points of coordinated management and financial control throughout the company. Each control point was responsible both for a profit river and for each profit stream within it. Each profit stream had its own profit stack, profit projections, and resource budget.

This structure allowed the company's financial managers to develop profit stream by profit stream, and profit river by profit river budgets and projections, and to juxtapose this bottom-up information with their view of the company's top-down needs in order to arrive at a set of extremely grounded, granular budgets that would grow profits while funding the company's repositioning.

Transaction-based profit metrics and analytics were essential to the success of this financial planning and budgeting process. This capability enabled the company's managers to perform detailed analysis and planning for each profit river and profit stream. It was imperative that the system was designed to be flexible enough to accommodate changing definitions of profit rivers and profit streams and to develop very granular profit contours for each. This served as the basis for the company's financial planning and budgeting process, along with its management control system, which aligned the company's activities.

This process is particularly important for companies undergoing repositioning, simultaneously building risk-managed Profit Peaks and developing a new strategic paradigm. These companies need to plan and track their progress carefully—by profit river and profit stream, and profit contour node by profit contour node within each. This will enable them to make the midcourse adjustments and corrections that they will inevitably need in order to succeed in a dynamic process like this one.

CHOOSE, ALIGN, AND MANAGE

Once you have chosen your customer, aligning your functions and managing your organization are especially important at this point in the late transition from the Age of Mass Markets to the Age of Diverse Markets.

In the past, when markets were homogeneous and pursuit of economies of scale was the core management objective, companies needed to be managed from the top down in a highly centralized way. Today, when markets are diverse and changing rapidly, decentralization with local control has to be the management mode. This means that managers have to manage at the right level; they have to be organized around the company's diverse profit rivers; and the company's metrics have to reflect their new units of responsibility and accountability.

Managing at the right level is today's business imperative. It is the key to aligning and managing your company for strategic success and profit acceleration.

THINGS TO THINK ABOUT

1. Do you have a strategic road map to invest in systems and processes that leverage transaction-based profit data?

2. Do you have a plan to manage this information at the right level?

3. Are you encouraging your organization toward decentralized segment-based decision-making?

4. Have you strategically focused on your strengths?

9

BECOME A VALUE ENTREPRENEUR

The Age of Diverse Markets is already here, and it will never go away. The era of stable mass markets is gone, and it will not return. Constant change is now the norm, the pace of change will only accelerate, and the digital giants and other aggressive innovators are bearing down on wide swaths of the market.

CONSTANT CHANGE IS NOW THE NORM

Today's new age of business requires a new way to manage your company. Now is the time to adopt this new management imperative. Tomorrow is already too late.

The Age of Diverse Markets is completely different from the prior mass markets era in three important ways.

First, both markets and businesses have transformed from monolithic, homogeneous entities to fragmented, heterogeneous domains.

In the past, big companies served big markets in a largely all-the-same way. Today, the big markets have fragmented into a host of smaller markets, all with different characteristics and needs. Successful companies today have to choose their customer carefully, being very selective about whom they serve; they must tightly coordinate how they package and manage their products and services to meet widely differing customer needs; and they must develop an organization and set of management processes that enable them to accomplish this.

Consider Li & Fung, which we profiled in the prior chapter. This company developed a powerful new strategic group based on its dispersed manufacturing innovation that enabled it to create a revolutionary new value footprint both downstream for its customers and upstream for its suppliers.

The company did not even try to compete with digital B2B exchanges, but instead it prospered by **choosing** the set of customers that fit its highly differentiated strategy; by **aligning** its customer, product, and supply chain functions; and, by **managing** its organization and management processes to flawlessly produce its value proposition.

Second, the speed of change is increasing at a rapidly accelerating pace.

In the past, markets were basically slow changing, so big companies could organize and manage their businesses primarily with functional departments. Strategic planning took place at the highest levels of a company, and it was largely a matter of coordinating functional department tactics for meeting different aspects of monolithic customer needs (for example, selling, manufacturing, distributing), with occasional larger choices of product and market focus. Standardized execution was the key success factor.

Successful companies today face fragmented customer market segments that are themselves transforming rapidly. They must be fully capable of meeting diverse customer needs in a multifunctional way, staying in front of those needs, and constantly restructuring their portfolio of products, markets, and services. Responsiveness and flexibility make all the difference.

Third, important ongoing technology revolutions are accelerating both customer needs and company capabilities.

For most of the past mass market era, companies were managed without computers. Only in the second half of the prior century did companies start to automate even their administrative and bookkeeping functions.

Today's ubiquitous internet and automated manufacturing were absent in this period.

Successful companies today are completely computerized and highly automated. They rely heavily on the internet and on *enterprise resource planning* (ERP) *systems*, increasingly coupled with artificial intelligence and machine learning. As these technological innovations improve at an accelerating pace, the companies that fully utilize these capabilities are accelerating their innovations as well—in turn, transforming their leading customers' expectations for more and more sophisticated services.

This process is rapidly upping the ante for all companies. Those who can't keep pace are already falling further and further behind.

Currents of Change

This transition to the new business era is playing out in a select number of major currents of change that are transforming industry after industry, creating new sets of industry-leading companies, while leaving scores of failing companies with household names in its wake.

These major currents of change cluster into four areas: metrics and analytics, technology, competitive dynamics, and consumer behavior.

Metrics and Analytics

In the past, when markets were large, homogeneous, and slow changing, companies needed only a set of broad analytics to shape their all-the-same offerings in order to attract a maximum number of customers. Because economies of scale were prevalent, successful companies had a primary incentive to get big. This enabled them to reduce their unit costs and, consequently, to make more profits.

These big companies could accommodate some early market segmentation through marginal differentiation in areas like advertising and packaging. But they correctly defined success as maximizing revenues, while keeping costs under reasonable control. Aggregate accounting categories, like revenue, gross margins, and operating costs, that spanned the whole enterprise were fully adequate for success in this era.

All this has changed in today's Age of Diverse Markets. As markets have fragmented and competitors have begun to position to pick off the most lucrative market segments, leading managers have increasingly found it necessary to gauge the profitability of the increasingly granular and diverse segments of their company's business.

Moreover, while mass markets were characterized by relatively uniform prices and costs to serve, today's increasingly fragmented markets feature prices and costs to serve that vary widely from customer to customer and from product to product (even within customers). This has dramatically increased the need for a new set of effective, granular metrics and analytics.

This new situation has rendered the older aggregate mass market era metrics obsolete and often misleading. A pressing need has arisen for a new set of metrics and analytics that are both extremely granular and very flexible. These new metrics have to show the relative profitability of microsegments of a company, along with the P&L components of each segment.

In response to this critical new need, we invented transaction-based profit metrics and analytics in the 1980s, and we have been using this to increase the profitable growth of tens of billions of dollars of client revenues in the nearly 35 years since then. Because the transaction (invoice line) is the financial atom of the company, we developed a rigorous way to create a full P&L, which we call a *profit stack*, for each and every transaction of a complex modern company.

When these transactions are analyzed using sophisticated proprietary data structures designed for transaction-based profitability analysis, they can be combined and recombined to show the profitability and profit stack components of any segment of a company, from an individual transaction, to a set of customers or products, to a channel, and so on, along any dimension. The related analytics and management processes make this complex information extremely manageable and actionable.

The difference between the aggregate broad metrics and analytics of the mass market era and today's transaction-based profit metrics and analytics is analogous to the difference between medical imaging in the pre-x-ray era and today. In the pre-x-ray era, physicians could only observe a body and try to infer what was causing distress. Today, physicians have a host of powerful tests, like CT scans, MRI scans, blood tests, and DNA analytics, to pinpoint the exact problem within the body's internal systems and structures and to administer the precise intervention to fix the patient's problem.

Similarly, in the past, managers could observe broad measures of their companies' performance only as a whole. Today, transaction-based profit metrics and analytics enable managers to exactly pinpoint their Profit Peaks, Profit Drains, and Profit Deserts, enabling them to double the peaks, eliminate the drains, and move their resources to the most productive uses.

Not only does this radically improve a manager's understanding and ability to create quantum, sustainable profit improvements surprisingly quickly, but importantly, it also enables a manager to project, under various assumptions, the profitability of microsegments of the company's current and potential market segments, as the industry transforms. This creates a double benefit: accelerating profitable growth, even while the company repositions into industry dominance in its transformed industry.

In this way, transaction-based profit metrics and analytics have provided managers a CT scan of their companies and markets, and they have created a road map to both sustained profitable growth and industry strategic dominance as their industry transforms and changes.

Technology

Technology innovation has been one of the primary underlying drivers of transformation in industry after industry. This is the answer to the implicit question: why is all this change occurring now?

Three areas of technological change, in particular, stand out as critical factors: computers, internet, and automation.

Computers have transformed nearly every facet of life and business today, from the home, to the office, to phones, to driving. All this has occurred at astonishing speed. This is why industry after industry is undergoing revolutionary change in such a short period of time.

Computer power has driven the fragmentation of markets as customers increasingly can access the niche products that best meet their evolving needs, and it has fueled the capability of companies to mass customize products and services. It has made transaction-based profit metrics and analytics both possible and necessary to enable companies to maximize their profitability and strategic positioning as they move to select and serve new portfolios of diverse, evolving markets.

Within companies, computer power has enabled firms to manage complexity. For example, through the *profit crossroads*, it is now possible to coordinate product management, sales management, and supply chain management in order to identify and provide tightly coordinated packages of products and services to meet the evolving needs of specific segments of today's fragmenting markets. This allows companies to achieve diverse operations without sacrificing economies of scale, operating instead in mass-customization mode.

Similarly, computer power has enabled supply chain managers to construct specific order cycles and product flow pathways to optimize their operating costs even while increasing their service to diverse markets. Market managers can create market development and promotional programs to discover their Profit Desert customers with the potential to grow into Profit Peak customers and to provide them with custom-tailored materials that will grow their purchases and profitability. Category managers can optimize their products' profitability by tailoring product mix and pricing to individual customers' buyer behavior.

Even in today's crisis, managers can create surprisingly large profit gains by identifying and growing their profit core—selectively increasing the profitability of their current book of business. This has enormous leverage.

In most companies, 10 to 15 percent of the customers (Profit Peaks) generate 150 to 200 percent of the reported profits, while 15 to 20 percent of the customers (Profit Drains) erode 50 percent or more of these profits. The remaining 65 to 75 percent of the customers (Profit Deserts) produce only minimal profits or losses.

This profit segmentation is the key to growing your profit core because each segment needs a different growth game plan.

For example, if a typical company increases its Profit Peaks by 20 percent and converts 20 percent of its Profit Drains to Profit Peaks, it will boost its net profits by over 50 percent. This affects only 10 to 15 percent of the customers.

The internet is as ubiquitous and powerful as computers. We recall talking with the CEO of a major telecommunications company that declined to invest in a widespread wireless network because it was unimaginable to assert that it would be financially viable to build a network so that middle school and high school children could text each other across a schoolyard. How much and how fast times have changed! Facebook was developed just over 15 years ago, and now the service has billions of active users. Apple, Amazon, and Microsoft—all relatively young companies—have posted market caps approaching or exceeding a trillion dollars (not a typo).

The internet is transforming business. It is enabling manufacturers and other companies to access their customers directly, and it is allowing new competitors to sweep into B2B industries using sets of powerful techniques honed in the fast-paced world of B2C. Chief among these powerful capabilities are artificial intelligence and machine learning, which enable companies to sense and shape the buyer behavior of millions of customers in real time.

From a broader perspective, these new capabilities are creating a business environment in which the lines that separated industries and incumbents are being blurred, with new companies rising to dominance in a decade or less and powerful incumbents moving into new industries in which the traditional players are still focused on tuning up yesterday's tactics. Today, leading managers are creating and executing breathtaking new strategies in record time, while over half of the well-established companies in industry after industry plunge into darkness.

Automation is the third critical technological factor driving change. For example, for several years, Amazon has employed robotics to optimize its DC operations, and it is now developing robotic pickers, drones, and self-driving vehicles. A number of companies that were driven offshore by high labor costs are now substituting automation for labor in an effort to return home.

In a related manufacturing innovation, additive manufacturing is revolutionizing important segments of the manufacturing industry. These new techniques are replacing traditional subtractive manufacturing in a number of high-value segments. In other fields, innovative technologies are exploding economies of scale by lowering the unit cost of small-batch production. These innovations are transforming the cost of many complex processes, including sequencing a person's genes.

Competitive Dynamics

The currents of change are profoundly changing the competitive dynamics in most industries. New technologies stemming from computer and internet capabilities are now available to all firms at very low costs, and both well-funded private equity firms and activist investors are fueling their captive companies' growth into the most lucrative market segments at a breakneck pace.

These destabilizing forces are disrupting the long-standing competitive equilibrium in most industries. Incumbent companies are now facing extremely innovative, aggressive new competitors with deep funding and a mandate to grow at rates that are many times greater than the traditional industry norm.

Importantly, many of these competitors have a clear understanding of the profitability of their market segments. They are aiming squarely at the incumbent firms' Profit Peaks. Many traditional firms, meanwhile, are scrambling to protect all of their revenues rather than channeling their resources to protect and grow the segments that are competitively differentiated and produce most of their profits—both now and in their transformed industry.

This process is rapidly creating a vortex of Profit Drains in companies that do not utilize transaction-based profit metrics and analytics to manage their business. In a vicious cycle, these companies struggle to maintain their sales across the board, but steadily lose their cash flow and profits. Many of their traditional measures of success are telling them that they are doing the right things, but their bottom-line performance is dropping at an accelerating rate. Soon, they will take their place among the industry's roster of formerly great companies that have faltered or failed.

Consumer Behavior

The world of consumers is bifurcating. The watershed line separates those who grew up after personal computers and similar devices came into widespread use and those who predated this revolution.

The millennial buyers, who have only known a world of pervasive internet availability and computer power, expect to have full information availability and a full range of easily accessible choices within easy reach. They expect many viable options and transparent pricing. These consumers turn quickly to online reviews and Q&A sites for full information, and are willing to buy from anyone who quickly and seamlessly meets their expectations and needs.

This trend is transforming consumer loyalty and with it, many firms' selling process. Companies like Amazon specialize in providing one-stop shopping in an easily accessible, information-rich environment. They are outcompeting many traditional vendors who are product specialists.

Yet most of these aggressive competitors focus on a narrow set of competitive dimensions, typically digital services to small customers, often with network effects—leaving a large, open playing field even in the same industry. This underscores the life-or-death importance of choosing your customer—understanding and building a fortress presence in the most lucrative portions of a defensible strategic group.

Older customers, on the other hand, are accustomed to older modes of buying in which vendor and brand loyalty are important. Yet many are migrating to the new purchasing mode. These traditional customers can still provide a relatively secure customer base to traditional firms, but this group is steadily switching to the new purchasing processes that are ubiquitous, convenient, and effective. Traditional competitors who stake their success on tuning up their traditional competitive positioning and selling processes will see their sales erode and their profitability plunge.

For firms that continue to employ traditional channels, like stores and sales reps, new omnichannel selling modes are increasingly determining the difference between success and failure. Effective omnichannel selling "follows the customer" from channel to channel, using artificial intelligence and machine learning to sense, probe, and shape consumer behavior.

These new artificial intelligence and machine-learning technologies enable a company to conduct these sensing, probing, and shaping activities uniquely for each and every customer. In companies that utilize transaction-based profit metrics and analytics, this process allows the company's managers to maximize not just revenue but instead the profitability of every transaction in every customer in real time.

With this information, a company can focus its resources on growing and maximizing the profits from its Profit Peak customers—both those in the current business and those in the transformed industry. At the same time, companies like Baxter, Nalco, and SKF Bearings have developed powerful, innovative ways to integrate with their key customers, developing decisively differentiated extended products.

In these ways, capable companies can shape their go-to-market activities and product mix to maximize their penetration into their most lucrative market segment and, in the process, generate both accelerating profitable growth and a long-term dominant strategic position.

VALUE ENTREPRENEURSHIP

Value entrepreneurship, our term, is the process of managing a company in a way that embodies your deep capability and experience in the three imperatives that we outlined in Chapter 1: (1) **choose**—define a defensible strategic group that your company can dominate; (2) **align**—identify and build the cornerstones that will enable your company to achieve high sustained profitability in your target strategic group; and (3) **manage**—develop your organization to enable your managers to seamlessly coordinate in understanding and meeting your customers' diverse and rapidly evolving needs.

In order to succeed in the Age of Diverse Markets, the Manager of the Future needs to master these imperatives.

In the final session of Jonathan's MIT graduate course every year, he explains to the graduating students and executives the deep historical meaning of graduating with a master's degree. The origin of universities dates back to the guild system of the Middle Ages, and many of the core principles of universities still reflect this heritage. The guild system featured three levels of practitioner proficiency.

The first level was apprentice. An *apprentice* was a young person who wanted to learn the guild's craft. He apprenticed himself to an expert practitioner and spent several years learning the craft's skills.

After this period, when the apprentice was judged to be capable of practicing the craft, he was approved to leave the expert's shop and travel around offering the craft's products. This was called the *journeyman* stage.

The third, and highest, stage of excellence in the craft was the *master*. After several years of practicing the craft as a journeyman, the guild certified the practitioner as a master. This process involved demonstrating excellence in the guild's craft by producing a work of supreme refinement—many of the world's museums have silver pieces and other artifacts produced by the old masters. These are called *masterpieces*, which is where the term came from.

The contemporary master's degree, which many young people earn, is the direct descendent of this process. The reason why the ceremony for the awarding of university degrees is called "commencement" rather than "graduation" is that it is essentially the university's certification that the graduates are skilled enough to be masters and to commence practicing their craft. A *master's thesis* is literally the student's masterpiece.

To succeed as a master in the guild system, a person had to be expert at two things: first, creating masterpieces of ever better refinement and excellence and, second, teaching apprentices to learn the craft. Like the masters of old, the Managers of the Future have to demonstrate mastery of these two realms. They have to masterfully position their companies in a rapidly changing world—choosing your customer—and they have to masterfully manage their organizations' functional alignment and management processes to enable and guide the managers beneath them to produce consistently excellent results.

Ultimately, they need to train the upcoming Managers of the Future to become masters at the three imperatives that are essential to success.

Choose Your Customer

Choosing your customer refers to the process of identifying and selecting the strategic group in which you choose to compete. To succeed, a manager must choose a target group that will be lucrative and defensible, even as the industry transforms and changes, while ensuring that the company is not dragged by its history into trying to be everything to everyone.

Today's aggressive competitors, including the digital giants, are terrific at what they do, but an important enabling factor is that they maintain a tight, disciplined focus on their target strategic group—generally digital, arm's-length services with network effects to relatively small customers. This leaves a wide-open set of very lucrative, defensible strategic groups that even a giant digital competitor with Big Data and machine learning cannot address.

Three principles are essential in carving out a dominant position in a lucrative strategic group:

- **It is all about customer value.** The customer value you create both positions you against your competitors and provides the basis for compensatory pricing.

- **Strategy is defined by what you say no to.** If you treat all revenues as equally desirable, you don't have a strategy. Strategy is about making choices. The failure to make choices is the root cause of so many companies failing today.

- **You have to be best at something.** If you are not the best at creating a winning customer value footprint and focusing your resources on developing your target market, you are destined to be overtaken by a competitor who can. This is a moving target—you must constantly improve your customer value footprint and refine your customer targeting in a defensible portion of the market, or you will be left in the dust by competitors who can.

In order to choose your customer, you need to do two things: (1) select your strategic group and (2) target the market segments, and customers, who are the most lucrative, defensible prospects.

Your company's strategy and risk management processes enable you to accomplish the first task. The starting point in strategy and risk management is to systematically assess your current company. This requires transaction-based profit metrics and analytics, which show the granular profitability of every nook and cranny of your company.

With this baseline understanding, you can organize your profit landscape into a set of profit contours showing the profitability and characteristics of the intersections of each *customer* Profit Peak, Profit Drain, and Profit Desert segment with each *product* Profit Peak, Profit Drain, and Profit Desert segment. Together, this shows exactly where a company is making money and where it is losing money, and it can be refined down to each individual product in every customer.

Armed with this knowledge, managers can systematically assess the likely impact of the currents of change that we discussed in Chapter 2. They can perform a *sensitivity analysis*, or simulation, of the opportunities and risks that each force introduces. This enables them to design and quantify possible strategic initiatives and risk mitigation measures, both in terms of the likely results and the resources required.

The information that this process develops shows managers which of their Profit Peaks will continue to prosper, which will decline, and which prospective customers and products could grow into this category. Similarly, it shows which Profit Drains will be attractive in the near term or long term if their operating costs are improved. Finally, it shows which Profit Deserts have the potential to develop into Profit Peaks.

In the process of building out a lucrative, defensible strategic group, it is very helpful to focus on ways to improve the value-to-cost relationship of your major profit segments—Profit Peaks, Profit Drains, and Profit Deserts—both in your current industry and in your transformed business. The action question is this: how can you enhance your customer value footprint, reduce your cost, or both, providing an effective new base for competitive advantage? The cases in this book illustrate the range of possibilities:

- **Edison Furniture** illustrates how a company can increase its value footprint for its Profit Peak customers.

- **Baxter** illustrates how a company can both increase its value footprint and lower its cost for its Profit Peak customers.

- **Nalco** illustrates how a company can increase its value footprint for its Profit Drain customers, turning them into Profit Peaks.

- **Healthcare provider's minority blood pressure innovation,** a case later in this chapter, illustrates how a company can lower its cost for its Profit Drain customers, turning them into Profit Peaks.

- **Adrian Enterprises** illustrates how a company can lower its cost for its Profit Drain customers, turning them into Profit Peaks.

- **SKF Bearings** illustrates how a company can increase its value footprint for its Profit Desert customers, turning them into Profit Peaks.

- **Craft beer distributor** illustrates how a company can lower its cost for its Profit Desert customers, turning them into Profit Peaks.

- **Amazon** illustrates how a company can both increase its value footprint and lower its cost for its Profit Desert customers, turning them into Profit Peaks.

- **George Roberts,** a case later in this chapter, illustrates how a company can both increase its value footprint and lower its cost for both its Profit Peak and Profit Desert customers, turning the latter into Profit Peaks as well.

A company's profit landscape inevitably involves a relatively small number of profit rivers, essentially "profit SBUs," that are essential management units within the company. Several *profit streams*—sets of customers and products that are somewhat similar within each profit river—also can be identified. These form the basis for aligning the company's capabilities and resources in a finite, manageable way.

Align Your Cornerstone Functions

A company's go-to-market strategy is formed by a combination of products, customers, and supply chain activities. As today's markets are fragmenting into diverse segments, companies need to align their companies' products, customers, and supply chain activities to address their respective profit rivers and profit streams.

In Chapter 5, we explained the importance of *extended products*—the package of physical products and related services that is increasingly becoming the unit of building your customer value. *Strategic category management*—the process of building your value footprint—enables you to position your product set at the center of your customers' evolving business.

Extended products can be designed in very creative ways. Consider the major healthcare problem of controlling minority adult blood pressure.

The healthcare industry in the United States has been undergoing enormous change, driven by a combination of forces that are transforming the industry and fundamentally affecting every participant. The fundamental driver of change is relentless cost pressure coming from payers (that is, insurers, HMOs, and government).

A few years ago, the federal government passed a comprehensive healthcare program commonly known as Obamacare, which, among other things, mandated that healthcare institutions had to lower their cost to serve by about 25 percent over a three-year period. In parallel, insurers and HMOs have been negotiating aggressively with healthcare institutions to lower their cost.

These forces, and more, are creating a tsunami of change that is sweeping through the industry. This has a major impact on payers and patients. The payer is the customer for healthcare institutions, while the patient is the actual consumer of the healthcare services.

In minority communities, many adults have chronically high blood pressure and do not go to doctors for regular checkups. This leads to a host of very problematic, chronic diseases like stroke and heart disease. The payers have a strong incentive to find effective ways to address this problem early.

A recent study by researchers at Cedars-Sinai Hospital in Los Angeles of how to lower the chronic high blood pressure among minority individuals took a very innovative approach. The hospital researchers worked with a number of barbershops that served adult males in minority communities. They trained the barbers to take the customers' blood pressure when they came in for their regular monthly haircuts. A large proportion of the customers needed blood pressure medications, but they had not been previously tested. Each barbershop had a nearby pharmacy trained to help the customers that needed medications, and the barbers referred their customers with high blood pressure to these nearby pharmacies.

In a parallel effort, another study did the same for minority women who attended church each week (they had their blood pressure taken at church). These studies were strikingly effective, with a major measured impact on over 25 percent of the population, providing an outstanding example of the power of devising a creative extended product—the process of reaching and identifying at-risk patients before chronic problems arose.

Your account management process differs significantly by customer profit segment. Profit Peak customers require and warrant dedicated multifunctional teams that are expert in developing enhanced customer value footprints that increasingly build switching costs, tying them into these critical profit-generating customers. We refer to these teams as *trusted profit partners*.

Profit Drain customers should have a very different set of dedicated multifunctional teams that are analogous to bank workout groups assigned to problem loans. Most of the time, pricing is not the source of Profit Drains, but instead, the issue usually is high operating costs stemming from hidden factors like overly frequent ordering, which are costly for both the customer and for the supplier. The team needs to be expert in both identifying the problem (which is easy with the company-specific profit stack) and in managing change within the customer.

Profit Deserts are small, low-profit customers. A few may be large companies where you are a minor supplier; these customers may have the potential to be developed into Profit Peaks. However, most are simply small companies. The objective of account management in this segment is to drive down the cost to serve to match these companies' profit potential through menu-based selections and automated customer service measures. It is important to note, however, that these customers can be a very lucrative target for a company like Amazon that specializes in this segment.

Supply chain activities also need to be aligned with a company's product and customer management programs, often on a segment-by-segment and even customer-by-customer basis. The core processes for doing this are a company's relationship hierarchy, market mapping process, and service differentiation plan.

The most effective companies define a *relationship hierarchy*, which is a set of a few standardized customer relationships, typically ranging from arm's length to highly integrated, that can be offered to customers. Each relationship is carefully defined both in terms of the qualification factors and the supporting infrastructure. This prevents the company from experiencing the cost explosion that comes from a host of one-off customer requests. It also provides sales reps with a set of clearly differentiated customer relationship alternatives to sell to customers.

Market mapping is a joint process of sales, marketing, and supply chain managers. The objective is to define the relationship that each customer *should have*, not what it initially wants. The task of these multifunctional account teams is to sell the customer into the relationship that best fits it.

Service differentiation refers to the set of activities that each relationship entails. These range from planning to integrated operations like vendor-managed inventory. Because these are standardized, the company can produce the services with economies of scale and scope.

George Roberts, a disguised national company that is a manufacturer and distributor of automobile accessories, illustrates this process. The company provides an important optional accessory that is typically installed on-site at auto dealerships by the company's installers just after a car is purchased, before the customer takes it home (the dealer gets a commission for the sale of the device). After a period of growing sales, the company found that its sales and profit growth were leveling off. The company's CEO decided to form a team to investigate what was causing this change and to recommend corrective actions.

The team started by confirming the company's basic strategic premise: they had to provide excellent, fast service in very tight time windows because new car buyers wanted to take their new vehicles home as quickly as possible.

In a second step, the team looked carefully at the profitability and growth of the company's customer market segments using transaction-based profit metrics and analytics.

When the team assembled and analyzed this information, they were surprised to find that the company was relatively unprofitable in largely rural areas and that the profit picture was distinctly mixed in the urban and suburban areas. (In the past, they had looked at revenues and gross margins on a regional basis, which combined urban and rural areas, and most sales reps were given territories that combined urban and nearby rural areas.)

In order to identify the problem, the team disaggregated this information and looked closely at their customers relative to the market in a sample of rural and urban areas.

They saw that in the rural areas, the car dealers were scattered widely. This made it hard for their sales reps to cover their accounts regularly, so the reps tended to concentrate mostly on the urban and suburban dealers and to give only occasional attention to the others.

The installers had an even bigger problem: the company had simply assumed that all customers should have the same relationship and customer service process. Because they had no control over the geographic pattern of the product sales, they were forced to drive for an hour or more to get to most installation sites. This was very problematic both because it was costly to spend a large proportion of their time driving around and because the dealers perceived that the company was failing to provide the rapid service that would enable a dealer to deliver a new car to a waiting customer in a short period of time. The result was a situation marked by high costs, poor service, low profits, and declining sales.

The urban and suburban areas had a different problem. The sales reps could get to their urban customers much easier than to their rural customers. They used what seemed to be a good, logical rule, based on dealer sales of the company's product, to allocate their time to customer visits: they visited their large A accounts weekly, their medium-sales B customers every few weeks, and their low-volume C dealers monthly or less.

The installers were stationed in a centralized location and dispatched to the urban or suburban customers in response to dealer calls. This required a lot of driving, especially in traffic-prone regions, which lowered profits, hurt their service, and required that they keep extra personnel on call to meet their unpredictable peak needs.

When the team assessed the situation, they recommended very different customer relationships for the company's main market segments—rural versus urban areas—essentially creating two distinct profit rivers.

In the rural areas, they recommended that the company replace their sales reps with sets of contract sales agents who represented other products as well, which would enable them to increase the frequency and breadth of account coverage. The company developed a thorough training program for the agents, focused metrics, and a set of dedicated managers who specialized in this segment.

In a similar vein, they replaced their installers with local independent installers who also had other devices to install. This gave the contract installers the critical mass to offer rapid service in relatively small geographic areas. Again, the company developed a special training program, metrics, and dedicated managers specifically for these contract installers.

The net result was to markedly increase the company's sales coverage, and to rapidly reduce its installation costs, even while increasing the service level. Both sales and profits rose dramatically.

In the urban and suburban areas, the company faced a very different problem, and developed a very different solution.

In the past, sales reps had allocated their time for dealer visits proportionately to the dealer's sales level of the company's product. When the team looked carefully at the sample markets, however, they found that a surprisingly large number of major dealers were relatively uncovered because they were low-volume C accounts (in terms of their sales of the company's product), even though they actually sold more vehicles than many of the A accounts. These Profit Desert accounts had all the right characteristics to become Profit Peak customers.

When the team talked to the sales reps about why so many large car dealers were uncovered, the reps had a variety of reasons, including "They don't like us," "We used to do business with them, but our service lagged, and we lost the account," and "I'm too busy with my good customers."

When the team asked the sales reps what they could do to rejuvenate the relationships, the reps replied that it would be impractical because it would take perhaps a dozen visits over a period of a few months, and about

$10,000 in promotional funds. The team quickly saw that the breakeven on this would be three to four months.

They developed a training program to focus the sales reps on increasing sales in large, underpenetrated accounts (Profit Desert customers with the potential to become Profit Peak accounts). Every sales rep was assigned five high-potential underpenetrated accounts to develop. They were given sales quota relief for this and a bonus when an account reached a threshold level of production. When an account was producing, the rep got another underpenetrated account. This kept the reps laser focused on a few specific development accounts. Consequently, sales rose rapidly and kept growing.

The installation process changed as well. In the past, the installers were based in a single location and sent to accounts in response to dealer calls. This required a significant portion of their time to drive around town, from customer to customer, often through heavy traffic. However, the team saw that in most towns and cities, the dealers tended to cluster geographically along a particular road or highway.

The team suggested that teams of installers be assigned to be resident in each dealer cluster, which transformed the customer relationship. This virtually eliminated the driving and service delays, creating a compelling extended product—speedy service—in the customers' eyes. In a further innovation, the team suggested that the sales reps' new account development efforts be focused on developing currently underpenetrated accounts located in the dealer clusters.

In essence, the company formed a set of profit streams, defined by the respective dealer clusters, as the core of its urban-suburban customer profit river. The team aligned the company's management structure with this configuration, assigning a manager to oversee both sales and installation in each major customer cluster and in each set of smaller customer clusters.

The reps could approach the underpenetrated accounts with the powerful argument that now the company had a team of installers resident in the cluster, so service would be immediate and extremely reliable. This new customer relationship convinced many currently underpenetrated customers to try the company again. When the team saw the success of the new set of relationships, they suggested that installers actually should be resident *inside* some of the particularly strong individual dealers (creating another set of profit rivers defined by individual major dealers, some of whom had multiple sales sites).

This program was extremely successful because strong customer relationships developed between the installers and the dealer personnel, who worked closely on a day-to-day basis. (This was similar to the relationship that developed between the on-site Baxter materials management coordinators and the head nurses that we described in Chapter 1, which was the driving force behind Baxter's remarkable sales increases.) In some cases, the dealer actually preinstalled the devices in their cars, making the purchase mandatory rather than optional. This further increased the value footprint of the company's speedy-service extended product.

Moreover, the sales reps could coordinate closely with the resident installers when planning to penetrate a dealer cluster, resulting in a new set of customer relationships with stronger sales, better service, lower costs, and high profit growth.

In this way, the team developed the right customer relationships—which aligned its customer targeting, service definition, and installation supply chain, as well as its organization and management processes—for each profit river and profit stream. The company reversed its sales and profit stagnation, and turned it into both strong profitable growth and a dominant positioning in the highest-potential profit rivers—and it was not vulnerable to incursions by digital giants.

Manage to Meet Your Customers' Needs

Managing at the right level is the most important element in effective management in the Age of Diverse Markets. This is a huge change. In the prior mass markets era, companies had homogeneous markets, so they needed to plan and coordinate only at the executive level, with the rest of the company's managers focusing on their respective functional specialties. Today's markets are rapidly becoming highly fragmented, reflecting diverse customer needs. This requires a much more decentralized set of management structures and processes, which strongly affects managers at all three levels of a company's organization.

Today, executive managers must be responsible for developing their company's positioning and capabilities in three to five years, the transition period for managing paradigmatic change. They bear responsibility for installing and overseeing the company's four cornerstone business processes—strategic positioning and risk management, profit river management, transition initiative management, and profit-driven process management.

Within this context, these top managers must take the lead in defining the company's strategic group through its strategy and risk management process, and they must oversee the company's profit river management process. Importantly, they have to mentor the company's VP- and director-level managers.

The VPs and directors group, working through their MPG Committee, is the locus of the company's profit-generating activities. They have to be fully fluent in transaction-based profit metrics and analytics, and they must use this knowledge to analyze and recommend to top management the company's strategy and risk trajectory. They need to determine and actively manage the company's profit rivers, and they need to define each profit river's profit streams. They also have to define and manage the company's transition initiatives and profit showcases.

Beside these high-level coordination activities, these upper-level managers need to mentor and develop the sales and operating managers below them, and they need to set up and oversee the profit crossroads that is essential to these managers' success in coordinating with each other.

The sales and operating managers run the company on a day-to-day basis, both by managing the company's core profit-driven processes and by coordinating with each other in tightly managed, multifunctional teams that manage the company's diverse, rapidly changing profit streams.

THE MANAGER OF THE FUTURE

In today's Age of Diverse Markets, managers' activities could not be more different from those required of managers in the prior mass market era. Successful managers today must be overwhelmingly broad and holistic in their perspective; their work is disruptive, innovative, and strategic; and they are primarily team oriented.

This difference in management is analogous to the difference between a good cook and a great chef. A good cook flawlessly follows a set of predetermined recipes, always creating very good meals. A great chef, on the other hand, has the vision and capability to *create* an increasingly superb set of innovative, new dishes that continually transform a cuisine—producing the recipes that good cooks follow.

A great chef is a master, in the sense of the guild masters of old. The Manager of the Future must reflect these attributes. Even at the day-to-day sales and operating level of a company, the Managers of the Future must coordinate with each other on multifunctional teams to identify and fulfill the emerging needs—often unrecognized even by the customers themselves—of the company's increasingly diverse set of customers.

The Manager of the Future—the successful manager in the Age of Diverse Markets—needs a completely different development pathway:

- **Broad academic background:** Managers need to be immersed in examples of changing needs and changing fulfillment of needs. They need to understand best practice in the process and politics of change management, especially ways to speed change and increase its effectiveness. This means that they need a broad background in literature, history, political science, and even the history of science. Instead of spending years gaining a deep technical background in one functional area, they need to develop a broad high-level view of all of the functional areas of business, and how they interact with each other to create unique customer value.

- **Deep immersion in customers:** Managers today have to spend a significant amount of time actually physically in customers— walking in the customer's shoes. They must be involved in profit-showcase projects with customers, which are opportunities to develop new forms of their customer value footprint, learning by doing. The Baxter case and several others, described in earlier chapters, provide specific examples of this.

- **Understanding your profit landscape:** Managers at all levels need training and practice in understanding transaction-based profit information—not as technical specialists but rather, as informed, creative users of this information both for targeting customers and for shaping the extended products that are produced by the multicapability teams on which they will be integral participants.

- **Building relationships:** Managers today need to work closely with their peers on multifunctional teams. This means that they need to build close working relationships with their counterpart managers throughout the company well before these relationships are needed. They need to understand how their counterparts think, what they are trying to accomplish, and what barriers to successful change they are encountering.

- **Understanding the company's history:** The key to really understanding a company is to know that most often it is doing what it needed to do 5 to 10 (or more) years ago. These practices—including customer targeting and management, category management, and supply chain and operations management—get embedded in a company's culture and are passed along from manager to manager, year after year.

  This embedded operating paradigm is both tacit and pervasive, and it appears as simply "the way we do business." This is why the obsolete Age of Mass Markets paradigm has such an incredibly strong influence on managers today, becoming a sea anchor on most established companies' ability to respond quickly and ably to market opportunities, and explaining to a large extent why the most successful companies today did not exist 50 years ago, while nearly all of the most successful companies 50 years ago have fallen by the wayside.

- **Managing the change process:** Today's business world is changing and fragmenting at an accelerating pace. The currents of change are gathering speed; they do not embody a finite shift from one state to another, but rather, they scribe a trajectory of constant change.

This pathway means that managers need to be extremely flexible and capable of identifying these constant shifts, developing and delivering ever-changing packages of products and related services, and managing change—both inside their own companies, and in their customers and suppliers.

- **Training and mentoring others in this new mode:** The key to manager success is ultimately training subordinates to be effective. This means that successful managers not only have to be capable of managing in this new mode, but they also have to be capable of training their subordinates in the new mode as well. After all, a manager can rise in the organization only as fast as his or her subordinates become capable of taking his or her place.

BUILD YOUR FUTURE

Today, we are situated at a historically unique time. The old Age of Mass Markets is fading away, and the new Age of Diverse Markets is already generating tsunamis that are sweeping through industry after industry, transforming everything in their paths. Like Noah of old, today's value entrepreneur needs to pilot his or her company through the turbulent waters to the permanent safety of strategic high ground and accelerating profitability.

This widespread transformation is both a relentless source of peril and a once-in-a-lifetime source of strategic opportunity.

Managers who cling to their old tried-and-true management processes—tuning up old tactics—will be swept away by the floodwaters of change. But those managers who master the new management processes described in this book will discover a clear pathway to accelerating profitable growth and strategic dominance for years to come—and they will find their jobs much more interesting, creative, and satisfying.

Each and every manager today faces a stark choice: either try to hold on to the past or focus on building your future.

The choice is up to you.

THINGS TO THINK ABOUT

1. Are you choosing your customers? Who are your Profit Peak customers? Who will they be in three to five years?

2. Are you aligning your organization with your profit rivers?

3. Are you managing at the right level and with transaction-based profit metrics?

4. Do your managers have the skills and experience they need to be value entrepreneurs and to succeed in the Age of Diverse Markets?

INDEX

ABOUT THE AUTHORS

Jonathan L. S. Byrnes is a senior lecturer at MIT. He is also chairman of Profit Isle (https://www.profitisle.com), a highly successful MIT spin-off that is a software-as-a-service (SaaS) profit solutions company. Using its unique, proprietary profitability analytics and management process, Profit Isle helps organizations increase profits by 10 to 30 percent.

A widely followed innovator, thought leader, writer, and speaker on all aspects of profitable growth and innovative customer-supplier relationships, he developed the first widely followed vendor-managed inventory system that pioneered the movement to integrate the operations of customers and suppliers. He also invented the transaction-based profit analytics that have successfully transformed the profitability of hundreds of billions of dollars of company revenues.

Jonathan is a frequent speaker and writer on managing profitable growth, and he has advised over a hundred companies and institutions.

He served on the board of directors of MSC Industrial Direct (an NYSE company) for over 10 years, and he has also served on several private company boards.

He has been a senior lecturer at MIT for over 30 years. His MIT graduate student and executive program alumni number in the thousands and include numerous top executives and boards of directors members of major companies, including top executives at Amazon, Microsoft, Google, Apple, Dell, Nordstrom, Intel, Target, and IBM.

He earned a doctorate from Harvard Business School, and he has served as president of the Harvard Alumni Association and as a member of the Harvard Business School Alumni Board. He has served on the board of directors of *Harvard Magazine* and as editor in chief of the *Columbia Journal of World Business*. He wrote a very popular column, "The Bottom Line," with a readership of hundreds of thousands each month, for Harvard Business School's *Working Knowledge* for over four years.

He is the author of *Islands of Profit in a Sea of Red Ink*, which was an *Inc. Magazine* Best Book for Business Owners and was published in four languages.

John S. Wass is the CEO of Profit Isle. Under his leadership, the company has managed the profit acceleration of over $100 billion in client revenues across multiple industries, and it has become the preeminent SaaS software company specializing in managing profitable growth.

Previously, John was a key member of the management team that grew Staples from three stores to over a thousand stores nationwide, serving as a senior vice president. In this capacity, he developed many of the marketing and supply chain innovations that are cornerstones of the retail industry today, including focused stores, loyalty cards, and flow-through supply chains linking factories in Asia with store shelves around the world. He developed the first system for digital marketing connecting Staples' stores and internet offerings, creating the foundation for today's omnichannel marketing. He was instrumental in developing much of the software that enables these systems to succeed.

John also served as CEO of WaveMark, an innovative multimillion-dollar company that pioneered radio frequency identification (RFID) tracking for medical devices. The company was acquired by Cardinal Health, and it is now a central element in Cardinal's hospital strategy.

A graduate of Princeton University and MIT, John has held an appointment as a visiting scholar at MIT, and he has lectured at MIT for over a decade. He is a well-known thought leader, writer, and speaker.

Visit profitisle.com.